KANT'S PROLEGOMENA

TO ANY FUTURE METAPHYSICS

EDITED IN ENGLISH

BY

DR. PAUL CARUS

REPRINT EDITION

WITH AN ESSAY ON KANT'S PHILOSOPHY, AND
OTHER SUPPLEMENTARY MATERIAL
FOR THE STUDY OF KANT

CHICAGO ::: LONDON
THE OPEN COURT PUBLISHING COMPANY
1949

Printed in the United States of America
By PAQUIN PRINTERS, Chicago

PUBLISHERS' PREFACE.

K ANT'S *Prolegomena*,[1] although a small book, is indubitably
the most important of his writings. It furnishes us with a
key to his main work, *The Critique of Pure Reason ;* in fact, it
is an extract containing all the salient ideas of Kant's system. It
approaches the subject in the simplest and most direct way, and
is therefore best adapted as an introduction into his philosophy.
For this reason, The Open Court Publishing Company has deemed
it advisable to bring out a new edition of the work, keeping in
view its broader use as a preliminary survey and explanation of
Kant's philosophy in general. In order to make the book useful
for this broader purpose, the editor has not only stated his own
views concerning the problem underlying the *Prolegomena* (see
page 167 et seq.), but has also collected the most important materials which have reference to Kant's philosophy, or to the recep-
tion which was accorded to it in various quarters (see page 241 et
seq.). The selections have not been made from a partisan standpoint, but have been chosen with a view to characterising the attitude of different minds, and to directing the student to the best
literature on the subject.

It is not without good reasons that the appearance of the
Critique of Pure Reason is regarded as the beginning of a new
era in the history of philosophy ; and so it seems that a comprehension of Kant's position, whether we accept or reject it, is indispensable to the student of philosophy. It is not his solution which

---

1 *Prolegomena* means literally prefatory or introductory remarks. It is
the neuter plural of the present passive participle of προλέγειν, *to speak before*,
i e., to make introductory remarks before beginning one's regular discourse.

makes the sage of Königsberg the initiator of modern thought, but his formulation of the problem.

*   *   *

The present translation is practically new, but it goes without saying that the editor utilised the labors of his predecessors, among whom Prof. John P. Mahaffy and John H. Bernard deserve special credit. Richardson's translation of 1818 may be regarded as superseded and has not been consulted, but occasional reference has been made to that of Prof. Ernest Belfort Bax. Considering the difficulties under which even these translators labored we must recognise the fact that they did their work well, with painstaking diligence, great love of the subject, and good judgment. The editor of the present translation has the advantage of being to the manor born; moreover, he is pretty well versed in Kant's style; and wherever he differs from his predecessors in the interpretation of a construction, he has deviated from them not without good reasons. Nevertheless there are some passages which will still remain doubtful, though happily they are of little consequence.

As a *curiosum* in Richardson's translation Professor Mahaffy mentions that the words *widersinnig gewundene Schnecken*, which simply means "symmetric helices,"[1] are rendered by "snails rolled up contrary to all sense"—a wording that is itself contrary to all sense and makes the whole paragraph unintelligible. We may add an instance of another mistake that misses the mark. Kant employs in the Appendix a word that is no longer used in German. He speaks of the *Cento der Metaphysik* as having *neue Lappen* and *einen veränderten Zuschnitt*. Mr. Bax translates *Cento* by "body," *Lappen* by "outgrowths," and *Zuschnitt* by "figure." His mistake is perhaps not less excusable than Richardson's; it is certainly not less comical, and it also destroys the sense, which in the present case is a very striking simile.

---

1 Mahaffy not incorrectly translates "spirals winding opposite ways," and Mr. Bax follows him *verbatim* even to the repetition of the footnote.

Cento is a Latin word[1] derived from the Greek κέντρων,[2] meaning "a garment of many patches sewed together," or, as we might now say, "a crazy quilt."

    * * *

  In the hope that this book will prove useful, The Open Court Publishing Company offers it as a help to the student of philosophy.

              P. C.

[1] The French *centon* is still in use.

[2] κέντρων, (1) one that bears the marks of the κέντρον, goad; a rogue, (2) a patched cloth; (3) any kind of patchwork, especially verses made up of scraps from other authors.

TABLE OF CONTENTS.

KANT'S PROLEGOMENA.

INTRODUCTION.

THESE Prolegomena are destined for the use, not of pupils, but of future teachers, and even the latter should not expect that they will be serviceable for the systematic exposition of a ready-made science, but merely for the discovery of the science itself.

There are scholarly men, to whom the history of philosophy (both ancient and modern) is philosophy itself; for these the present Prolegomena are not written. They must wait till those who endeavor to draw from the fountain of reason itself have completed their work; it will then be the historian's turn to inform the world of what has been done. Unfortunately, nothing can be said, which in their opinion has not been said before, and truly the same prophecy applies to all future time; for since the human reason has for many centuries speculated upon innumerable objects in various ways, it is hardly to be expected that we should not be able to discover analogies for every new idea among the old sayings of past ages.

My object is to persuade all those who think Metaphysics worth studying, that it is absolutely necessary to pause a moment, and, neglecting all that has been done, to propose first the preliminary question, 'Whether such a thing as metaphysics be at all possible?'

If it be a science, how comes it that it cannot, like other sciences, obtain universal and permanent recognition? If not, how can it maintain its pretensions, and keep the human mind in suspense with hopes, never ceasing, yet never fulfilled? Whether then we demonstrate our knowledge or our ignorance in this field, we must come once for all to a definite conclusion respecting the nature of this so-called science, which cannot possibly remain on its present footing. It seems almost ridiculous, while every other science is continually advancing, that in this, which pretends to be Wisdom incarnate, for whose oracle every one inquires, we should constantly move round the same spot, without gaining a single step. And so its followers having melted away, we do not find men confident of their ability to shine in other sciences venturing their reputation here, where everybody, however ignorant in other matters, may deliver a final verdict, as in this domain there is as yet no standard weight and measure to distinguish sound knowledge from shallow talk.

After all it is nothing extraordinary in the elaboration of a science, when men begin to wonder how far it has advanced, that the question should at last occur, whether and how such a science is possible? Human reason so delights in constructions, that it has several times built up a tower, and then razed it to examine the nature of the foundation. It is never too late to become wise; but if the change comes late, there is always more difficulty in starting a reform.

The question whether a science be possible, presupposes a doubt as to its actuality. But such a doubt offends the men whose whole possessions consist of this supposed jewel; hence he who raises the doubt must expect opposition from all sides. Some, in the proud consciousness of their possessions, which are ancient, and therefore considered legitimate, will take their metaphysical compendia in their hands, and look down on him with contempt; others, who never see anything except it be identical with what they have seen before, will not understand him, and everything will remain for a time, as if nothing had happened to excite the concern, or the hope, for an impending change.

Nevertheless, I venture to predict that the independent reader of these Prolegomena will not only doubt his previous science, but ultimately be fully persuaded, that it cannot exist unless the demands here stated on which its possibility depends, be satisfied ; and, as this has never been done, that there is, as yet, no such thing as Metaphysics. But as it can never cease to be in demand,[1]—since the interests of common sense are intimately interwoven with it, he must confess that a radical reform, or rather a new birth of the science after an original plan, are unavoidable, however men may struggle against it for a while.

Since the Essays of Locke and Leibnitz, or rather since the origin of metaphysics so far as we know its history, nothing has ever happened which was more decisive to its fate than the attack made upon it by David Hume. He threw no light on this species of knowledge, but he certainly struck a spark from

[1] Says Horace :

      " Rusticus expectat, dum defluat amnis, at ille
        Labitur et labetur in omne volubilis aevum;"

    " A rustic fellow waiteth on the shore
      For the river to flow away,
      But the river flows, and flows on as before,
      And it flows forever and aye."

which light might have been obtained, had it caught
some inflammable substance and had its smouldering
fire been carefully nursed and developed.

Hume started from a single but important concept
in Metaphysics, viz., that of Cause and Effect (including its derivatives force and action, etc.). He
challenges reason, which pretends to have given birth
to this idea from herself, to answer him by what right
she thinks anything to be so constituted, that if that
thing be posited, something else also must necessarily
be posited; for this is the meaning of the concept of
cause. He demonstrated irrefutably that it was perfectly impossible for reason to think *a priori* and by
means of concepts a combination involving necessity.
We cannot at all see why, in consequence of the existence of one thing, another must necessarily exist,
or how the concept of such a combination can arise
a priori. Hence he inferred, that reason was altogether deluded with reference to this concept, which
she erroneously considered as one of her children,
whereas in reality it was nothing but a bastard of imagination, impregnated by experience, which subsumed certain representations under the Law of Asso-
ciation, and mistook the subjective necessity of habit
for an objective necessity arising from insight. Hence
he inferred that reason had no power to think such
combinations, even generally, because her concepts
would then be purely fictitious, and all her pretended
a priori cognitions nothing but common experiences
marked with a false stamp. In plain language there
is not, and cannot be, any such thing as metaphysics
at all.[1]

---

[1] Nevertheless Hume called this very destructive science metaphysics
and attached to it great value. Metaphysics and morals [he declares in the

However hasty and mistaken Hume's conclusion may appear, it was at least founded upon investigation, and this investigation deserved the concentrated attention of the brighter spirits of his day as well as determined efforts on their part to discover, if possible, a happier solution of the problem in the sense proposed by him, all of which would have speedily resulted in a complete reform of the science.

But Hume suffered the usual misfortune of metaphysicians, of not being understood. It is positively painful to see how utterly his opponents, Reid, Oswald, Beattie, and lastly Priestley, missed the point of the problem; for while they were ever taking for granted that which he doubted, and demonstrating with zeal and often with impudence that which he never thought of doubting, they so misconstrued his valuable suggestion that everything remained in its old condition, as if nothing had happened.

The question was not whether the concept of cause was right, useful, and even indispensable for our knowledge of nature, for this Hume had never doubted; but whether that concept could be thought by reason *a priori*, and consequently whether it possessed an inner truth, independent of all experience, implying a wider application than merely to the objects of experience. This was Hume's problem. It was a question concerning the *origin*, not concerning the *indispensable need* of the concept. Were the former

fourth part of his Essays] are the most important branches of science; mathematics and physics are not nearly so important. But the acute man merely regarded the negative use arising from the moderation of extravagant claims of speculative reason, and the complete settlement of the many endless and troublesome controversies that mislead mankind. He overlooked the positive injury which results, if reason be deprived of its most important prospects, which can alone supply to the will the highest aim for all its endeavor.

decided, the conditions of the use and the sphere of
its valid application would have been determined as
a matter of course.

But to satisfy the conditions of the problem, the
opponents of the great thinker should have penetrated
very deeply into the nature of reason, so far as it is
concerned with pure thinking,—a task which did not
suit them.   They found a more convenient method of
being defiant without any insight, viz., the appeal to
common sense.   It is indeed a great gift of God, to possess right, or (as they now call it) plain common
sense.   But this common sense must be shown practically, by well-considered and reasonable thoughts
and words, not by appealing to it as an oracle, when
no rational justification can be advanced.   To appeal
to common sense, when insight and science fail, and
no sooner—this is one of the subtile discoveries of
modern times, by means of which the most superficial
ranter can safely enter the lists with the most thorough
thinker, and hold his own.   But as long as a particle
of insight remains, no one would think of having recourse to this subterfuge.   For what is it but an appeal to the opinion of the multitude, of whose ap-
plause the philosopher is ashamed, while the popular
charlatan glories and confides in it?   I should think
that Hume might fairly have laid as much claim to
common sense as Beattie, and in addition to a critical
reason (such as the latter did not possess), which
keeps common sense in check and prevents it from
speculating, or, if speculations are under discussion,
restrains the desire to decide because it cannot satisfy
itself concerning its own arguments.   By this means
alone can common sense remain sound.   Chisels and
hammers may suffice to work a piece of wood, but for

steel-engraving we require an engraver's needle. Thus common sense and speculative understanding are each serviceable in their own way, the former in judgments which apply immediately to experience, the latter when we judge universally from mere concepts, as in metaphysics, where sound common sense, so called in spite of the inapplicability of the word, has no right to judge at all.

I openly confess, the suggestion of David Hume was the very thing, which many years ago first interrupted my dogmatic slumber, and gave my investigations in the field of speculative philosophy quite a new direction. I was far from following him in the conclusions at which he arrived by regarding, not the whole of his problem, but a part, which by itself can give us no information. If we start from a well-founded, but undeveloped, thought, which another has bequeathed to us, we may well hope by continued reflection to advance farther than the acute man, to whom we owe the first spark of light.

1 therefore first tried whether Hume's objection could not be put into a general form, and soon found that the concept of the connexion of cause and effect was by no means the only idea by which the understanding thinks the connexion of things *a priori*, but rather that metaphysics consists altogether of such connexions. I sought to ascertain their number, and when I had satisfactorily succeeded in this by starting from a single principle, I proceeded to the deduction of these concepts, which I was now certain were not deduced from experience, as Hume had apprehended, but sprang from the pure understanding. This deduction (which seemed impossible to my acute predecessor, which had never even occurred to any one

else, though no one had hesitated to use the concepts without investigating the basis of their objective validity) was the most difficult task ever undertaken in the service of metaphysics; and the worst was that metaphysics, such as it then existed, could not assist me in the least, because this deduction alone can render metaphysics possible. But as soon as I had succeeded in solving Hume's problem not merely in a particular case, but with respect to the whole faculty of pure reason, I could proceed safely, though slowly, to determine the whole sphere of pure reason completely and from general principles, in its circumference as well as in its contents. This was required for metaphysics in order to construct its system according to a reliable method.

But I fear that the execution of Hume's problem in its widest extent (viz., my Critique of the Pure Reason) will fare as the problem itself fared, when first proposed. It will be misjudged because it is misunderstood, and misunderstood because men choose to skim through the book, and not to think through it—a disagreeable task, because the work is dry, obscure, opposed to all ordinary notions, and moreover long-winded. I confess, however, I did not expect to hear from philosophers complaints of want of popularity, entertainment, and facility, when the existence of a highly prized and indispensable cognition is at stake, which cannot be established otherwise, than by the strictest rules of methodic precision. Popularity may follow, but is inadmissible at the beginning. Yet as regards a certain obscurity, arising partly from the diffuseness of the plan, owing to which the principal points of the investigation are easily lost sight of, the

complaint is just, and I intend to remove it by the
present Prolegomena.

The first-mentioned work, which discusses the pure
faculty of reason in its whole compass and bounds,
will remain the foundation, to which the Prolegomena,
as a preliminary exercise, refer; for our critique must
first be established as a complete and perfected science, before we can think of letting Metaphysics appear on the scene, or even have the most distant hope
of attaining it.

We have been long accustomed to seeing anti-
quated knowledge produced as new by taking it out
of its former context, and reducing it to system in a
new suit of any fancy pattern under new titles. Most
readers will set out by expecting nothing else from
the Critique; but these Prolegomena may persuade
him that it is a perfectly new science, of which no
one has ever even thought, the very idea of which
was unknown, and for which nothing hitherto accomplished can be of the smallest use, except it be the
suggestion of Hume's doubts. Yet even he did not
suspect such a formal science, but ran his ship ashore,
for safety's sake, landing on scepticism, there to let it
lie and rot; whereas my object is rather to give it a
pilot, who, by means of safe astronomical principles
drawn from a knowledge of the globe, and provided
with a complete chart and compass, may steer the
ship safely, whither he listeth.

If in a new science, which is wholly isolated and
unique in its kind, we started with the prejudice that
we can judge of things by means of our previously
acquired knowledge, which is precisely what has first
to be called in question, we should only fancy we saw
everywhere what we had already known, the expres-

sions, having a similar sound, only that all would ap
pear utterly metamorphosed, senseless and unintelligible, because we should have as a foundation our
own notions, made by long habit a second nature, instead of the author's.   But the longwindedness of the
work, so far as it depends on the subject, and not the
exposition, its consequent unavoidable dryness and
its scholastic precision are qualities which can only
benefit the science, though they may discredit the
book.

Few writers are gifted with the subtilty, and at the
same time with the grace, of David Hume, or with
the depth, as well as the elegance, of Moses Mendelssohn.   Yet I flatter myself I might have made my
own exposition popular, had my object been merely to
sketch out a plan and leave its completion to others,
instead of having my heart in the welfare of the science, to which I had devoted myself so long ; in truth,
it required no little constancy, and even self-denial,
to postpone the sweets of an immediate success to
the prospect of a slower, but more lasting, reputation.

Making plans is often the occupation of an opu-
lent and boastful mind, which thus obtains the reputation of a creative genius, by demanding what it
cannot itself supply; by censuring, what it cannot
improve ; and by proposing, what it knows not where
to find.   And yet something more should belong to a
sound plan of a general critique of pure reason than
mere conjectures, if this plan is to be other than the
usual declamations of pious aspirations.   But pure
reason is a sphere so separate and self-contained, that
we cannot touch a part without affecting all the rest.
We can therefore do nothing without first determining the position of each part, and its relation to the

rest; for, as our judgment cannot be corrected by anything without, the validity and use of every part depends upon the relation in which it stands to all the rest within the domain of reason.

So in the structure of an organized body, the end of each member can only be deduced from the full conception of the whole. It may, then, be said of such a critique that it is never trustworthy except it be perfectly complete, down to the smallest elements of pure reason. In the sphere of this faculty you can determine either everything or nothing.

But although a mere sketch, preceding the Critique of Pure Reason, would be unintelligible, unreliable, and useless, it is all the more useful as a sequel. For so we are able to grasp the whole, to examine in detail the chief points of importance in the science, and to improve in many respects our exposition, as compared with the first execution of the work.

After the completion of the work I offer here such a plan which is sketched out after an analytical method, while the work itself had to be executed in the synthetical style, in order that the science may present all its articulations, as the structure of a peculiar cognitive faculty, in their natural combination. But should any reader find this plan, which I publish as the Prolegomena to any future Metaphysics, still obscure, let him consider that not every one is bound to study Metaphysics, that many minds will succeed very well, in the exact and even in deep sciences, more closely allied to practical experience,[1] while they

---

[1] The term *Anschauung* here used means sense-perception. It is that which is given to the senses and apprehended immediately, as an object is seen by merely looking at it. The translation *intuition*, though etymologically correct, is misleading. In the present passage the term is not used in its technical significance but means " practical experience."—*Ed*.

cannot succeed in investigations dealing exclusively with abstract concepts. In such cases men should apply their talents to other subjects. But he who undertakes to judge, or still more, to construct, a system of Metaphysics, must satisfy the demands here made, either by adopting my solution, or by thoroughly refuting it, and substituting another. To evade it is impossible.

In conclusion, let it be remembered that this much-abused obscurity (frequently serving as a mere pretext under which people hide their own indolence or dullness) has its uses, since all who in other sciences observe a judicious silence, speak authoritatively in metaphysics and make bold decisions, because their ignorance is not here contrasted with the knowledge of others. Yet it does contrast with sound critical principles, which we may therefore commend in the words of Virgil:

"Ignavum, fucos, pecus a præsepibus arcent."
'Bees are defending their hives against drones, those indolent creatures."

PROLEGOMENA.

PREAMBLE ON THE PECULIARITIES OF ALL META-PHYSICAL COGNITION.

§ 1. *Of the Sources of Metaphysics.*

IF it becomes desirable to formulate any cognition as science, it will be necessary first to determine accurately those peculiar features which no other science has in common with it, constituting its characteristics; otherwise the boundaries of all sciences become confused, and none of them can be treated thoroughly according to its nature.

The characteristics of a science may consist of a simple difference of object, or of the sources of cognition, or of the kind of cognition, or perhaps of all three conjointly. On this, therefore, depends the idea of a possible science and its territory.

First, as concerns the sources of metaphysical cognition, its very concept implies that they cannot be empirical. Its principles (including not only its maxims but its basic notions) must never be derived from experience. It must not be physical but metaphysical knowledge, viz., knowledge lying beyond experience. It can therefore have for its basis neither external experience, which is the source of physics proper, nor internal, which is the basis of empirical psychology. It is therefore *a priori* knowledge, coming from pure Understanding and pure Reason.

But so far Metaphysics would not be distinguishable from pure Mathematics; it must therefore be called pure philosophical cognition; and for the meaning of this term I refer to the Critique of the Pure Reason (II. "Method of Transcendentalism," Chap. I., Sec. i), where the distinction between these two employments of the reason is sufficiently explained. So far concerning the sources of metaphysical cognition.

§ 2. *Concerning the Kind of Cognition which can alone be called Metaphysical.*

a. *Of the Distinction between Analytical and Synthetical Judgments in general.*—The peculiarity of its sources demands that metaphysical cognition must consist of nothing but *a priori* judgments. But whatever be their origin, or their logical form, there is a distinction in judgments, as to their content, according to which they are either merely explicative, adding nothing to the content of the cognition, or expansive, increasing the given cognition: the former may be called analytical, the latter synthetical, judgments.

Analytical judgments express nothing in the predicate but what has been already actually thought in the concept of the subject, though not so distinctly or with the same (full) consciousness. When I say: All bodies are extended, I have not amplified in the least my concept of body, but have only analysed it, as extension was really thought to belong to that concept before the judgment was made, though it was not expressed; this judgment is therefore analytical. On the contrary, this judgment, All bodies have weight, contains in its predicate something not actually thought in the general concept of the body; it amplifies my knowledge by adding something to my concept, and must therefore be called synthetical.

b. The Common Principle of all Analytical Judgments is the Law of Contradiction.—All analytical judgments depend wholly on the law of Contradiction, and are in their nature *a priori* cognitions, whether the concepts that supply them with matter be empirical or not. For the predicate of an affirmative analytical judgment is already contained in the concept of the subject, of which it cannot be denied without contradiction. In the same way its opposite is necessarily denied of the subject in an analytical, but negative, judgment, by the same law of contradiction. Such is the nature of the judgments: all bodies are extended, and no bodies are unextended (i. e., simple).

For this very reason all analytical judgments are *a priori* even when the concepts are empirical, as, for example, Gold is a yellow metal; for to know this I require no experience beyond my concept of gold as a yellow metal: it is, in fact, the very concept, and I need only analyse it, without looking beyond it elsewhere.

c. Synthetical Judgments require a different Principle from the Law of Contradiction.—There are synthetical *a posteriori* judgments of empirical origin; but there are also others which are proved to be certain *a priori*, and which spring from pure Understanding and Reason. Yet they both agree in this, that they cannot possibly spring from the principle of analysis, viz., the law of contradiction, alone; they require a quite different principle, though, from whatever they may be deduced, they must be subject to the law of contradiction, which must never be violated, even though everything cannot be deduced from it. I shall first classify synthetical judgments.

1. *Empirical Judgments* are always synthetical. For it would be absurd to base an analytical judgment on experience, as our concept suffices for the purpose without requiring any testimony from experience. That body is extended, is a judgment established *a priori*, and not an empirical judgment. For before appealing to experience, we already have all the conditions of the judgment in the concept, from which we have but to elicit the predicate according to the law of contradiction, and thereby to become conscious of the necessity of the judgment, which experience could not even teach us.

2. *Mathematical Judgments* are all synthetical. This fact seems hitherto to have altogether escaped the observation of those who have analysed human reason; it even seems directly opposed to all their conjectures, though incontestably certain, and most important in its consequences. For as it was found that the conclusions of mathematicians all proceed according to the law of contradiction (as is demanded by all apodeictic certainty), men persuaded themselves that the fundamental principles were known from the same law. This was a great mistake, for a synthetical proposition can indeed be comprehended according to the law of contradiction, but only by presupposing another synthetical proposition from which it follows, but never in itself.

First of all, we must observe that all proper mathematical judgments are *a priori*, and not empirical, because they carry with them necessity, which cannot be obtained from experience. But if this be not conceded to me, very good; I shall confine my assertion to *pure Mathematics*, the very notion of which implies that it contains pure *a priori* and not empirical cognitions.

It might at first be thought that the proposition $7 + 5 = 12$ is a mere analytical judgment, following from the concept of the sum of seven and five, according to the law of contradiction. But on closer examination it appears that the concept of the sum of $7 + 5$ contains merely their union in a single number, without its being at all thought what the particular number is that unites them. The concept of twelve is by no means thought by merely thinking of the combination of seven and five; and analyse this possible sum as we may, we shall not discover twelve in the concept. We must go beyond these concepts, by calling to our aid some concrete image (*Anschauung*), i.e., either our five fingers, or five points (as Segner has it in his Arithmetic), and we must add successively the units of the five, given in some concrete image (*Anschauung*), to the concept of seven. Hence our concept is really amplified by the proposition $7 + 5 = 12$, and we add to the first a second, not thought in it. Arithmetical judgments are therefore synthetical, and the more plainly according as we take larger numbers; for in such cases it is clear that, however closely we analyse our concepts without calling visual images (*Anschauung*) to our aid, we can never find the sum by such mere dissection.

All principles of geometry are no less analytical. That a straight line is the shortest path between two points, is a synthetical proposition. For my concept of straight contains nothing of quantity, but only a quality. The attribute of shortness is therefore altogether additional, and cannot be obtained by any analysis of the concept. Here, too, visualisation (*Anschauung*) must come to aid us. It alone makes the synthesis possible.

Some other principles, assumed by geometers, are indeed actually analytical, and depend on the law of contradiction; but they only serve, as identical propositions, as a method of concatenation, and not as principles, e. g., $a = a$, the whole is equal to itself, or $a + b > a$, the whole is greater than its part. And yet even these, though they are recognised as valid from mere concepts, are only admitted in mathematics, because they can be represented in some visual form (*Anschauung*). What usually makes us believe that the predicate of such apodeictic[1] judgments is already contained in our concept, and that the judgment is therefore analytical, is the duplicity of the expression, requesting us to think a certain predicate as of necessity implied in the thought of a given concept, which necessity attaches to the concept. But the question is not what we are requested to join in thought *to* the given concept, but what we actually think together with and in it, though obscurely; and so it appears that the predicate belongs to these concepts necessarily indeed, yet not directly but indirectly by an added visualisation (*Anschauung*).

§ 3. *A Remark on the General Division of Judgments into Analytical and Synthetical.*

This division is indispensable, as concerns the Critique of human understanding, and therefore de-

[1] The term *apodeictic* is borrowed by Kant from Aristotle who uses it in the sense of "certain beyond dispute." The word is derived from ἀποδείκνυμι (=*I show*) and is contrasted to dialectic propositions, i. e., such statements as admit of controversy.—*Ed.*

serves to be called classical, though otherwise it is of
little use, but this is the reason why dogmatic philosophers, who always seek the sources of metaphysical
judgments in Metaphysics itself, and not apart from
it, in the pure laws of reason generally, altogether
neglected this apparently obvious distinction. Thus
the celebrated Wolf, and his acute follower Baumgarten, came to seek the proof of the principle of
Sufficient Reason, which is clearly synthetical, in the
principle of Contradiction. In Locke's Essay, however, I find an indication of my division. For in the
fourth book (chap. iii. § 9, seq.), having discussed
the various connexions of representations in judgments, and their sources, one of which he makes
"identity and contradiction" (analytical judgments),
and another the coexistence of representations in a
subject, he confesses (§ 10) that our *a priori* knowledge of the latter is very narrow, and almost nothing.
But in his remarks on this species of cognition, there
is so little of what is definite, and reduced to rules,
that we cannot wonder if no one, not even Hume, was
led to make investigations concerning this sort of
judgments. For such general and yet definite principles are not easily learned from other men, who
have had them obscurely in their minds. We must
hit on them first by our own reflexion, then we find
them elsewhere, where we could not possibly have
found them at first, because the authors themselves
did not know that such an idea lay at the basis of
their observations. Men who never think independently have nevertheless the acuteness to discover
everything, after it has been once shown them, in
what was said long since, though no one ever saw it
there before.

§ 4. *The General Question of the Prolegomena.—Is Metaphysics at all Possible?*

Were a metaphysics, which could maintain its place as a science, really in existence; could we say, here is metaphysics, learn it, and it will convince you irresistibly and irrevocably of its truth: this question would be useless, and there would only remain that other question (which would rather be a test of our acuteness, than a proof of the existence of the thing itself), "How is the science possible, and how does reason come to attain it?" But human reason has not been so fortunate in this case. There is no single book to which you can point as you do to Euclid, and say: This is Metaphysics; here you may find the noblest objects of this science, the knowledge of a highest Being, and of a future existence, proved from principles of pure reason. We can be shown indeed many judgments, demonstrably certain, and never questioned; but these are all analytical, and rather concern the materials and the scaffolding for Metaphysics, than the extension of knowledge, which is our proper object in studying it (§ 2). Even supposing you produce synthetical judgments (such as the law of Sufficient Reason, which you have never proved, as you ought to, from pure reason *a priori*, though we gladly concede its truth), you lapse when they come to be employed for your principal object, into such doubtful assertions, that in all ages one Metaphysics has contradicted another, either in its assertions, or their proofs, and thus has itself destroyed its own claim to lasting assent. Nay, the very attempts to set up such a science are the main cause

of the early appearance of scepticism, a mental attitude in which reason treats itself with such violence
that it could never have arisen save from complete
despair of ever satisfying our most important aspirations. For long before men began to inquire into nature methodically, they consulted abstract reason,
which had to some extent been exercised by means of
ordinary experience; for reason is ever present, while
laws of nature must usually be discovered with labor.
So Metaphysics floated to the surface, like foam, which
dissolved the moment it was scooped off. But immediately there appeared a new supply on the surface,
to be ever eagerly gathered up by some, while others,
instead of seeking in the depths the cause of the phenomenon, thought they showed their wisdom by ridi-
culing the idle labor of their neighbors.

The essential and distinguishing feature of pure
mathematical cognition among all other *a priori* cognitions is, that it cannot at all proceed from concepts,
but only by means of the construction of concepts
(see Critique II., Method of Transcendentalism,
chap. I., sect. 1). As therefore in its judgments it
must proceed beyond the concept to that which its
corresponding visualisation (*Anschauung*) contains,
these judgments neither can, nor ought to, arise analytically, by dissecting the concept, but are all synthetical.

I cannot refrain from pointing out the disadvan-
tage resulting to philosophy from the neglect of this
easy and apparently insignificant observation. Hume
being prompted (a task worthy of a philosopher) to
cast his eye over the whole field of *a priori* cognitions
in which human understanding claims such mighty
possessions, heedlessly severed from it a whole, and

indeed its most valuable, province, viz., pure mathematics; for he thought its nature, or, so to speak,
the state-constitution of this empire, depended on
totally different principles, namely, on the law of
contradiction alone; and although he did not divide
judgments in this manner formally and universally as
I have done here, what he said was equivalent to this:
that mathematics contains only analytical, but metaphysics synthetical, *a priori* judgments. In this, however, he was greatly mistaken, and the mistake had a
decidedly injurious effect upon his whole conception.
But for this, he would have extended his question
concerning the origin of our synthetical judgments
far beyond the metaphysical concept of Causality,
and included in it the possibility of mathematics *a
priori* also, for this latter he must have assumed to
be equally synthetical. And then he could not have
based his metaphysical judgments on mere experience
without subjecting the axioms of mathematics equally
to experience, a thing which he was far too acute to
do. The good company into which metaphysics would
thus have been brought, would have saved it from
the danger of a contemptuous ill-treatment, for the
thrust intended for it must have reached mathematics,
which was not and could not have been Hume's intention. Thus that acute man would have been led
into considerations which must needs be similar to
those that now occupy us, but which would have
gained inestimably ʏ v his inimitably elegant style.

Metaphysical judgments, properly so called, are all
synthetical. We must distinguish judgments pertaining to metaphysics from metaphysical judgments
properly so called. Many of the former are analytical,
but they only afford the means for metaphysical judg-

ments, which are the whole end of the science, and which are always synthetical. For if there be concepts pertaining to metaphysics (as, for example, that of substance), the judgments springing from simple analysis of them also pertain to metaphysics, as, for example, substance is that which only exists as subject; and by means of several such analytical judgments, we seek to approach the definition of the concept. But as the analysis of a pure concept of the understanding pertaining to metaphysics, does not proceed in any different manner from the dissection of any other, even empirical, concepts, not pertaining to metaphysics (such as: air is an elastic fluid, the elasticity of which is not destroyed by any known degree of cold), it follows that the concept indeed, but not the analytical judgment, is properly metaphysical. This science has something peculiar in the production of its *a priori* cognitions, which must therefore be distinguished from the features it has in common with other rational knowledge. Thus the judgment, that all the substance in things is permanent, is a synthetical and properly metaphysical judgment.

If the *a priori* principles, which constitute the materials of metaphysics, have first been collected according to fixed principles, then their analysis will be of great value; it might be taught as a particular part (as a *philosophia definitiva*), containing nothing but analytical judgments pertaining to metaphysics, and could be treated separately from the synthetical which constitute metaphysics proper. For indeed these analyses are not elsewhere of much value, except in metaphysics, i. e., as regards the synthetical judgments, which are to be generated by these previously analysed concepts.

The conclusion drawn in this section then is, that metaphysics is properly concerned with synthetical propositions *a priori*, and these alone constitute its end, for which it indeed requires various dissections of its concepts, viz., of its analytical judgments, but wherein the procedure is not different from that in every other kind of knowledge, in which we merely seek to render our concepts distinct by analysis. But the generation of *a priori* cognition by concrete images as well as by concepts, in fine of synthetical propositions *a priori* in philosophical cognition, constitutes the essential subject of Metaphysics.

Weary therefore as well of dogmatism, which teaches us nothing, as of scepticism, which does not even promise us anything, not even the quiet state of a contented ignorance; disquieted by the importance of knowledge so much needed; and lastly, rendered suspicious by long experience of all knowledge which we believe we possess, or which offers itself, under the title of pure reason: there remains but one critical question on the answer to which our future procedure depends, viz., *Is Metaphysics at all possible?* But this question must be answered not by sceptical objections to the asseverations of some actual system of metaphysics (for we do not as yet admit such a thing to exist), but from the conception, as yet only problematical, of a science of this sort.

In the *Critique of Pure Reason* I have treated this question synthetically, by making inquiries into pure reason itself, and endeavoring in this source to determine the elements as well as the laws of its pure use according to principles. The task is difficult, and requires a resolute reader to penetrate by degrees into a system, based on no data except reason itself, and which therefore seeks, without resting upon any fact, to unfold knowledge from its original germs. *Prolegomena*, however, are designed for preparatory exercises; they are intended rather to point out what we have to do in order if possible to actualise a science, than to propound it. They must therefore rest upon something already known as trustworthy, from which we can set out with confidence, and ascend to sources as yet unknown, the discovery of which will not only explain to us what we knew, but exhibit a sphere of many cognitions which all spring from the same sources. The method of *Prolegomena*, especially of those designed as a preparation for future metaphysics, is consequently analytical.

But it happens fortunately, that though we cannot assume metaphysics to be an actual science, we can say with confidence that certain pure *a priori* synthetical cognitions, pure Mathematics and pure Physics are actual and given; for both contain propositions, which are thoroughly recognised as apodeictically certain, partly by mere reason, partly by general consent arising from experience, and yet as independent of experience. We have therefore some at least uncontested synthetical knowledge *a priori*, and need not ask *whether* it be possible, for it is actual, but *how* it is possible, in order that we may deduce from the principle which makes the given cognitions possible the possibility of all the rest.

The General Problem: How is Cognition from Pure Reason Possible?

§ 5. We have above learned the significant distinction between analytical and synthetical judgments. The possibility of analytical propositions was easily comprehended, being entirely founded on the law or Contradiction. The possibility of synthetical *a posteriori* judgments, of those which are gathered from experience, also requires no particular explanation; for experience is nothing but a continual synthesis of perceptions. There remain therefore only synthetical propositions *a priori*, of which the possibility must be sought or investigated, because they must depend upon other principles than the law of contradiction.

But here we need not first establish the possibility of such propositions so as to ask whether they are possible. For there are enough of them which indeed are of undoubted certainty, and as our present method is analytical, we shall start from the fact, that such synthetical but purely rational cognition actually exists; but we must now inquire into the reason of this possibility, and ask, *how* such cognition is possible, in order that we may from the principles of its possibility be enabled to determine the conditions of its use, its sphere and its limits. The proper problem upon which all depends, when expressed with scholastic precision, is therefore:

How are Synthetic Propositions a priori possible?

For the sake of popularity I have above expressed this problem somewhat differently, as an inquiry into purely rational cognition, which I could do for once without detriment to the desired comprehension, because, as we have only to do here with metaphysics and its sources, the reader will, I hope, after the foregoing remarks, keep in mind that when we speak of purely rational cognition, we do not mean analytical, but synthetical cognition.[1]

1 It is unavoidable that as knowledge advances, certain expressions which have become classical, after having been used since the infancy of science,

Metaphysics stands or falls with the solution of this problem : its very existence depends upon it. Let any one make metaphysical assertions with ever so much plausibility, let him overwhelm us with conclusions, if he has not previously proved able to answer this question satisfactorily, I have a right to say: this is all vain baseless philosophy and false wisdom. You speak through pure reason, and claim, as it were to create cognitions *a priori* by not only dissecting given concepts, but also by asserting connexions which do not rest upon the law of contradiction, and which you believe you conceive quite independently of all experience ; how do you arrive at this, and how will you justify your pretensions? An appeal to the consent of the common sense of mankind cannot be allowed ; for that is a witness whose authority depends merely upon rumor. Says Horace :

"Quodcunque ostendis mihi sic, incredulus odi."

" To all that which thou provest me thus, I refuse to give credence."

The answer to this question, though indispensable, is difficult ; and though the principal reason that it was not made long ago is, that the possibility of the question never occurred to anybody, there is yet another reason, which is this that a satisfactory answer

will be found inadequate and unsuitable, and a newer and more appropriate application of the terms will give rise to confusion. [This is the case with the term "analytical."] The analytical method, so far as it is opposed to the synthetical, is very different from that which constitutes the essence of analytical propositions : it signifies only that we start from what is sought, as if it were given, and ascend to the only conditions under which it is possible. In this method we often use nothing but synthetical propositions, as in mathematical analysis, and it were better to term it the regressive method, in contradistinction to the synthetic or progressive. A principal part of Logic too is distinguished by the name of Analytics, which here signifies the logic of truth in contrast to Dialectics, without considering whether the cognitions belonging to it are analytical or synthetical.

to this one question requires a much more persistent, profound, and painstaking reflexion, than the most diffuse work on Metaphysics, which on its first appearance promised immortality to its author. And every intelligent reader, when he carefully reflects what this problem requires, must at first be struck with its difficulty, and would regard it as insoluble and even impossible, did there not actually exist pure synthetical cognitions *a priori*. This actually happened to David Hume, though he did not conceive the question in its entire universality as is done here, and as must be done, should the answer be decisive for all Metaphysics. For how is it possible, says that acute man, that when a concept is given me, I can go beyond it and connect with it another, which is not contained in it, in such a manner as if the latter necessarily belonged to the former? Nothing but experience can furnish us with such connexions (thus he concluded from the difficulty which he took to be an impossibility), and all that vaunted necessity, or, what is the same thing, all cognition assumed to be *a priori*, is nothing but a long habit of accepting something as true, and hence of mistaking subjective necessity for objective.

Should my reader complain of the difficulty and the trouble which I occasion him in the solution of this problem, he is at liberty to solve it himself in an easier way. Perhaps he will then feel under obligation to the person who has undertaken for him a labor of so profound research, and will rather be surprised at the facility with which, considering the nature of the subject, the solution has been attained. Yet it has cost years of work to solve the problem in its whole universality (using the term in the mathematical sense.

viz., for that which is sufficient for all cases), and finally to exhibit it in the analytical form, as the reader finds it here.

All metaphysicians are therefore solemnly and legally suspended from their occupations till they shall have answered in a satisfactory manner the question, "How are synthetic cognitions *a priori* possible?" For the answer contains the only credentials which they must show when they have anything to offer in the name of pure reason. But if they do not possess these credentials, they can expect nothing else of reasonable people, who have been deceived so often, than to be dismissed without further ado.

If they on the other hand desire to carry on their business, not as a science, but as an art of wholesome oratory suited to the common sense of man, they cannot in justice be prevented. They will then speak the modest language of a rational belief, they will grant that they are not allowed even to conjecture, far less to know, anything which lies beyond the bounds of all possible experience, but only to assume (not for speculative use, which they must abandon, but for practical purposes only) the existence of something that is possible and even indispensable for the guidance of the understanding and of the will in life. In this manner alone can they be called useful and wise men, and the more so as they renounce the title of metaphysicians; for the latter profess to be speculative philosophers, and since, when judgments *a priori* are under discussion, poor probabilities cannot be admitted (for what is declared to be known *a priori* is thereby announced as necessary), such men cannot be permitted to play with conjectures, but their assertions must be either science, or are worth nothing at all.

It may be said, that the entire transcendental philosophy, which necessarily precedes all metaphysics, is nothing but the complete solution of the problem here propounded, in systematical order and completeness, and hitherto we have never had any transcendental philosophy; for what goes by its name is properly a part of metaphysics, whereas the former science is intended first to constitute the possibility of the latter, and must therefore precede all metaphysics. And it is not surprising that when a whole science, deprived of all help from other sciences, and consequently in itself quite new, is required to answer a single question satisfactorily, we should find the answer troublesome and difficult, nay even shrouded in obscurity.

As we now proceed to this solution according to the analytical method, in which we assume that such cognitions from pure reasons actually exist, we can only appeal to two sciences of theoretical cognition (which alone is under consideration here), pure mathematics and pure natural science (physics). For these alone can exhibit to us objects in a definite and actualisable form (*in der Anschauung*), and consequently (if there should occur in them a cognition *a priori*) can show the truth or conformity of the cognition to the object *in concreto*, that is, its actuality, from which we could proceed to the reason of its possibility by the analytic method. This facilitates our work greatly for here universal considerations are not only applied to facts, but even start from them, while in a synthetic procedure they must strictly be derived *in abstracto* from concepts.

But, in order to rise from these actual and at the same time well-grounded pure cognitions *a priori* to

such a possible cognition of the same as we are seeking, viz., to metaphysics as a science, we must comprehend that which occasions it, I mean the mere
natural, though in spite of its truth not unsuspected,
cognition *a priori* which lies at the bottom of that science, the elaboration of which without any critical investigation of its possibility is commonly called metaphysics. In a word, we must comprehend the natural
conditions of such a science as a part of our inquiry,
and thus the transcendental problem will be gradually
answered by a division into four questions :

1. *How is pure mathematics possible?*
2. *How is pure natural science possible?*
3. *How is metaphysics in general possible?*
4. *How is metaphysics as a science possible?*

It may be seen that the solution of these problems,
though chiefly designed to exhibit the essential matter
of the Critique, has yet something peculiar, which for
itself alone deserves attention. This is the search for
the sources of given sciences in reason itself, so that
its faculty of knowing something *a priori* may by its
own deeds be investigated and measured. By this
procedure these sciences gain, if not with regard to
their contents, yet as to their proper use, and while
they throw light on the higher question concerning
their common origin, they give, at the same time, an
occasion better to explain their own nature.

FIRST PART OF THE TRANSCEN-
DENTAL PROBLEM.

HOW IS PURE MATHEMATICS POSSIBLE?

§ 6.

HERE is a great and established branch of knowledge, encompassing even now a wonderfully
large domain and promising an unlimited extension in
the future. Yet it carries with it thoroughly apodeictical certainty, i. e., absolute necessity, which therefore
rests upon no empirical grounds. Consequently it is
a pure product of reason, and moreover is thoroughly
synthetical. [Here the question arises:]

"How then is it possible for human reason to produce a cognition of this nature entirely *a priori?*"

Does not this faculty [which produces mathemat-
ics], as it neither is nor can be based upon experience, presuppose some ground of cognition *a priori*,
which lies deeply hidden, but which might reveal itself by these its effects, if their first beginnings were
but diligently ferreted out?

§ 7. But we find that all mathematical cognition
has this peculiarity: it must first exhibit its concept
in a visual form (*Anschauung*) and indeed *a priori*,
therefore in a visual form which is not empirical, but
pure. Without this mathematics cannot take a single
step; hence its judgments are always visual, viz.,

"intuitive"; whereas philosophy must be satisfied with discursive judgments from mere concepts, and though it may illustrate its doctrines through a visual figure, can never derive them from it. This observation on the nature of mathematics gives us a clue to the first and highest condition of its possibility, which is, that some non-sensuous visualisation (called pure intuition, or *reine Anschauung*) must form its basis, in which all its concepts can be exhibited or constructed, *in concreto* and yet *a priori*. If we can find out this pure intuition and its possibility, we may thence easily explain how synthetical propositions *a priori* are possible in pure mathematics, and consequently how this science itself is possible. Empirical intuition [viz., sense-perception] enables us without difficulty to enlarge the concept which we frame of an object of intuition [or sense-perception], by new predicates, which intuition [i. e., sense-perception] itself presents synthetically in experience. Pure intuition [viz., the visualisation of forms in our imagination, from which every thing sensual, i. e., every thought of material qualities, is excluded] does so likewise, only with this difference, that in the latter case the synthetical judgment is *a priori* certain and apodeictical, in the former, only *a posteriori* and empirically certain; because this latter contains only that which occurs in contingent empirical intuition, but the former, that which must necessarily be discovered in pure intuition. Here intuition, being an intuition *a priori*, is *before all experience*, viz., before any perception of particular objects, inseparably conjoined with its concept.

§ 8. But with this step our perplexity seems rather to increase than to lessen. For the question now

is, "How is it possible to intuite [in a visual form]
anything *a priori?*" An intuition [viz., a visual sense-
perception] is such a representation as immediately
depends upon the presence of the object.   Hence it
seems impossible to intuite from the outset *a priori*, because intuition would in that event take place without
either a former or a present object to refer to, and by
consequence could not be intuition.   Concepts indeed
are such, that we can easily form some of them *a
priori*, viz., such as contain nothing but the thought
of an object in general; and we need not find ourselves in an immediate relation to the object.   Take,
for instance, the concepts of Quantity, of Cause, etc.
But even these require, in order to make them understood, a certain concrete use—that is, an application
to some sense-experience (*Anschauung*), by which an
object of them is given us.   But how can the intuition of the object [its visualisation] precede the object itself?

§ 9. If our intuition [i. e., our sense-experience]
were perforce of such a nature as to represent things
as they are in themselves, there would not be any intuition *a priori*, but intuition would be always empirical. For I can only know what is contained in the object in itself when it is present and given to me.   It is
indeed even then incomprehensible how the visualising (*Anschauung*) of a present thing should make me
know this thing as it is in itself, as its properties cannot migrate into my faculty of representation.   But
even granting this possibility, a visualising of that
sort would not take place *a priori*, that is, before the
object were presented to me; for without this latter
fact no reason of a relation between my representa-

tion and the object can be imagined, unless it depend upon a direct inspiration.

Therefore in one way only can my intuition (*Anschauung*) anticipate the actuality of the object, and be a cognition *a priori*, viz.: if my intuition contains nothing but the form of sensibility, antedating in my subjectivity all the actual impressions through which I am affected by objects. For that objects of sense can only be intuited according to this form of sensibility I can know *a priori*. Hence it follows: that propositions, which concern this form of sensuous intuition only, are possible and valid for objects of the senses; as also, conversely, that intuitions which are possible *a priori* can never concern any other things than objects of our senses.[1]

§ 10. Accordingly, it is only the form of sensuous intuition by which we can intuite things *a priori*, but by which we can know objects only as they *appear* to us (to our senses), not as they are in themselves; and this assumption is absolutely necessary if synthetical propositions *a priori* be granted as possible, or if, in case they actually occur, their possibility is to be comprehended and determined beforehand.

Now, the intuitions which pure mathematics lays at the foundation of all its cognitions and judgments which appear at once apodeictic and necessary are Space and Time. For mathematics must first have all its concepts in intuition, and pure mathematics in pure intuition, that is, it must construct them. If it proceeded in any other way, it would be impossible to make any headway, for mathematics proceeds, not

1 This whole paragraph (§ 9) will be better understood when compared with Remark I., following this section, appearing in the present edition on page 40.—*Ed.*

analytically by dissection of concepts, but synthetically, and if pure intuition be wanting, there is nothing
in which the matter for synthetical judgments *a priori*
can be given. Geometry is based upon the pure intuition of space. Arithmetic accomplishes its concept
of number by the successive addition of units in time;
and pure mechanics especially cannot attain its concepts of motion without employing the representation
of time. Both representations, however, are only intuitions; for if we omit from the empirical intuitions
of bodies and their alterations (motion) everything
empirical, or belonging to sensation, space and time
still remain, which are therefore pure intuitions that
lie *a priori* at the basis of the empirical. Hence they
can never be omitted, but at the same time, by their
being pure intuitions *a priori*, they prove that they are
mere forms of our sensibility, which must precede all
empirical intuition, or perception of actual objects,
and conformably to which objects can be known *a
priori*, but only as they appear to us.

§ 11. The problem of the present section is therefore solved. Pure mathematics, as synthetical cognition *a priori*, is only possible by referring to no other
objects than those of the senses. At the basis of their
empirical intuition lies a pure intuition (of space and
of time) which is *a priori*. This is possible, because
the latter intuition is nothing but the mere form of
sensibility, which precedes the actual appearance of
the objects, in that it, in fact, makes them possible.
Yet this faculty of intuiting *a priori* affects not the
matter of the phenomenon (that is, the sense-element
in it, for this constitutes that which is empirical), but
its form, viz., space and time. Should any man venture to doubt that these are determinations adhering

not to things in themselves, but to their relation to
our sensibility, I should be glad to know how it can
be possible to know the constitution of things *a priori*,
viz., before we have any acquaintance with them and
before they are presented to us. Such, however, is
the case with space and time. But this is quite comprehensible as soon as both count for nothing more
than formal conditions of our sensibility, while the
objects count merely as phenomena ; for then the form
of the phenomenon, i. e., pure intuition, can by all
means be represented as proceeding from ourselves,
that is, *a priori*.

§ 12. In order to add something by way of illus-
tration and confirmation, we need only watch the
ordinary and necessary procedure of geometers. All
proofs of the complete congruence of two given figures (where the one can in every respect be substi-
tuted for the other) come ultimately to this that they
may be made to coincide; which is evidently nothing else than a synthetical proposition resting upon
immediate intuition, and this intuition must be pure,
or given *a priori*, otherwise the proposition could not
rank as apodeictically certain, but would have empirical certainty only. In that case, it could only be
said that it is always found to be so, and holds good
only as far as our perception reaches. That everywhere space (which [in its entirety] is itself no longer
the boundary of another space) has three dimensions,
and that space cannot in any way have more, is based
on the proposition that not more than three lines can
intersect at right angles in one point; but this proposition cannot by any means be shown from concepts,
but rests immediately on intuition, and indeed on pure
and *a priori* intuition, because it is apodeictically cer-

tain. That we can require a line to be drawn to infinity (*in indefinitum*), or that a series of changes (for
example, spaces traversed by motion) shall be infinitely continued, presupposes a representation of
space and time, which can only attach to intuition,
namely, so far as it in itself is bounded by nothing,
for from concepts it could never be inferred. Consequently, the basis of mathematics actually are pure
intuitions, which make its synthetical and apodeictically valid propositions possible. Hence our transcendental deduction of the notions of space and of
time explains at the same time the possibility of pure
mathematics. Without some such deduction its truth
may be granted, but its existence could by no means
be understood, and we must assume "that everything
which can be given to our senses (to the external
senses in space, to the internal one in time) is intuited
by us as it appears to us, not as it is in itself."

§ 13. Those who cannot yet rid themselves of the
notion that space and time are actual qualities inhering in things in themselves, may exercise their acumen
on the following paradox. When they have in vain
attempted its solution, and are free from prejudices
at least for a few moments, they will suspect that the
degradation of space and of time to mere forms of
our sensuous intuition may perhaps be well founded.

If two things are quite equal in all respects as
much as can be ascertained by all means possible,
quantitatively and qualitatively, it must follow, that
the one can in all cases and under all circumstances
replace the other, and this substitution would not occasion the least perceptible difference. This in fact
is true of plane figures in geometry; but some spherical figures exhibit, notwithstanding a complete in-

ternal agreement, such a contrast in their external relation, that the one figure cannot possibly be put in the place of the other. For instance, two spherical triangles on opposite hemispheres, which have an arc of the equator as their common base, may be quite equal, both as regards sides and angles, so that nothing is to be found in either, if it be described for itself alone and completed, that would not equally be applicable to both; and yet the one cannot be put in the place of the other (being situated upon the opposite hemisphere). Here then is an internal difference between the two triangles, which difference our understanding cannot describe as internal, and which only manifests itself by external relations in space.

But I shall adduce examples, taken from common life, that are more obvious still.

What can be more similar in every respect and in every part more alike to my hand and to my ear, than their images in a mirror? And yet I cannot put such a hand as is seen in the glass in the place of its archetype; for if this is a right hand, that in the glass is a left one, and the image or reflexion of the right ear is a left one which never can serve as a substitute for the other. There are in this case no internal differences which our understanding could determine by thinking alone. Yet the differences are internal as the senses teach, for, notwithstanding their complete equality and similarity, the left hand cannot be enclosed in the same bounds as the right one (they are not congruent); the glove of one hand cannot be used for the other. What is the solution? These objects are not representations of things as they are in themselves, and as the pure understanding would cognise them, but sensuous intuitions, that is, appearances, the possibility of which rests upon the relation of certain things unknown in themselves to something else, viz., to our sensibility. Space is the form of the external intuition of this sensibility, and the internal determination of every space is only possible by the determination of its external relation to the whole space, of which it is a part (in other words, by its relation to the external sense). That is to say, the part is only possible through the whole, which is never the case with things in themselves, as objects of the mere understanding, but with appearances only. Hence the difference between similar and equal things, which are yet not congruent (for instance, two symmetric helices), cannot be made intelligible by any concept, but only by the relation to the right and the left hands which immediately refers to intuition.

Remark I.

Pure Mathematics, and especially pure geometry, can only have objective reality on condition that they refer to objects of sense. But in regard to the latter the principle holds good, that our sense representation is not a representation of things in themselves, but of the way in which they appear to us. Hence it follows, that the propositions of geometry are not the results of a mere creation of our poetic imagination, and that therefore they cannot be referred with assurance to actual objects; but rather that they are necessarily valid of space, and consequently of all that may be found in space, because space is nothing else than the form of all external appearances, and it is this form alone in which objects of sense can be given. Sensibility, the form of which is the basis of geometry, is that upon which the possibility of external appearance depends.   Therefore these appearances can never contain anything but what geometry prescribes to them.

It would be quite otherwise if the senses were so constituted as to represent objects as they are in themselves.   For then it would not by any means follow from the conception of space, which with all its properties serves to the geometer as an *a priori* foundation, together with what is thence inferred, must be so in nature.   The space of the geometer would be considered a mere fiction, and it would not be credited with objective validity, because we cannot see how things must of necessity agree with an image of them, which we make spontaneously and previous to our acquaintance with them.   But if this image, or rather this formal intuition, is the essential property of our sensibility, by means of which alone objects are given to us, and if this sensibility represents not things in themselves, but their appearances: we shall easily comprehend, and at the same time indisputably prove, that all external objects of our world of sense must necessarily coincide in the most rigorous way with the propositions of geometry; because sensibility by means of its form of external intuition, viz., by space, the same with which the geometer is occupied, makes those objects at all possible as mere appearances.

It will always remain a remarkable phenomenon in the history of philosophy, that there was a time, when even mathematicians, who at the same time were philosophers, began to doubt, not of the accuracy of their geometrical propositions so far as they concerned space, but of their objective validity and the applicability of this concept itself, and of all its corol laries, to nature. They showed much concern whether a line in nature might not consist of physical points, and consequently that true space in the object might consist of simple [discrete] parts, while the space which the geometer has in his mind [being continuous] cannot be such. They did not recognise that this mental space renders possible the physical space, i. e., the extension of matter; that this pure space is not at all a quality of things in themselves, but a form of our sensuous faculty of representation; and that all objects in space are mere appearances, i. e., not things in themselves but representations of our sensuous intuition. But such is the case, for the space of the geometer is exactly the form of sensuous intuition which we find *a priori* in us, and contains the ground of the possibility of all external appearances (according to their form), and the latter must necessarily and most rigidly agree with the propositions of the geometer, which he draws not from any fictitious concept, but from the subjective basis of all external phenomena, which is sensibility itself. In this and no other way can geometry be made secure as to the undoubted objective reality of its propositions against all the intrigues of a shallow Metaphysics, which is surprised at them [the geometrical propositions], because it has not traced them to the sources of their concepts.

REMARK II.

Whatever is given us as object, must be given us in intuition. All our intuition however takes place by means of the senses only; the understanding intuites nothing, but only reflects. And as we have just shown that the senses never and in no manner enable us to know things in themselves, but only their appearances, which are mere representations of the sensibility, we conclude that 'all bodies, together with the space in which they are, must be considered nothing but mere representations in us, and exist nowhere but in our thoughts.' You will say: Is not this manifest idealism?

Idealism consists in the assertion, that there are none but thinking beings, all other things, which we think are perceived in intuition, being nothing but representations in the thinking beings, to which no object external to them corresponds in fact. Whereas I say, that things as objects of our senses existing outside us are given, but we know nothing of what they may be in themselves, knowing only their appearances, i. e., the representations which they cause in us by affecting our senses. Consequently I grant by all means that there are bodies without us, that is, things which, though quite unknown to us as to what they are in themselves, we yet know by the representations which their influence on our sensibility procures us, and which we call bodies, a term signifying merely the appearance of the thing which is unknown to us, but not therefore less actual. Can this be termed idealism? It is the very contrary.

Long before Locke's time, but assuredly since him, it has been generally assumed and granted without detriment to the actual existence of external things, that many of their predicates may be said to belong not to the things in themselves, but to their appearances, and to have no proper existence outside our representation. Heat, color, and taste, for instance, are of this kind. Now, if I go farther, and for weighty reasons rank as mere appearances the remaining qualities of bodies also, which are called primary, such as extension, place, and in general space, with all that which belongs to it (impenetrability or materiality, space, etc.)—no one in the least can adduce the reason of its being inadmissible. As little as the man who admits colors not to be properties of the object in itself, but only as modifications of the sense of sight, should on that account be called an idealist, so little can my system be named idealistic, merely because I find that more, nay,

All the properties which constitute the intuition of a body belong merely to its appearance.

The existence of the thing that appears is thereby not destroyed, as in genuine idealism, but it is only shown, that we cannot possibly know it by the senses as it is in itself.

I should be glad to know what my assertions must be in order to avoid all idealism. Undoubtedly, I should say, that the representation of space is not only perfectly conformable to the relation which our sensibility has to objects—that I have said—but that it is quite similar to the object,—an assertion in which I can find as little meaning as if I said that the sensation of red has a similarity to the property of vermilion, which in me excites this sensation.

Remark III.

Hence we may at once dismiss an easily foreseen but futile objection, "that by admitting the ideality of space and of time the whole sensible world would be turned into mere sham." At first all philosophical insight into the nature of sensuous cognition was spoiled, by making the sensibility merely a confused mode of representation, according to which we still know things as they are, but without being able to reduce everything in this our representation to a clear consciousness; whereas proof is offered by us that sensibility consists, not in this logical distinction of clearness and obscurity, but in the genetical one of the origin of cognition itself. For sensuous perception represents things not at all as they are, but only the mode in which they affect our senses, and consequently by sensuous perception appearances only and not things themselves are given to the understanding for reflexion. After this necessary corrective, an objection rises from an unpardonable and almost intentional misconception, as if my doctrine turned all the things of the world of sense into mere illusion.

When an appearance is given us, we are still quite free as to how we should judge the matter. The appearance depends upon the senses, but the judgment upon the understanding, and the only question is, whether in the determination of the object there is truth or not. But the difference between truth and dreaming is not ascertained by the nature of the representations, which are referred to objects (for they are the same in both cases), but by their connexion according to those rules, which determine the coherence of the representations in the concept of an object, and by ascertaining whether they can subsist together in experience or not. And it is not the fault of the appearances if our cognition takes illusion for truth, i. e., if the intuition, by which an object is given us, is considered a concept of the thing or of its existence also, which the understanding can only think. The senses represent to us the paths of the planets as now progressive, now retrogressive, and herein is neither falsehood nor truth, because as long as we hold this path to be nothing but appearance, we do not judge of the objective nature of their motion. But as a false judgment may easily arise when the understanding is not on its guard against this subjective mode of representation being considered objective, we say they appear to move backward; it is not the senses however which must be charged with the illusion, but the understanding, whose province alone it is to give an objective judgment on appearances.

Thus, even if we did not at all reflect on the origin of our representations, whenever we connect our intuitions of sense (whatever they may contain), in space and in time, according to the rules of the coherence of all cognition in experience, illusion or truth will arise according as we are negligent or careful. It is merely a question of the use of sensuous representations in the understanding, and not of their origin. In the same way, if I consider all the representations of the senses, together with their form, space and time, to be nothing but appearances, and space and time to be a mere form of the sensibility, which is not to be met with in objects out of it, and if I make use of these representations in reference to possible experience only, there is nothing in my regarding them as appearances that can lead astray or cause illusion. For all that they can correctly cohere according to rules of truth in experience. Thus all the propositions of geometry hold good of space as well as of all the objects of the senses, consequently of all possible experience, whether I consider space as a mere form of the sensibility, or as something cleaving to the things themselves. In the former case however I comprehend how I can know *a priori* these propositions concerning all the objects of external intuition. Otherwise, everything else as regards all possible experience remains just as if I had not departed from the vulgar view.

But if I venture to go beyond all possible experience with my notions of space and time, which I cannot refrain from doing if I proclaim them qualities inherent in things in themselves (for what should prevent me from letting them hold good of the same things, even though my senses might be different, and unsuited to them?), then a grave error may arise due to illusion, for thus I would proclaim to be universally valid what is merely a subjective condition of the intuition of things and sure only for all objects of sense, viz., for all possible experience; I would refer this condition to things in themselves, and do not limit it to the conditions of experience.

My doctrine of the ideality of space and of time, therefore, far from reducing the whole sensible world to mere illusion, is the only means of securing the application of one of the most important cognitions (that which mathematics propounds *a priori*) to actual objects, and of preventing its being regarded as mere illusion. For without this observation it would be quite impossible to make out whether the intuitions of space and time, which we borrow from no experience, and which yet lie in our representation *a priori*, are not mere phantasms of our brain, to which objects do not correspond, at least not adequately, and consequently, whether we have been able to show its unquestionable validity with regard to all the objects of the sensible world just because they are mere appearances.

Secondly, though these my principles make appearances of the representations of the senses, they are so far from turning the truth of experience into mere illusion, that they are rather the only means of preventing the transcendental illusion, by which metaphysics has hitherto been deceived, leading to the childish endeavor of catching at bubbles, because appearances, which are mere representations, were taken for things in themselves. Here originated the remarkable event of the antimony of Reason which I shall mention by and by, and which is destroyed by the single observation, that appearance, as long as it is employed in experience, produces truth, but the moment it transgresses the bounds of experience, and consequently becomes transcendent, produces nothing but illusion.

Inasmuch, therefore, as I leave to things as we obtain them by the senses their actuality, and only limit our sensuous intuition of these things to this, that they represent in no respect, not even in the pure intuitions of space and of time, anything more than mere appearance of those things, but never their constitution in themselves, this is not a sweeping illusion invented for nature by me. My protestation too against all charges of idealism is so valid and clear as even to seem superfluous, were there not incompetent judges, who, while they would have an old name for every deviation from their perverse though common opinion, and never judge of the spirit of philosophic nomenclature, but cling to the letter only, are ready to put their own conceits in the place of well-defined notions, and thereby deform and distort them. I have myself given this my theory the name of transcendental idealism, but that cannot authorise any one to confound it either with the empirical idealism of Descartes, (indeed, his was only an insoluble problem, owing to which he thought every one at liberty to deny the existence of the corporeal world, because it could never be proved satisfactorily), or with the mystical and visionary idealism of Berkeley, against which and other similar phantasms our Critique contains the proper antidote. My idealism concerns not the existence of things (the doubting of which, however, constitutes idealism in the ordinary sense), since it never came into my head to doubt it, but it concerns the sensuous representation of things, to which space and time especially belong. Of these [viz., space and time], consequently of all appearances in general, I have only shown, that they are neither things (but mere modes of representation), nor determinations belonging to things in themselves. But the word "transcendental," which with me means a reference of our cognition, i. e., not to things, but only to the cognitive faculty, was meant to obviate this misconception. Yet rather than give further occasion to it by this word, I now retract it, and desire this idealism of mine to be called critical. But if it be really an objectionable idealism to convert actual things (not appearances) into mere representations, by what name shall we call him who conversely changes mere representations to things? It may, I think, be called "dreaming idealism," in contradistinction to the former, which may be called "visionary," both of which are to be refuted by my transcendental, or, better, critical idealism.

SECOND PART OF THE TRANSCEN-
DENTAL PROBLEM.

HOW IS THE SCIENCE OF NATURE POSSIBLE?

§ 14.

NATURE is the existence of things, so far as it is determined according to universal laws. Should nature signify the existence of things in themselves, we could never cognise it either *a priori* or *a posteriori*. Not *a priori*, for how can we know what belongs to things in themselves, since this never can be done by the dissection of our concepts (in analytical judgments)? We do not want to know what is contained in our concept of a thing (for the [concept describes what] belongs to its logical being), but what is in the actuality of the thing superadded to our concept, and by what the thing itself is determined in its existence outside the concept. Our understanding, and the conditions on which alone it can connect the determinations of things in their existence, do not prescribe any rule to things themselves; these do not conform to our understanding, but it must conform itself to them; they must therefore be first given us in order to gather these determinations from them, wherefore they would not be cognised *a priori*.

A cognition of the nature of things in themselves *a posteriori* would be equally impossible. For, if experience is to teach us laws, to which the existence of things is subject, these laws, if they regard things in themselves, must belong to them of necessity even outside our experience. But experience teaches us what exists and how it exists, but never that it must necessarily exist so and not otherwise. Experience therefore can never teach us the nature of things in themselves.

§ 15. We nevertheless actually possess a pure science of nature in which are propounded, *a priori* and with all the necessity requisite to apodeictical propositions, laws to which nature is subject. I need only call to witness that propædeutic of natural science which, under the title of the universal Science of Nature, precedes all Physics (which is founded upon empirical principles). In it we have Mathematics applied to appearance, and also merely discursive principles (or those derived from concepts), which constitute the philosophical part of the pure cognition of nature. But there are several things in it, which are not quite pure and independent of empirical sources: such as the concept of *motion*, that of *impenetrability* (upon which the empirical concept of matter rests), that of *inertia*, and many others, which prevent its being called a perfectly pure science of nature. Besides, it only refers to objects of the external sense, and therefore does not give an example of a universal science of nature, in the strict sense, for such a science must reduce nature in general, whether it regards the object of the external or that of the internal sense (the object of Physics as well as Psychology), to universal laws. But among the principles of this universal physics there are a few which actually have the required universality; for instance, the proposi-

tions that "substance is permanent," and that "every
event is determined by a cause according to constant
laws," etc.   These are actually universal laws of nature, which subsist completely *a priori*.   There is then
in fact a pure science of nature, and the question
arises, *How is it possible?*

§ 16.   The word "nature" assumes yet another
meaning, which determines the object, whereas in the
former sense it only denotes the conformity to law
[*Gesetzmässigkeit*] of the determinations of the existence of things generally.   If we consider it *materialiter*
(i. e., in the matter that forms its objects) "nature is
the complex of all the objects of experience."   And
with this only are we now concerned, for besides,
things which can never be objects of experience, if
they must be cognised as to their nature, would oblige
us to have recourse to concepts whose meaning could
never be given *in concreto* (by any example of possible
experience).   Consequently we must form for ourselves
a list of concepts of their nature, the reality whereof
(i. e., whether they actually refer to objects, or are
mere creations of thought) could never be determined.
The cognition of what cannot be an object of experience would be hyperphysical, and with things hyperphysical we are here not concerned, but only with
the cognition of nature, the actuality of which can be
confirmed by experience, though it [the cognition of
nature] is possible *a priori* and precedes all experience.

§ 17.   The formal [aspect] of nature in this narrower sense is therefore the conformity to law of all
the objects of experience, and so far as it is cognised
a priori, their necessary conformity.   But it has just
been shown that the laws of nature can never be cog-

nised *a priori* in objects so far as they are considered not in reference to possible experience, but as things in themselves. And our inquiry here extends not to things in themselves (the properties of which we pass by), but to things as objects of possible experience, and the complex of these is what we properly designate as nature. And now I ask, when the possibility of a cognition of nature *a priori* is in question, whether it is better to arrange the problem thus: How can we cognise *a priori* that things as objects of experience necessarily conform to law? or thus: How is it possible to cognise *a priori* the necessary conformity to law of experience itself as regards all its objects generally?

Closely considered, the solution of the problem, represented in either way, amounts, with regard to the pure cognition of nature (which is the point of the question at issue), entirely to the same thing. For the subjective laws, under which alone an empirical cognition of things is possible, hold good of these things, as objects of possible experience (not as things in themselves, which are not considered here). Either of the following statements means quite the same:

A judgment of observation can never rank as experience, without the law, that "whenever an event is observed, it is always referred to some antecedent, which it follows according to a universal rule."

"Everything, of which experience teaches that it happens, must have a cause."

It is, however, more commendable to choose the first formula. For we can *a priori* and previous to all given objects have a cognition of those conditions, on which alone experience is possible, but never of the laws to which things may in themselves be subject, without reference to possible experience. We cannot therefore study the nature of things *a priori* otherwise than by investigating the conditions and the universal (though subjective) laws, under which alone such a cognition as experience (as to mere form) is possible, and we determine accordingly the possibility of things, as objects of experience. For if I should choose the second formula, and seek the conditions *a priori*, on which nature as an object of experience is possible, I might easily fall into error, and fancy that I was speaking of nature as a thing in itself, and then move round in endless circles, in a vain search for laws concerning things of which nothing is given me.

Accordingly we shall here be concerned with experience only, and the universal conditions of its possibility which are given *a priori*. Thence we shall determine nature as the whole object of all possible experience. I think it will be understood that I here do not mean the rules of the observation of a nature that is already given, for these already presuppose experience. I do not mean how (through experience) we can study the laws of nature; for these would not then be laws *a priori*, and would yield us no pure science of nature; but [I mean to ask] how the conditions *a priori* of the possibility of experience are at the same time the sources from which all the universal laws of nature must be derived.

§ 18. In the first place we must state that, while all judgments of experience (*Erfahrungsurtheile*) are empirical (i. e., have their ground in immediate sense-perception), *vice versa*, all empirical judgments (*empirische Urtheile*) are not judgments of experience, but, besides the empirical, and in general besides what is given to the sensuous intuition, particular concepts must yet be superadded—concepts which have their origin quite *a priori* in the pure under-standing, and under which every perception must be first of all subsumed and then by their means changed into experience.[1]

Empirical judgments, so far as they have objective validity, are **judgments of experience**; but those which are only subjectively valid, I name mere **judgments of perception**. The latter require no pure concept of the understanding, but only the logical connexion of perception in a thinking subject. But the former always require, besides the representation of the sensuous intuition, particular *concepts originally begotten in the understanding*, which produce the objective validity of the judgment of experience.

All our judgments are at first merely judgments of perception; they hold good only for us (i. e., for our subject), and we do not till afterwards give them a new reference (to an object), and desire that they shall always hold good for us and in the same way for everybody else; for when a judgment agrees with an object, all judgments concerning the same object must likewise agree among themselves, and thus the objective validity of the judgment of experience signifies nothing else than its necessary universality of application. And conversely when we have reason to consider a judgment necessarily universal (which never depends upon perception, but upon the pure concept of the understanding, under which the perception is subsumed), we must consider it objective

[1] Empirical judgments (*empirische Urtheile*) are either mere statements of fact, viz., records of a perception, or statements of a natural law, implying a causal connexion between two facts. The former Kant calls "judgments of perception" (*Wahrnehmungsurtheile*), the latter "judgments of experience" (*Erfahrungsurtheile*).—*Ed.*

also, that is, that it expresses not merely a reference
of our perception to a subject, but a quality of the
object.   For there would be no reason for the judgments of other men necessarily agreeing with mine, if
it were not the unity of the object to which they all
refer, and with which they accord ; hence they must
all agree with one another.

§ 19. Therefore objective validity and necessary
universality (for everybody) are equivalent terms, and
though we do not know the object in itself, yet when
we consider a judgment as universal, and also necessary, we understand it to have objective validity.   By
this judgment we cognise the object (though it remains
unknown as it is in itself) by the universal and necessary connexion of the given perceptions.   As this is
the case with all objects of sense, judgments of experience take their objective validity not from the immediate cognition of the object (which is impossible),
but from the condition of universal validity in empirical judgments, which, as already said, never rests
upon empirical, or, in short, sensuous conditions, but
upon a pure concept of the understanding.   The object always remains unknown in itself ; but when by
the concept of the understanding the connexion of the
representations of the object, which are given to our
sensibility, is determined as universally valid, the object is determined by this relation, and it is the judgment that is objective.

To illustrate the matter : When we say, "the room
is warm, sugar sweet, and wormwood bitter,"[1]—we

---

[1] I freely grant that these examples do not represent such judgments of
perception as ever could become judgments of experience, even though a
concept of the understanding were superadded, because they refer merely
to feeling, which everybody knows to be merely subjective, and which of
course can never be attributed to the object, and consequently never become

have only subjectively valid judgments. I do not at all expect that I or any other person shall always find it as I now do; each of these sentences only expresses a relation of two sensations to the same subject, to myself, and that only in my present state of perception; consequently they are not valid of the object. Such are judgments of perception. Judgments of experience are of quite a different nature. What experience teaches me under certain circumstances, it must always teach me and everybody; and its validity is not limited to the subject nor to its state at a particular time. Hence I pronounce all such judgments as being objectively valid. For instance, when I say the air is elastic, this judgment is as yet a judgment of perception only—I do nothing but refer two of my sensations to one another. But, if I would have it called a judgment of experience, I require this connexion to stand under a condition, which makes it universally valid. I desire therefore that I and everybody else should always connect necessarily the same perceptions under the same circumstances.

§ 20. We must consequently analyse experience in order to see what is contained in this product of the senses and of the understanding, and how the judgment of experience itself is possible. The foundation is the intuition of which I become conscious, i. e., perception (*perceptio*), which pertains merely to the senses. But in the next place, there are acts of judging (which belong only to the understanding). But this judging may be twofold—first, I may merely

objective. I only wished to give here an example of a judgment that is merely subjectively valid, containing no ground for universal validity, and thereby for a relation to the object. An example of the judgments of perception, which become judgments of experience by superadded concepts of the understanding, will be given in the next note.

compare perceptions and connect them in a particular state of my consciousness; or, secondly, I may connect them in consciousness generally. The former judgment is merely a judgment of perception, and of subjective validity only: it is merely a connexion of perceptions in my mental state, without reference to the object. Hence it is not, as is commonly imagined, enough for experience to compare perceptions and to connect them in consciousness through judgment; there arises no universality and necessity, for which alone judgments can become objectively valid and be called experience.

Quite another judgment therefore is required before perception can become experience. The given intuition must be subsumed under a concept, which determines the form of judging in general relatively to the intuition, connects its empirical consciousness in consciousness generally, and thereby procures universal validity for empirical judgments. A concept of this nature is a pure *a priori* concept of the Understanding, which does nothing but determine for an intuition the general way in which it can be used for judgments. Let the concept be that of cause, then it determines the intuition which is subsumed under it, e. g., that of air, relative to judgments in general, viz., the concept of air serves with regard to its expansion in the relation of antecedent to consequent in a hypothetical judgment. The concept of cause accordingly is a pure concept of the understanding, which is totally disparate from all possible perception, and only serves to determine the representation subsumed under it, relatively to judgments in general, and so to make a universally valid judgment possible.

Before, therefore, a judgment of perception can

become a judgment of experience, it is requisite that the perception should be subsumed under some such a concept of the understanding; for instance, air ranks under the concept of causes, which determines our judgment about it in regard to its expansion as hypothetical.[1] Thereby the expansion of the air is represented not as merely belonging to the perception of the air in my present state or in several states of mine, or in the state of perception of others, but as belonging to it necessarily. The judgment, "the air is elastic," becomes universally valid, and a judgment of experience, only by certain judgments preceding it, which subsume the intuition of air under the concept of cause and effect: and they thereby determine the perceptions not merely as regards one another in me, but relatively to the form of judging in general, which is here hypothetical, and in this way they render the empirical judgment universally valid.

If all our synthetical judgments are analysed so far as they are objectively valid, it will be found that they never consist of mere intuitions connected only (as is commonly believed) by comparison into a judgment; but that they would be impossible were not a pure concept of the understanding superadded to the concepts abstracted from intuition, under which concept these latter are subsumed, and in this manner only combined into an objectively valid judgment.

[1] As an easier example, we may take the following: "When the sun shines on the stone, it grows warm." This judgment, however often I and others may have perceived it, is a mere judgment of perception, and contains no necessity; perceptions are only usually conjoined in this manner. But if I say, "The sun warms the stone," I add to the perception a concept of the understanding, viz., that of cause, which connects with the concept of sunshine that of heat as a necessary consequence, and the synthetical judgment becomes of necessity universally valid, viz., objective, and is converted from a perception into experience.

Even the judgments of pure mathematics in their simplest axioms are not exempt from this condition. The principle, "a straight line is the shortest between two points," presupposes that the line is subsumed under the concept of quantity, which certainly is no mere intuition, but has its seat in the understanding alone, and serves to determine the intuition (of the line) with regard to the judgments which may be made about it, relatively to their quantity, that is, to plurality (as *judicia plurativa*).[1] For under them it is understood that in a given intuition there is contained a plurality of homogenous parts.

§ 21. To prove, then, the possibility of experience so far as it rests upon pure concepts of the understanding *a priori*, we must first represent what belongs to judgments in general and the various functions of the understanding, in a complete table. For the pure concepts of the understanding must run parallel to these functions, as such concepts are nothing more than concepts of intuitions in general, so far as these are determined by one or other of these functions of judging, in themselves, that is, necessarily and universally. Hereby also the *a priori* principles of the possibility of all experience, as of an objectively valid empirical cognition, will be precisely determined. For they are nothing but propositions by which all perception is (under certain universal conditions of intuition) subsumed under those pure concepts of the understanding.

---

[1] This name seems preferable to the term *particularia*, which is used for these judgments in logic. For the latter implies the idea that they are not universal. But when I start from unity (in single judgments) and so proceed to universality, I must not [even indirectly and negatively] imply any reference to universality. I think plurality merely without universality, and not the exception from universality. This is necessary, if logical considerations shall form the basis of the pure concepts of the understanding. However, there is no need of making changes in logic.

Logical Table of Judgments.

1.

As to Quantity.
Universal.
Particular.
Singular.

2.

As to Quality.
Affirmative.
Negative.
Infinite.

3.

As to Relation.
Categorical.
Hypothetical.
Disjunctive.

4.

As to Modality.
Problematical.
Assertorical.
Apodeictical.

Transcendental Table of the Pure Concepts of the Understanding.

1.

As to Quantity.
Unity (the Measure).
Plurality (the Quantity).
Totality (the Whole).

2.

As to Quality.
Reality.
Negation.
Limitation.

3.

As to Relation.
Substance.
Cause.
Community.

4.

As to Modality.
Possibility.
Existence.
Necessity.

Pure Physiological Table of the Universal Principles of the Science of Nature.

1.

Axioms of Intuition.

2.

Anticipations of Perception.

3.

Analogies of Experience.

4.

Postulates of Empirical Thinking
generally.

§ 21a. In order to comprise the whole matter in one idea, it is first necessary to remind the reader that we are discussing not the origin of experience, but of that which lies in experience. The former pertains to empirical psychology, and would even then never be adequately explained without the latter, which belongs to the Critique of cognition, and particularly of the understanding.

Experience consists of intuitions, which belong to the sensibility, and of judgments, which are entirely a work of the understanding. But the judgments, which the understanding forms alone from sensuous intuitions, are far from being judgments of experience. For in the one case the judgment connects only the perceptions as they are given in the sensuous intuition, while in the other the judgments must express what experience in general, and not what the mere perception (which possesses only subjective validity) contains. The judgment of experience must therefore add to the sensuous intuition and its logical connexion in a judgment (after it has been rendered universal by comparison) something that determines the synthetical judgment as necessary and therefore as universally valid. This can be nothing else than that concept which represents the intuition as determined in itself with regard to one form of judgment rather than another, viz., a concept of that synthetical unity of intuitions which can only be represented by a given logical function of judgments.

§ 22. The sum of the matter is this: the business of the senses is to intuite—that of the understanding is to think. But thinking is uniting representations in one consciousness. This union originates either merely relative to the subject, and is accidental and subjective, or is absolute, and is necessary or objective. The union of representations in one consciousness is judgment. Thinking therefore is the same as judging, or referring representations to judgments in general. Hence judgments are either merely subjective, when representations are referred to a consciousness in one subject only, and united in it, or objective, when they are united in a consciousness generally, that is, necessarily. The logical functions of all judgments are but various modes of uniting representations in consciousness. But if they serve for concepts, they are concepts of their necessary union in a consciousness, and so principles of objectively valid judgments. This union in a consciousness is either analytical, by identity, or synthetical, by the combination and addition of various representations one to another. Experience consists in the synthetical connexion of phenomena (perceptions) in consciousness, so far as this connexion is necessary. Hence the pure concepts of the understanding are those under which all perceptions must be subsumed ere they can serve for judgments of experience, in which the synthetical unity of the perceptions is represented as necessary and universally valid.[1]

---

[1] But how does this proposition, "that judgments of experience contain necessity in the synthesis of perceptions," agree with my statement so often before inculcated, that "experience as cognition *a posteriori* can afford contingent judgments only?" When I say that experience teaches me something, I mean only the perception that lies in experience,—for example, that heat always follows the shining of the sun on a stone; consequently the proposition of experience is always so far accidental. That this heat necessarily follows the shining of the sun is contained indeed in the judgment of experience (by means of the concept of cause), yet is a fact not learned by experience; for conversely, experience is first of all generated by this addition of the concept of the understanding (of cause) to perception. How perception attains this addition may be seen by referring in the *Critique* itself to the section on the Transcendental faculty of Judgment [viz., in the first edition, *Von dem Schematismus der reinen Verstandsbegriffe*].

§ 23. Judgments, when considered merely as the condition of the union of given representations in a consciousness, are rules.   These rules, so far as they represent the union as necessary, are rules *a priori*, and so far as they cannot be deduced from higher rules, are fundamental principles.   But in regard to the possibility of all experience, merely in relation to the form of thinking in it, no conditions of judgments of experience are higher than those which bring the phenomena, according to the various form of their intuition, under pure concepts of the understanding, and render the empirical judgment objectively valid. These concepts are therefore the *a priori* principles of possible experience.

The principles of possible experience are then at the same time universal laws of nature, which can be cognised *a priori*.   And thus the problem in our second question, "How is the pure Science of Nature possible?" is solved.   For the system which is required for the form of a science is to be met with in perfection here, because, beyond the above-mentioned formal conditions of all judgments in general offered in logic, no others are possible, and these constitute a logical system.   The concepts grounded thereupon, which contain the *a priori* conditions of all synthetical and necessary judgments, accordingly constitute a transcendental system.   Finally the principles, by means of which all phenomena are subsumed under these concepts, constitute a physical[1] system, that is, a system of nature, which precedes all empirical cognition of nature, makes it even possible, and hence

[1] [Kant uses the term physiological in its etymological meaning as "pertaining to the science of physics," i. e., nature in general, not as we use the term now as "pertaining to the functions of the living body." Accordingly it has been translated "physical."—*Ed.*]

may in strictness be denominated the universal and pure science of nature.

§ 24. The first one[1] of the physiological principles subsumes all phenomena, as intuitions in space and time, under the concept of Quantity, and is so far a principle of the application of Mathematics to experience. The second one subsumes the empirical element, viz., sensation, which denotes the real in intuitions, not indeed directly under the concept of quantity, because sensation is not an intuition that contains either space or time, though it places the respective object into both. But still there is between reality (sense-representation) and the zero, or total void of intuition in time, a difference which has a quantity. For between every given degree of light and of darkness, between every degree of heat and of absolute cold, between every degree of weight and of absolute lightness, between every degree of occupied space and of totally void space, diminishing degrees can be conceived, in the same manner as between consciousness and total unconsciousness (the darkness of a psychological blank) ever diminishing degrees obtain. Hence there is no perception that can prove an absolute absence of it; for instance, no psychological darkness that cannot be considered as a kind of consciousness, which is only outbalanced by a stronger consciousness. This occurs in all cases of sensation, and so the understanding can anticipate even sensations, which constitute the peculiar quality of empirical representations (appearances), by means of the principle: "that they all have (consequently that

---

[1] The three following paragraphs will hardly be understood unless reference be made to what the *Critique* itself says on the subject of the Principles; they will, however, be of service in giving a general view of the Principles, and in fixing the attention on the main points.

what is real in all phenomena has) a degree." Here is the second application of mathematics (*mathesis intensorum*) to the science of nature.

§ 25. Anent the relation of appearances merely with a view to their existence, the determination is not mathematical but dynamical, and can never be objectively valid, consequently never fit for experience, if it does not come under *a priori* principles by which the cognition of experience relative to appearances becomes even possible. Hence appearances must be subsumed under the concept of Substance, which is the foundation of all determination of existence, as a concept of the thing itself; or secondly— so far as a succession is found among phenomena, that is, an event—under the concept of an Effect with reference to Cause; or lastly—so far as coexistence is to be known objectively, that is, by a judgment of experience—under the concept of Community (action and reaction).[1] Thus *a priori* principles form the basis of objectively valid, though empirical judgments, that is, of the possibility of experience so far as it must connect objects as existing in nature. These principles are the proper laws of nature, which may be termed dynamical.

Finally the cognition of the agreement and connexion not only of appearances among themselves in experience, but of their relation to experience in general, belongs to the judgments of experience. This relation contains either their agreement with the formal conditions, which the understanding cognises, or their coherence with the materials of the senses and of perception, or combines both into one concept. Consequently it contains Possibility, Actuality, and

1 [Kant uses here the equivocal term *Wechselwirkung.—Ed.*]

Necessity according to universal laws of nature; and this constitutes the physical doctrine of method, or the distinction of truth and of hypotheses, and the bounds of the certainty of the latter.

§ 26. The third table of Principles drawn from the nature of the understanding itself after the critical method, shows an inherent perfection, which raises it far above every other table which has hitherto though in vain been tried or may yet be tried by analysing the objects themselves dogmatically. It exhibits all synthetical *a priori* principles completely and according to one principle, viz., the faculty of judging in general, constituting the essence of experience as regards the understanding, so that we can be certain that there are no more such principles, which affords a satisfaction such as can never be attained by the dogmatical method. Yet is this not all: there is a still greater merit in it.

We must carefully bear in mind the proof which shows the possibility of this cognition *a priori*, and at the same time limits all such principles to a condition which must never be lost sight of, if we desire it not to be misunderstood, and extended in use beyond the original sense which the understanding attaches to it. This limit is that they contain nothing but the conditions of possible experience in general so far as it is subjected to laws *a priori*. Consequently I do not say, that things *in themselves* possess a quantity, that their actuality possesses a degree, their existence a connexion of accidents in a substance, etc. This nobody can prove, because such a synthetical connexion from mere concepts, without any reference to sensuous intuition on the one side, or connexion of it in a possible experience on the other, is absolutely impos-

sible. The essential limitation of the concepts in
these principles then is : That all things stand necessarily *a priori* under the afore-mentioned conditions,
as objects of experience only.

Hence there follows secondly a specifically peculiar mode of proof of these principles : they are not
directly referred to appearances and to their relations,
but to the possibility of experience, of which appearances constitute the matter only, not the form. Thus
they are referred to objectively and universally valid
synthetical propositions, in which we distinguish
judgments of experience from those of perception.
This takes place because appearances, as mere intuitions, occupying a part of space and time, come under the concept of Quantity, which unites their multiplicity *a priori* according to rules synthetically. Again,
so far as the perception contains, besides intuition,
sensibility, and between the latter and nothing (i. e.,
the total disappearance of sensibility), there is an
ever-decreasing transition, it is apparent that that
which is in appearances must have a degree, so far
as it (viz., the perception) does not itself occupy
any part of space or of time.[1] Still the transition to
actuality from empty time or empty space is only
possible in time ; consequently though sensibility, as

1 Heat and light are in a small space just as large as to degree as in a
large one ; in like manner the internal representations, pain, consciousness
in general, whether they last a short or a long time, need not vary as to the
degree. Hence the quantity is here in a point and in a moment just as great
as in any space or time however great. Degrees are therefore capable of increase, but not in intuition, rather in mere sensation (or the quantity of the
degree of an intuition). Hence they can only be estimated quantitatively by
the relation of 1 to 0, viz., by their capability of decreasing by infinite intermediate degrees to disappearance, or of increasing from naught through infinite gradations to a determinate sensation in a certain time. *Quantitas
qualitatis est gradus* [i. e., the degrees of quality must be measured by
equality].

the quality of empirical intuition, can never be cognised *a priori*, by its specific difference from other
sensibilities, yet it can, in a possible experience in
general, as a quantity of perception be intensely distinguished from every other similar perception. Hence
the application of mathematics to nature, as regards
the sensuous intuition by which nature is given to us,
becomes possible and is thus determined.

Above all, the reader must pay attention to the
mode of proof of the principles which occur under
the title of Analogies of experience. For these do
not refer to the genesis of intuitions, as do the principles of applied mathematics, but to the connexion
of their existence in experience; and this can be
nothing but the determination of their existence in
time according to necessary laws, under which alone
the connexion is objectively valid, and thus becomes
experience. The proof therefore does not turn on
the synthetical unity in the connexion of things in
themselves, but merely of perceptions, and of these
not in regard to their matter, but to the determination
of time and of the relation of their existence in it, according to universal laws. If the empirical determination in relative time is indeed objectively valid (i. e.,
experience), these universal laws contain the necessary determination of existence in time generally (viz.,
according to a rule of the understanding *a priori*).

In these Prolegomena I cannot further descant on
the subject, but my reader (who has probably been
long accustomed to consider experience a mere empirical synthesis of perceptions, and hence not considered that it goes much beyond them, as it imparts
to empirical judgments universal validity, and for
that purpose requires a pure and *a priori* unity of the

understanding) is recommended to pay special attention to this distinction of experience from a mere aggregate of perceptions, and to judge the mode of proof
from this point of view.

§ 27. Now we are prepared to remove Hume's
doubt. He justly maintains, that we cannot comprehend by reason the possibility of Causality, that is, of
the reference of the existence of one thing to the existence of another, which is necessitated by the former. I add, that we comprehend just as little the
concept of Subsistence, that is, the necessity that at
the foundation of the existence of things there lies a
subject which cannot itself be a predicate of any other
thing ; nay, we cannot even form a notion of the possibility of such a thing (though we can point out examples of its use in experience). The very same incomprehensibility affects the Community of things, as
we cannot comprehend how from the state of one
thing an inference to the state of quite another thing
beyond it, and *vice versa*, can be drawn, and how substances which have each their own separate existence
should depend upon one another necessarily. But I
am very far from holding these concepts to be derived
merely from experience, and the necessity represented
in them, to be imaginary and a mere illusion produced
in us by long habit. On the contrary, I have amply
shown, that they and the theorems derived from them
are firmly established *a priori*, or before all experience,
and have their undoubted objective value, though
only with regard to experience.

§ 28. Though I have no notion of such a connexion of things in themselves, that they can either exist
as substances, or act as causes, or stand in community with others (as parts of a real whole), and I can

just as little conceive such properties in appearances as such (because those concepts contain nothing that lies in the appearances, but only what the understanding alone must think): we have yet a notion of such a connexion of representations in our understanding, and in judgments generally; consisting in this that representations appear in one sort of judgments as subject in relation to predicates, in another as reason in relation to consequences, and in a third as parts, which constitute together a total possible cognition. Besides we cognise *a priori* that without considering the representation of an object as determined in some of these respects, we can have no valid cognition of the object, and, if we should occupy ourselves about the object in itself, there is no possible attribute, by which I could know that it is determined under any of these aspects, that is, under the concept either of substance, or of cause, or (in relation to other substances) of community, for I have no notion of the possibility of such a connexion of existence. But the question is not how things in themselves, but how the empirical cognition of things is determined, as regards the above aspects of judgments in general, that is, how things, as objects of experience, can and shall be subsumed under these concepts of the understanding. And then it is clear, that I completely comprehend not only the possibility, but also the necessity of subsuming all phenomena under these concepts, that is, of using them for principles of the possibility of experience.

§ 29. When making an experiment with Hume's problematical concept (his *crux metaphysicorum*), the concept of cause, we have, in the first place, given *a priori*, by means of logic, the form of a conditional

judgment in general, i. e., we have one given cognition as antecedent and another as consequence. But
it is possible, that in perception we may meet with a
rule of relation, which runs thus : that a certain phenomenon is constantly followed by another (though
not conversely), and this is a case for me to use the
hypothetical judgment, and, for instance, to say, if
the sun shines long enough upon a body, it grows
warm. Here there is indeed as yet no necessity of
connexion, or concept of cause. But I proceed and
say, that if this proposition, which is merely a subjective connexion of perceptions, is to be a judgment of
experience, it must be considered as necessary and
universally valid. Such a proposition would be, "the
sun is by its light the cause of heat." The empirical
rule is now considered as a law, and as valid not
merely of appearances but valid of them for the purposes of a possible experience which requires universal and therefore necessarily valid rules. I therefore
easily comprehend the concept of cause, as a concept
necessarily belonging to the mere form of experience,
and its possibility as a synthetical union of perceptions in consciousness generally; but I do not at all
comprehend the possibility of a thing generally as a
cause, because the concept of cause denotes a condition not at all belonging to things, but to experience.
It is nothing in fact but an objectively valid cognition
of appearances and of their succession, so far as the
antecedent can be conjoined with the consequent according to the rule of hypothetical judgments.

§ 30. Hence if the pure concepts of the understanding do not refer to objects of experience but to
things in themselves (*noumena*), they have no signification whatever. They serve, as it were, only to de-

cipher appearances, that we may be able to read them as experience. The principles which arise from their reference to the sensible world, only serve our understanding for empirical use. Beyond this they are arbitrary combinations, without objective reality, and we can neither cognise their possibility *a priori*, nor verify their reference to objects, let alone make it intelligible by any example ; because examples can only be borrowed from some possible experience, consequently the objects of these concepts can be found nowhere but in a possible experience.

This complete (though to its originator unexpected) solution of Hume's problem rescues for the pure concepts of the understanding their *a priori* origin, and for the universal laws of nature their validity, as laws of the understanding, yet in such a way as to limit their use to experience, because their possibility depends solely on the reference of the understanding to experience, but with a completely reversed mode of connexion which never occurred to Hume, not by deriving them from experience, but by deriving experience from them.

This is therefore the result of all our foregoing inquiries : "All synthetical principles *a priori* are nothing more than principles of possible experience, and can never be referred to things in themselves, but to appearances as objects of experience. And hence pure mathematics as well as a pure science of nature can never be referred to anything more than mere appearances, and can only represent either that which makes experience generally possible, or else that which, as it is derived from these principles, must always be capable of being represented in some possible experience."

§ 31. And thus we have at last something definite, upon which to depend in all metaphysical enterprises, which have hitherto, boldly enough but always at random, attempted everything without discrimination. That the aim of their exertions should be so near, struck neither the dogmatical thinkers nor those who, confident in their supposed sound common sense, started with concepts and principles of pure reason (which were legitimate and natural, but destined for mere empirical use) in quest of fields of knowledge, to which they neither knew nor could know any determinate bounds, because they had never reflected nor were able to reflect on the nature or even on the possibility of such a pure understanding.

Many a naturalist of pure reason (by which I mean the man who believes he can decide in matters of metaphysics without any science) may pretend, that he long ago by the prophetic spirit of his sound sense, not only suspected, but knew and comprehended, what is here propounded with so much ado, or, if he likes, with prolix and pedantic pomp: "that with all our reason we can never reach beyond the field of experience." But when he is questioned about his rational principles individually, he must grant, that there are many of them which he has not taken from experience, and which are therefore independent of it and valid *a priori*. How then and on what grounds will he restrain both himself and the dogmatist, who makes use of these concepts and principles beyond all possible experience, because they are recognised to be independent of it? And even he, this adept in sound sense, in spite of all his assumed and cheaply acquired wisdom, is not exempt from wandering inadvertently beyond objects of experience into the field of chimeras. He is often deeply enough involved in them, though in announcing everything as mere probability, rational conjecture, or analogy, he gives by his popular language a color to his groundless pretensions.

§ 32. Since the oldest days of philosophy inquirers into pure reason have conceived, besides the things of sense, or appearances (phenomena), which make up the sensible world, certain creations of the understanding (*Verstandeswesen*), called noumena, which should constitute an intelligible world. And as appearance and illusion were by those men identified (a thing which we may well excuse in an undeveloped epoch), actuality was only conceded to the creations of thought.

And we indeed, rightly considering objects of sense as mere appearances, confess thereby that they are based upon a thing in itself, though we know not this thing in its internal constitution, but only know its appearances, viz., the way in which our senses are affected by this unknown something. The understanding therefore, by assuming appearances, grants the existence of things in themselves also, and so far we may say, that the representation of such things as form the basis of phenomena, consequently of mere creations of the understanding, is not only admissible, but unavoidable.

Our critical deduction by no means excludes things of that sort (noumena), but rather limits the principles of the Aesthetic (the science of the sensibility) to this, that they shall not extend to all things, as everything would then be turned into mere appearance, but that they shall only hold good of objects of possible experience. Hereby then objects of the understanding are granted, but with the inculcation of this rule which admits of no exception: "that we neither know nor can know anything at all definite of these pure objects of the understanding, because our pure concepts of the understanding as well as our pure intuitions extend to nothing but objects of possible experience, consequently to mere things of sense, and as soon as we leave this sphere these concepts retain no meaning whatever."

§ 33. There is indeed something seductive in our pure concepts of the understanding, which tempts us to a transcendent use,—a use which transcends all possible experience. Not only are our concepts of substance, of power, of action, of reality, and others, quite independent of experience, containing nothing of sense appearance, and so apparently applicable to things in themselves (noumena), but, what strengthens this conjecture, they contain a necessity of determination in themselves, which experience never attains. The concept of cause implies a rule, according to which one state follows another necessarily; but experience can only show us, that one state of things often, or at most, commonly, follows another, and therefore affords neither strict universality, nor necessity.

Hence the Categories seem to have a deeper meaning and import than can be exhausted by their empirical use, and so the understanding inadvertently adds for itself to the house of experience a much more extensive wing, which it fills with nothing but creatures of thought, without ever observing that it has transgressed with its otherwise lawful concepts the bounds of their use.

§ 34. Two important, and even indispensable,

though very dry, investigations had therefore become indispensable in the Critique of Pure Reason,—viz., the two chapters "Vom Schematismus der reinen Verstandsbegriffe," and "Vom Grunde der Unterscheidung aller Verstandesbegriffe überhaupt in Phänomena und Noumena." In the former it is shown, that the senses furnish not the pure concepts of the understanding *in concreto*, but only the schedule for their use, and that the object conformable to it occurs only in experience (as the product of the understanding from materials of the sensibility). In the latter it is shown, that, although our pure concepts of the understanding and our principles are independent of experience, and despite of the apparently greater sphere of their use, still nothing whatever can be thought by them beyond the field of experience, because they can do nothing but merely determine the logical form of the judgment relatively to given intuitions. But as there is no intuition at all beyond the field of the sensibility, these pure concepts, as they cannot possibly be exhibited *in concreto*, are void of all meaning; consequently all these noumena, together with their complex, the intelligible world,[1] are nothing but representation of a problem, of which the object in itself is possible, but the solution, from the nature of our understanding, totally impossible. For our understanding is not a faculty of intuition, but of

---

1 We speak of the "intelligible world," not (as the usual expression is) "intellectual world." For cognitions are intellectual through the understanding, and refer to our world of sense also; but objects, so far as they can be represented merely by the understanding, and to which none of our sensible intuitions can refer, are termed "intelligible." But as some possible intuition must correspond to every object, we would have to assume an understanding that intuites things immediately; but of such we have not the least notion, nor have we of the *things of the understanding* [Verstandeswesen], to which it should be applied.

the connexion of given intuitions in experience.   Experience must therefore contain all the objects for our concepts; but beyond it no concepts have any significance, as there is no intuition that might offer them a foundation.

§ 35. The imagination may perhaps be forgiven for occasional vagaries, and for not keeping carefully within the limits of experience, since it gains life and vigor by such flights, and since it is always easier to moderate its boldness, than to stimulate its languor. But the understanding which ought to *think* can never be forgiven for indulging in vagaries; for we depend upon it alone for assistance to set bounds, when necessary, to the vagaries of the imagination.

But the understanding begins its aberrations very innocently and modestly. It first elucidates the elementary cognitions, which inhere in it prior to all experience, but yet must always have their application in experience. It gradually drops these limits, and what is there to prevent it, as it has quite freely derived its principles from itself? And then it proceeds first to newly-imagined powers in nature, then to beings outside nature; in short to a world, for whose construction the materials cannot be wanting, because fertile fiction furnishes them abundantly, and though not confirmed, is never refuted, by experience. This is the reason that young thinkers are so partial to metaphysics of the truly dogmatical kind, and often sacrifice to it their time and their talents, which might be otherwise better employed.

But there is no use in trying to moderate these fruitless endeavors of pure reason by all manner of cautions as to the difficulties of solving questions so occult, by complaints of the limits of our reason, and by degrading our assertions into mere conjectures. For if their impossibility is not distinctly shown, and reason's cognition of its own essence does not become a true science, in which the field of its right use is distinguished, so to say, with mathematical certainty from that of its worthless and idle use, these fruitless efforts will never be abandoned for good.

§ 36. *How is Nature itself possible?*

This question—the highest point that transcendental philosophy can ever reach, and to which, as its boundary and completion, it must proceed—properly contains two questions.

FIRST: How is nature at all possible in the material sense, by intuition, considered as the totality of appearances; how are space, time, and that which fills both—the object of sensation, in general possible? The answer is: By means of the constitution of our Sensibility, according to which it is specifically affected by objects, which are in themselves unknown to it, and totally distinct from those phenomena. This answer is given in the *Critique* itself in the transcendental Aesthetic, and in these *Prolegomena* by the solution of the first general problem.

SECONDLY: How is nature possible in the formal sense, as the totality of the rules, under which all phenomena must come, in order to be thought as connected in experience? The answer must be this: It is only possible by means of the constitution of our Understanding, according to which all the above representations of the sensibility are necessarily referred to a consciousness, and by which the peculiar way in which we think (viz., by rules), and hence experience also, are possible, but must be clearly distinguished from an insight into the objects in themselves. This answer is given in the *Critique* itself in the transcendental Logic, and in these *Prolegomena,* in the course of the solution of the second main problem.

But how this peculiar property of our sensibility itself is possible, or that of our understanding and of the apperception which is necessarily its basis and that of all thinking, cannot be further analysed or answered, because it is of them that we are in need for all our answers and for all our thinking about objects.

There are many laws of nature, which we can only know by means of experience; but conformity to law in the connexion of appearances, i. e., in nature in general, we cannot discover by any experience, because experience itself requires laws which are *a priori* at the basis of its possibility.

The possibility of experience in general is therefore at the same time the universal law of nature, and the principles of the experience are the very laws of nature. For we do not know nature but as the totality of appearances, i. e., of representations in us, and hence we can only derive the laws of its connexion from the principles of their connexion in us, that is, from the conditions of their necessary union in consciousness, which constitutes the possibility of experience.

Even the main proposition expounded throughout this section—that universal laws of nature can be distinctly cognised *a priori*—leads naturally to the proposition: that the highest legislation of nature must lie in ourselves, i. e., in our understanding, and that we must not seek the universal laws of nature in nature by means of experience, but conversely must seek nature, as to its universal conformity to law, in the conditions of the possibility of experience, which lie in our sensibility and in our understanding. For how were it otherwise possible to know *a priori* these laws, as they are not rules of analytical cognition, but truly synthetical extensions of it?

Such a necessary agreement of the principles of possible experience with the laws of the possibility of nature, can only proceed from one of two reasons: either these laws are drawn from nature by means of experience, or conversely nature is derived from the laws of the possibility of experience in general, and is quite the same as the mere universal conformity to law of the latter. The former is self-contradictory, for the universal laws of nature can and must be cognised *a priori* (that is, independent of all experience), and be the foundation of all empirical use of the understanding; the latter alternative therefore alone remains.[1]

But we must distinguish the empirical laws of nature, which always presuppose particular perceptions, from the pure or universal laws of nature, which, without being based on particular perceptions, contain merely the conditions of their necessary union in experience. In relation to the latter, nature and possible experience are quite the same, and as the conformity to law here depends upon the necessary connexion of appearances in experience (without which we cannot cognise any object whatever in the sensible world), consequently upon the original laws

[1] Crusius alone thought of a compromise: that a Spirit, who can neither err nor deceive, implanted these laws in us originally. But since false principles often intrude themselves, as indeed the very system of this man shows in not a few examples, we are involved in difficulties as to the use of such a principle in the absence of sure criteria to distinguish the genuine origin from the spurious. as we never can know certainly what the Spirit of truth or the father of lies may have instilled into us.

of the understanding, it seems at first strange, but is not the less certain, to say:

The understanding does not derive its laws (a priori) from, but prescribes them to, nature.

§ 37. We shall illustrate this seemingly bold proposition by an example, which will show, that laws, which we discover in objects of sensuous intuition (especially when these laws are cognised as necessary), are commonly held by us to be such as have been placed there by the understanding, in spite of their being similar in all points to the laws of nature, which we ascribe to experience.

§ 38. If we consider the properties of the circle, by which this figure combines so many arbitrary determinations of space in itself, at once in a universal rule, we cannot avoid attributing a constitution (*eine Natur*) to this geometrical thing.   Two right lines, for example, which intersect one another and the circle, howsoever they may be drawn, are always divided so that the rectangle constructed with the segments of the one is equal to that constructed with the segments of the other.   The question now is: Does this law lie in the circle or in the understanding, that is, Does this figure, independently of the understanding, contain in itself the ground of the law, or does the understanding, having constructed according to its concepts (according to the quality of the radii) the figure itself, introduce into it this law of the chords cutting one another in geometrical proportion? When we follow the proofs of this law, we soon perceive, that it can only be derived from the condition on which the understanding founds the construction of this figure, and which is that of the equality of the radii.   But, if we enlarge this concept, to pursue further the unity of various properties of geometrical figures under common laws, and consider the circle as a conic section, which of course is subject to the same fundamental conditions of construction as other conic sections, we shall find that all the chords which intersect within the ellipse, parabola, and hyperbola, always intersect so that the rectangles of their segments are not indeed equal, but always bear a constant ratio to one another. If we proceed still farther, to the fundamental laws of physical astronomy, we find a physical law of reciprocal attraction diffused over all material nature, the rule of which is: ''that it decreases inversely as the square of the distance from each attracting point, i. e., as the spherical surfaces increase, over which this force spreads,'' which law seems to be necessarily inherent in the very nature of things, and hence is usually propounded as cognisable *a priori*. Simple as the sources of this law are, merely resting upon the relation of spherical surfaces of different radii, its consequences are so valuable with regard to the variety of their agreement and its regularity, that not only are all possible orbits of the celestial bodies conic sections, but such a relation of these orbits to each other results, that no other law of attraction, than that of the inverse square of the distance, can be imagined as fit for a cosmical system.

Here accordingly is a nature that rests upon laws which the understanding cognises *a priori*, and chiefly from the universal principles of the determination of space. Now I ask :

Do the laws of nature lie in space, and does the understanding learn them by merely endeavoring to find out the enormous wealth of meaning that lies in space ; or do they inhere in the understanding and in the way in which it determines space according to the conditions of the synthetical unity in which its concepts are all centred?

Space is something so uniform and as to all particular properties so indeterminate, that we should certainly not seek a store of laws of nature in it. Whereas that which determines space to assume the form of a circle or the figures of a cone and a sphere, is the understanding, so far as it contains the ground of the unity of their constructions.

The mere universal form of intuition, called space, must therefore be the substratum of all intuitions determinable to particular objects, and in it of course the condition of the possibility and of the variety of these intuitions lies. But the unity of the objects is entirely determined by the understanding, and on conditions which lie in its own nature; and thus the understanding is the origin of the universal order of nature, in that it comprehends all appearances under its own laws, and thereby first constructs, *a priori*, experience (as to its form), by means of which whatever is to be cognised only by experience, is necessarily subjected to its laws. For we are not now concerned with the nature of things in themselves, which is independent of the conditions both of our sensibility and our understanding, but with nature, as an object of possible experience, and in this case the understanding, whilst it makes experience possible, thereby insists that the sensuous world is either not an object of experience at all, or must be nature [viz., an existence of things, determined according to universal laws [1]].

1 The definition of nature is given in the beginning of the Second Part of the "Transcendental Problem," in § 14.

APPENDIX TO THE PURE SCIENCE OF NATURE.

§ 39. *Of the System of the Categories.*

There can be nothing more desirable to a philosopher, than to be able to derive the scattered multiplicity of the concepts or the principles, which had occurred to him in concrete use, from a principle *a priori,* and to unite everything in this way in one cognition. He formerly only believed that those things, which remained after a certain abstraction, and seemed by comparison among one another to constitute a particular kind of cognitions, were completely collected; but this was only an Aggregate. Now he knows, that just so many, neither more nor less, can constitute the mode of cognition, and perceives the necessity of his division, which constitutes comprehension; and now only he has attained a *System.*

To search in our daily cognition for the concepts, which do not rest upon particular experience, and yet occur in all cognition of experience, where they as it were constitute the mere form of connexion, presupposes neither greater reflexion nor deeper insight, than to detect in a language the rules of the actual use of words generally, and thus to collect elements for a grammar. In fact both researches are very nearly related, even though we are not able to give a reason why each language has just this and no other formal constitution, and still less why an exact number of such formal determinations in general are found in it.

Aristotle collected ten pure elementary concepts under the name of Categories.[1] To these, which are also called predicaments, he found himself obliged afterwards to add five post-predicaments,[2] some of which however (*prius*, *simul*, and *motus*) are contained in the former; but this random collection must be considered (and commended) as a mere hint for future inquirers, not as a regularly developed idea, and hence it has, in the present more advanced state of philosophy, been rejected as quite useless.

After long reflexion on the pure elements of human knowledge (those which contain nothing empirical), I at last succeeded in distinguishing with certainty and in separating the pure elementary notions of the Sensibility (space and time) from those of the Understanding. Thus the 7th, 8th, and 9th Categories had to be excluded from the old list. And the others were of no service to me; because there was no principle [in them], on which the understanding could be investigated, measured in its completion, and all the functions, whence its pure concepts arise, determined exhaustively and with precision.

But in order to discover such a principle, I looked about for an act of the understanding which comprises all the rest, and is distinguished only by various modifications or phases, in reducing the multiplicity of representation to the unity of thinking in general: I found this act of the understanding to consist in judging. Here then the labors of the logicians were ready at hand, though not yet quite free from defects, and with this help I was enabled to exhibit a complete

---

[1] 1. *Substantia.* 2. *Qualitas.* 3. *Quantitas.* 4. *Relatio.* 5. *Actio.* 6. *Passio.* 7. *Quando.* 8. *Ubi.* 9. *Situs.* 10. *Habitus.*

[2] *Oppositum. Prius. Simul. Motus. Habere.*

table of the pure functions of the understanding,
which are however undetermined in regard to any object. I finally referred these functions of judging to
objects in general, or rather to the condition of determining judgments as objectively valid, and so there
arose the pure concepts of the understanding, concerning which I could make certain, that these, and
this exact number only, constitute our whole cognition of things from pure understanding. I was justified in calling them by their old name, *Categories,*
while I reserved for myself the liberty of adding, under the title of "Predicables," a complete list of all
the concepts deducible from them, by combinations
whether among themselves, or with the pure form of
the appearance, i. e., space or time, or with its matter, so far as it is not yet empirically determined (viz.,
the object of sensation in general), as soon as a system of transcendental philosophy should be completed
with the construction of which I am engaged in the
Critique of Pure Reason itself.

Now the essential point in this system of Categories, which distinguishes it from the old rhapsodical
collection without any principle, and for which alone
it deserves to be considered as philosophy, consists
in this: that by means of it the true significance of
the pure concepts of the understanding and the condition of their use could be precisely determined. For
here it became obvious that they are themselves nothing but logical functions, and as such do not produce
the least concept of an object, but require some sensuous intuition as a basis. They therefore only serve
to determine empirical judgments, which are otherwise undetermined and indifferent as regards all functions of judging, relatively to these functions, thereby

procuring them universal validity, and by means of them making judgments of experience in general possible.

Such an insight into the nature of the categories, which limits them at the same time to the mere use of experience, never occurred either to their first author, or to any of his successors; but without this insight (which immediately depends upon their derivation or deduction), they are quite useless and only a miserable list of names, without explanation or rule for their use. Had the ancients ever conceived such a notion, doubtless the whole study of the pure rational knowledge, which under the name of metaphysics has for centuries spoiled many a sound mind, would have reached us in quite another shape, and would have enlightened the human understanding, instead of actually exhausting it in obscure and vain speculations, thereby rendering it unfit for true science.

This system of categories makes all treatment of every object of pure reason itself systematic, and affords a direction or clue how and through what points of inquiry every metaphysical consideration must proceed, in order to be complete; for it exhausts all the possible movements (*momenta*) of the understanding, among which every concept must be classed. In like manner the table of Principles has been formulated, the completeness of which we can only vouch for by the system of the categories. Even in the division of the concepts,[1] which must go beyond the physical application of the understanding, it is always the very same clue, which, as it must always be deter-

1 See the two tables in the chapters *Von den Paralogismen der reinen Vernunft* and the first division of the Antinomy of Pure Reason, *System der kosmologischen Ideen.*

mined *a priori* by the same fixed points of the human understanding, always forms a closed circle. There is no doubt that the object of a pure conception either of the understanding or of reason, so far as it is to be estimated philosophically and on *a priori* principles, can in this way be completely cognised. I could not therefore omit to make use of this clue with regard to one of the most abstract ontological divisions, viz., the various distinctions of "the notions of something and of nothing," and to construct accordingly (*Critique*, p. 207) a regular and necessary table of their divisions.[1]

And this system, like every other true one founded on a universal principle, shows its inestimable value in this, that it excludes all foreign concepts, which might otherwise intrude among the pure concepts of the understanding, and determines the place of every cognition. Those concepts, which under the name of "concepts of reflexion" have been likewise arranged in a table according to the clue of the categories, intrude, without having any privilege or title to be

[1] On the table of the categories many neat observations may be made, for instance : (1) that the third arises from the first and the second joined in one concept; (2) that in those of Quantity and of Quality there is merely a progress from unity to totality or from something to nothing (for this purpose the categories of Quality must stand thus : reality, limitation. total negation), without *correlata* or *opposita*, whereas those of Relation and of Modality have them ; (3) that, as in *Logic* categorical judgments are the basis of all others, so the category of Substance is the basis of all concepts of actual things; (4) that as Modality in the judgment is not a particular predicate, so by the modal concepts a determination is not superadded to things, etc., etc   Such observations are of great use. If we besides enumerate all the predicables, which we can find pretty completely in any good ontology (for example, Baumgarten's), and arrange them in classes under the categories, in which operation we must not neglect to add as complete a dissection of all these concepts as possible, there will then arise a merely analytical part of metaphysics, which does not contain a single synthetical proposition, which might precede the second (the synthetical), and would by its precision and completeness be not only useful, but, in virtue of its system, be even to some extent elegant.

among the pure concepts of the understanding in Ontology. They are concepts of connexion, and thereby
of the objects themselves, whereas the former are only
concepts of a mere comparison of concepts already
given, hence of quite another nature and use. By
my systematic division[1] they are saved from this confusion. But the value of my special table of the categories will be still more obvious, when we separate the
table of the transcendental concepts of Reason from
the concepts of the understanding. The latter being
of quite another nature and origin, they must have
quite another form than the former. This so necessary separation has never yet been made in any system of metaphysics for, as a rule, these rational concepts all mixed up with the categories, like children
of one family, which confusion was unavoidable in the
absence of a definite system of categories.

[1] See *Critique of Pure Reason, Von der Amphibolie der Reflexbegriffe.*

THIRD PART OF THE MAIN TRANSCENDENTAL PROBLEM.

HOW IS METAPHYSICS IN GENERAL POSSIBLE?

§ 40.

PURE mathematics and pure science of nature had no occasion for such a deduction, as we have made of both, for their own safety and certainty. For the former rests upon its own evidence; and the latter (though sprung from pure sources of the understanding) upon experience and its thorough confirmation. Physics cannot altogether refuse and dispense with the testimony of the latter; because with all its certainty, it can never, as philosophy, rival mathematics. Both sciences therefore stood in need of this inquiry, not for themselves, but for the sake of another science, metaphysics.

Metaphysics has to do not only with concepts of nature, which always find their application in experience, but also with pure rational concepts, which never can be given in any possible experience. Consequently the objective reality of these concepts (viz., that they are not mere chimeras), and the truth or falsity of metaphysical assertions, cannot be discovered or confirmed by any experience. This part of metaphysics however is precisely what constitutes its essential end, to which the rest is only a means, and thus this science is in need of such a deduction for its own sake. The third question now proposed relates therefore as it were to the root and essential difference of metaphysics, i. e., the occupation of Reason with itself, and the supposed knowledge of objects arising immediately from this incubation of its own concepts, without requiring, or indeed being able to reach that knowledge through, experience.[1]

Without solving this problem reason never is justified. The empirical use to which reason limits the pure understanding, does not fully satisfy the proper destination of the latter. Every single experience is only a part of the whole sphere of its domain, but the absolute totality of all possible experience is itself not experience. Yet it is a necessary [concrete] problem for reason, the mere representation of which requires concepts quite different from the categories, whose use is only immanent, or refers to experience, so far as it can be given. Whereas the concepts of reason aim at the completeness, i. e., the collective unity of all possible experience, and thereby transcend every given experience. Thus they become *transcendent*.

As the understanding stands in need of categories for experience, reason contains in itself the source of ideas, by which I mean necessary concepts, whose object cannot be given in any experience. The latter are inherent in the nature of reason, as the former are in that of the understanding. While the former carry with them an illusion likely to mislead, the illu-

1 If we can say, that a science is actual at least in the idea of all men, as soon as it appears that the problems which lead to it are proposed to everybody by the nature of human reason, and that therefore many (though faulty) endeavors are unavoidably made in its behalf, then we are bound to say that metaphysics is subjectively (and indeed necessarily) actual, and therefore we justly ask, how is it (objectively) possible.

sion of the latter is inevitable, though it certainly can be kept from misleading us.

Since all illusion consists in holding the subjective ground of our judgments to be objective, a self-knowledge of pure reason in its transcendent (exaggerated) use is the sole preservative from the aberrations into which reason falls when it mistakes its destination, and refers that to the object transcendently, which only regards its own subject and its guidance in all immanent use.

§ 41. The distinction of ideas, that is, of pure concepts of reason, from categories, or pure concepts of the understanding, as cognitions of a quite distinct species, origin and use, is so important a point in founding a science which is to contain the system of all these *a priori* cognitions, that without this distinction metaphysics is absolutely impossible, or is at best a random, bungling attempt to build a castle in the air without a knowledge of the materials or of their fitness for any purpose. Had the *Critique of Pure Reason* done nothing but first point out this distinction, it had thereby contributed more to clear up our conception of, and to guide our inquiry in, the field of metaphysics, than all the vain efforts which have hitherto been made to satisfy the transcendent problems of pure reason, without ever surmising that we were in quite another field than that of the understanding, and hence classing concepts of the understanding and those of reason together, as if they were of the same kind.

§ 42. All pure cognitions of the understanding have this feature, that their concepts present themselves in experience, and their principles can be confirmed by it; whereas the transcendent cognitions of

reason cannot, either as ideas, appear in experience,
or as propositions ever be confirmed or refuted by it.
Hence whatever errors may slip in unawares, can only
be discovered by pure reason itself—a discovery of
much difficulty, because this very reason naturally
becomes dialectical by means of its ideas, and this
unavoidable illusion cannot be limited by any objective and dogmatical researches into things, but by a
subjective investigation of reason itself as a source of
ideas.

§ 43. In the *Critique of Pure Reason* it was always
my greatest care to endeavor not only carefully to distinguish the several species of cognition, but to derive concepts belonging to each one of them from
their common source. I did this in order that by
knowing whence they originated, I might determine
their use with safety, and also have the unanticipated
but invaluable advantage of knowing the completeness
of my enumeration, classification and specification of
concepts *a priori*, and therefore according to principles. Without this, metaphysics is mere rhapsody,
in which no one knows whether he has enough, or
whether and where something is still wanting. We
can indeed have this advantage only in pure philosophy, but of this philosophy it constitutes the very
essence.

As I had found the origin of the categories in the
four logical functions of all the judgments of the understanding, it was quite natural to seek the origin of
the ideas in the three functions of the syllogisms of
reason. For as soon as these pure concepts of reason (the transcendental ideas) are given, they could
hardly, except they be held innate, be found anywhere
else, than in the same activity of reason, which, so

far as it regards mere form, constitutes the logical element of the syllogisms of reason; but, so far as it represents judgments of the understanding with respect to the one or to the other form *a priori*, constitutes transcendental concepts of pure reason.

The formal distinction of syllogisms renders their division into categorical, hypothetical, and disjunctive necessary. The concepts of reason founded on them contained therefore, first, the idea of the complete subject (the substantial); secondly, the idea of the complete series of conditions; thirdly, the determination of all concepts in the idea of a complete complex of that which is possible.[1] The first idea is psychological, the second cosmological, the third theological, and, as all three give occasion to Dialectics, yet each in its own way, the division of the whole Dialects of pure reason into its Paralogism, its Antinomy, and its Ideal, was arranged accordingly. Through this deduction we may feel assured that all the claims of pure reason are completely represented, and that none can be wanting; because the faculty of reason itself, whence they all take their origin, is thereby completely surveyed.

§ 44. In these general considerations it is also remarkable that the ideas of reason are unlike the categories, of no service to the use of our understanding

---

[1] In disjunctive judgments we consider all possibility as divided in respect to a particular concept. By the ontological principle of the universal determination of a thing in general, I understand the principle that either the one or the other of all possible contradictory predicates must be assigned to any object. This is at the same time the principle of all disjunctive judgments, constituting the foundation of our conception of possibility, and in it the possibility of every object in general is considered as determined. This may serve as a slight explanation of the above proposition: that the activity of reason in disjunctive syllogisms is formally the same as that by which it fashions the idea of a universal conception of all reality, containing in itself that which is positive in all contradictory predicates.

in experience, but quite dispensable, and become even an impediment to the maxims of a rational cognition of nature. Yet in another aspect still to be determined they are necessary. Whether the soul is or is not a simple substance, is of no consequence to us in the explanation of its phenomena. For we cannot render the notion of a simple being intelligible by any possible experience that is sensuous or concrete. The notion is therefore quite void as regards all hoped-for insight into the cause of phenomena, and cannot at all serve as a principle of the explanation of that which internal or external experience supplies. So the cosmological ideas of the beginning of the world or of its eternity (*a parte ante*) cannot be of any greater service to us for the explanation of any event in the world itself. And finally we must, according to a right maxim of the philosophy of nature, refrain from all explanations of the design of nature, drawn from the will of a Supreme Being; because this would not be natural philosophy, but an acknowledgment that we have come to the end of it. The use of these ideas, therefore, is quite different from that of those categories by which (and by the principles built upon which) experience itself first becomes possible. But our laborious analytics of the understanding would be superfluous if we had nothing else in view than the mere cognition of nature as it can be given in experience; for reason does its work, both in mathematics and in the science of nature, quite safely and well without any of this subtle deduction. Therefore our Critique of the Understanding combines with the ideas of pure reason for a purpose which lies beyond the empirical use of the understanding; but this we have above declared to be in this aspect totally inadmissible, and without any object or meaning. Yet there must be a harmony between that of the nature of reason and that of the understanding, and the former must contribute to the perfection of the latter, and cannot possibly upset it.

The solution of this question is as follows : Pure reason does not in its ideas point to particular objects, which lie beyond the field of experience, but only requires completeness of the use of the understanding in the system of experience. But this completeness can be a completeness of principles only, not of intuitions (i. e., concrete atsights or *Anschauungen*) and of objects. In order however to represent the ideas definitely, reason conceives them after the fashion of the cognition of an object. The cognition is as far as these rules are concerned completely determined, but the object is only an idea invented for the purpose of bringing the cognition of the understanding as near as possible to the completeness represented by that idea.

Prefatory Remark to the Dialectics of Pure Reason.

§ 45. We have above shown in §§ 33 and 34 that the purity of the categories from all admixture of sensuous determinations may mislead reason into extending their use, quite beyond all experience, to things in themselves ; though as these categories themselves find no intuition which can give them meaning or sense *in concreto*, they, as mere logical functions, can represent a thing in general, but not give by themselves alone a determinate concept of anything. Such hyperbolical objects are distinguised by the appellation of *Noümena*, or pure beings of the understanding (or better, beings of thought), such as, for example, "substance," but conceived without permanence in time, or "cause," but not acting in time, etc. Here predicates, that only serve to make the conformity-to-law of experience possible, are applied to these concepts, and yet they are deprived of all the conditions of intuition, on which alone experience is possible, and so these concepts lose all significance.

There is no danger, however, of the understanding spontaneously making an excursion so very wantonly beyond its own bounds into the field of the mere creatures of thought, without being impelled by foreign laws. But when reason, which cannot be fully satisfied with any empirical use of the rules of the understanding, as being always conditioned, requires a completion of this chain of conditions, then the understanding is forced out of its sphere. And then it partly represents objects of experience in a series so extended that no experience can grasp, partly even (with a view to complete the series) it seeks entirely beyond it noumena, to which it can attach that chain, and so, having at last escaped from the conditions of experience, make its attitude as it were final. These are then the transcendental ideas, which, though according to the true but hidden ends of the natural determination of our reason, they may aim not at extravagant concepts, but at an unbounded extension of their empirical use, yet seduce the understanding by an unavoidable illusion to a transcendent use, which, though deceitful, cannot be restrained within the bounds of experience by any resolution, but only by scientific instruction and with much difficulty.

I. *The Psychological Idea.*[1]

§ 46. People have long since observed, that in all substances the proper subject, that which remains after all the accidents (as predicates) are abstracted, consequently that which forms the substance of things remains unknown, and various complaints have been made concerning these limits to our knowledge. But it will be well to consider that the human understanding is not to be blamed for its inability to know the substance of things, that is, to determine it by itself, but rather for requiring to cognise it which is a mere idea definitely as though it were a given object. Pure reason requires us to seek for every predicate of a thing its proper subject, and for this subject, which is itself necessarily nothing but a predicate, its subject, and so on indefinitely (or as far as we can reach). But hence it follows, that we must not hold anything, at which we can arrive, to be an ultimate subject, and that substance itself never can be thought by our understanding, however deep we may penetrate, even if all nature were unveiled to us. For the specific nature of our understanding consists in thinking everything discursively, that is, representing it by concepts, and so by mere predicates, to which therefore the absolute subject must always be wanting. Hence all the real properties, by which we cognise bodies, are mere accidents, not excepting impenetrability, which we can only represent to ourselves as the effect of a power of which the subject is unknown to us.

Now we appear to have this substance in the consciousness of ourselves (in the thinking subject), and indeed in an immediate intuition; for all the predi-

[1] See *Critique of Pure Reason, Von den Paralogismen der reinen Vernunft.*

cates of an internal sense refer to the *ego*, as a subject, and I cannot conceive myself as the predicate of
any other subject.   Hence completeness in the reference of the given concepts as predicates to a subject
—not merely an idea, but an object—that is, the absolute subject itself, seems to be given in experience.
But this expectation is disappointed.   For the ego is
not a concept,[1] but only the indication of the object
of the internal sense, so far as we cognise it by no
further predicate.   Consequently it cannot be in itself
a predicate of any other thing; but just as little can
it be a determinate concept of an absolute subject,
but is, as in all other cases, only the reference of the
internal phenomena to their unknown subject.   Yet
this idea (which serves very well, as a regulative principle, totally to destroy all materialistic explanations
of the internal phenomena of the soul) occasions by a
very natural misunderstanding a very specious argument, which, from this supposed cognition of the
substance of our thinking being, infers its nature, so
far as the knowledge of it falls quite without the complex of experience.

§ 47. But though we may call this thinking self
(the soul) substance, as being the ultimate subject of
thinking which cannot be further represented as the
predicate of another thing; it remains quite empty
and without significance, if permanence—the quality
which renders the concept of substances in experience
fruitful—cannot be proved of it.

But permanence can never be proved of the con-

1 Were the representation of the apperception (the Ego) a concept, by
which anything could be thought, it could be used as a predicate of other
things or contain predicates in itself. But it is nothing more than the feeling
of an existence without the least definite conception and is only the representation of that to which all thinking stands in relation (*relatione accidentis*).

cept of a substance, as a thing in itself, but for the purposes of experience only. This is sufficiently shown by the first Analogy of Experience,[1] and whoever will not yield to this proof may try for himself whether he can succeed in proving, from the concept of a subject which does not exist itself as the predicate of another thing, that its existence is thoroughly permanent, and that it cannot either in itself or by any natural cause originate or be annihilated. These synthetical *a priori* propositions can never be proved in themselves, but only in reference to things as objects of possible experience.

§ 48. If therefore from the concept of the soul as a substance, we would infer its permanence, this can hold good as regards possible experience only, not [of the soul] as a thing in itself and beyond all possible experience. But life is the subjective condition of all our possible experience, consequently we can only infer the permanence of the soul in life; for the death of man is the end of all experience which concerns the soul as an object of experience, except the contrary be proved, which is the very question in hand. The permanence of the soul can therefore only be proved (and no one cares for that) during the life of man, but not, as we desire to do, after death; and for this general reason, that the concept of substance, so far as it is to be considered necessarily combined with the concept of permanence, can be so combined only according to the principles of possible experience, and therefore for the purposes of experience only.[2]

---

[1] Cf. *Critique, Von den Analogien der Erfahrung.*

[2] It is indeed very remarkable how carelessly metaphysicians have always passed over the principle of the permanence of substances without ever

§ 49. That there is something real without us which not only corresponds, but must correspond, to our external perceptions, can likewise be proved to be not a connexion of things in themselves, but for the sake of experience. This means that there is something empirical, i. e., some phenomenon in space without us, that admits of a satisfactory proof, for we have nothing to do with other objects than those which belong to possible experience; because objects which cannot be given us in any experience, do not exist for us. Empirically without me is that which appears in space, and space, together with all the phenomena which it contains, belongs to the representations, whose connexion according to laws of experience proves their objective truth, just as the connexion of the phenomena of the internal sense proves the actuality of my soul (as an object of the internal sense). By means of external experience I am conscious of the actuality of bodies, as external phenomena in space, in the same manner as by means of the internal experience I am conscious of the existence of my

attempting a proof of it; doubtless because they found themselves abandoned by all proofs as soon as they began to deal with the concept of substance. Common sense, which felt distinctly that without this presupposition no union of perceptions in experience is possible, supplied the want by a postulate. From experience itself it never could derive such a principle, partly because substances cannot be so traced in all their alterations and dissolutions, that the matter can always be found undiminished, partly because the principle contains *necessity*, which is always the sign of an *a priori* principle. People then boldly applied this postulate to the concept of soul as a *substance*, and concluded a necessary continuance of the soul after the death of man (especially as the simplicity of this substance, which is inferred from the indivisibility of consciousness, secured it from destruction by dissolution). Had they found the genuine source of this principle—a discovery which requires deeper researches than they were ever inclined to make—they would have seen, that the law of the permanence of substances has place for the purposes of experience only, and hence can hold good of things so far as they are to be cognised and conjoined with others in experience, but never independently of all possible experience, and consequently cannot hold good of the soul after death.

soul in time, but this soul is only cognised as an object of the internal sense by phenomena that constitute an internal state, and of which the essence in itself, which forms the basis of these phenomena, is unknown. Cartesian idealism therefore does nothing but distinguish external experience from dreaming; and the conformity to law (as a criterion of its truth) of the former, from the irregularity and the false illusion of the latter. In both it presupposes space and time as conditions of the existence of objects, and it only inquires whether the objects of the external senses, which we when awake put in space, are as actually to be found in it, as the object of the internal sense, the soul, is in time; that is, whether experience carries with it sure criteria to distinguish it from imagination. This doubt, however, may easily be disposed of, and we always do so in common life by investigating the connexion of phenomena in both space and time according to universal laws of experience, and we cannot doubt, when the representation of external things throughout agrees therewith, that they constitute truthful experience. Material idealism, in which phenomena are considered as such only according to their connexion in experience, may accordingly be very easily refuted; and it is just as sure an experience, that bodies exist without us (in space), as that I myself exist according to the representation of the internal sense (in time): for the notion without us, only signifies existence in space. However as the Ego in the proposition, "I am," means not only the object of internal intuition (in time), but the subject of consciousness, just as body means not only external intuition (in space), but the thing-in-itself, which is the basis of this phenomenon; [as this is the case] the question, whether bodies (as phenomena of the external sense) exist as bodies apart from my thoughts, may without any hesitation be denied in nature. But the question, whether I myself as a phenomenon of the internal sense (the soul according to empirical psychology) exist apart from my faculty of representation in time, is an exactly similar inquiry, and must likewise be answered in the negative. And in this manner everything, when it is reduced to its true meaning, is decided and certain. The formal (which I have also called transcendental) actually abolishes the material, or Cartesian, idealism. For if space be nothing but a form of my sensibility, it is as a representation in me just as actual as I myself am, and nothing but the empirical truth of the representations in it remains for consideration. But, if this is not the case, if space and the phenomena in it are something existing without us, then all the criteria of experience beyond our perception can never prove the actuality of these objects without us.

II. *The Cosmological Idea.*[1]

§ 50. This product of pure reason in its transcendent use is its most remarkable curiosity. It serves as a very powerful agent to rouse philosophy from its dogmatic slumber, and to stimulate it to the arduous task of undertaking a *Critique of Reason* itself.

I term this idea cosmological, because it always takes its object only from the sensible world, and does not use any other than those whose object is given to sense, consequently it remains in this respect in its native home, it does not become transcendent, and is therefore so far not mere idea; whereas, to conceive

1 Cf. *Critique, Die Antinomie der reinen Vernunft.*

the soul as a simple substance, already means to conceive such an object (the simple) as cannot be presented to the senses. Yet the cosmological idea extends the connexion of the conditioned with its condition (whether the connexion is mathematical or dynamical) so far, that experience never can keep up with it. It is therefore with regard to this point always an idea, whose object never can be adequately given in any experience.

§ 51. In the first place, the use of a system of categories becomes here so obvious and unmistakable, that even if there were not several other proofs of it, this alone would sufficiently prove it indispensable in the system of pure reason. There are only four such transcendent ideas, as there are so many classes of categories; in each of which, however, they refer only to the absolute completeness of the series of the conditions for a given conditioned. In analogy to these cosmological ideas there are only four kinds of dialectical assertions of pure reason, which, as they are dialectical, thereby prove, that to each of them, on equally specious principles of pure reason, a contradictory assertion stands opposed. As all the metaphysical art of the most subtile distinction cannot prevent this opposition, it compels the philosopher to recur to the first sources of pure reason itself. This Antinomy, not arbitrarily invented, but founded in the nature of human reason, and hence unavoidable and never ceasing, contains the following four theses together with their antitheses:

I.

Thesis.

The World has, as to Time and Space, a Beginning (limit).

Antithesis.

The World is, as to Time and Space, infinite.

2.

Thesis.

Everything in the World consists of [elements that are] simple.

Antithesis.

There is nothing simple, but everything is composite.

3.

Thesis.

There are in the World Causes through Freedom.

Antithesis.

There is no Liberty, but all is Nature.

4.

Thesis.

In the Series of the World-Causes there is some necessary Being.

Antithesis.

There is Nothing necessary in the World, but in this Series All is incidental.

§ 52. *a.* Here is the most singular phenomenon of human reason, no other instance of which can be shown in any other use. If we, as is commonly done, represent to ourselves the appearances of the sensible world as things in themselves, if we assume the principles of their combination as principles universally valid of things in themselves and not merely of experience, as is usually, nay without our *Critique*, unavoidably done, there arises an unexpected conflict, which never can be removed in the common dogmatical way; because the thesis, as well as the antithesis, can be shown by equally clear, evident, and irresistible proofs—for I pledge myself as to the correctness of all these proofs—and reason therefore perceives that it is divided with itself, a state at which the sceptic rejoices, but which must make the critical philosopher pause and feel ill at ease.

§ 52. *b.* We may blunder in various ways in metaphysics without any fear of being detected in falsehood. For we never can be refuted by experience if we but avoid self-contradiction, which in synthetical, though purely fictitious propositions, may be done whenever the concepts, which we connect, are mere ideas, that cannot be given (in their whole content) in experience. For how can we make out by experience, whether the world is from eternity or had a beginning, whether matter is infinitely divisible or consists of simple parts? Such concept cannot be given in any experience, be it ever so extensive, and consequently the falsehood either of the positive or the negative proposition cannot be discovered by this touch-stone.

The only possible way in which reason could have revealed unintentionally its secret Dialectics, falsely announced as Dogmatics, would be when it were made to ground an assertion upon a universally admitted principle, and to deduce the exact contrary with the greatest accuracy of inference from another which is equally granted. This is actually here the case with regard to four natural ideas of reason, whence four assertions on the one side, and as many counter-assertions on the other arise, each consistently following from universally-acknowledged principles. Thus they reveal by the use of these principles the dialectical illusion of pure reason which would otherwise forever remain concealed.

This is therefore a decisive experiment, which must necessarily expose any error lying hidden in the assumptions of reason.[1] Contradictory propositions cannot both be false, except the concept, which is the subject of both, is self-contradictory; for example, the propositions, "a square circle is round, and a square circle is not round," are both false. For, as to the former it is false, that the circle is round, because it is quadrangular; and it is likewise false, that it is not round, that is, angular, because it is a circle. For the logical criterion of the impossibility of a concept consists in this, that if we presuppose it, two contradictory propositions both become false; consequently, as no middle between them is conceivable, nothing at all is thought by that concept.

§ 52. c. The first two antinomies, which I call mathematical, because they are concerned with the addition or division of the homogeneous, are founded on such a self-contradictory concept; and hence I explain how it happens, that both the Thesis and Antithesis of the two are false.

When I speak of objects in time and in space, it is not of things in themselves, of which I know nothing, but of things in appearance, that is, of experience, as the particular way of cognising objects which is afforded to man. I must not say of what I think in time or in space, that in itself, and independent of

---

[1] I therefore would be pleased to have the critical reader to devote to this antinomy of pure reason his chief attention, because nature itself seems to have established it with a view to stagger reason in its daring pretentions, and to force it to self-examination. For every proof, which I have given, as well of the thesis as of the antithesis, I undertake to be responsible, and thereby to show the certainty of the inevitable antinomy of reason. When the reader is brought by this curious phenomenon to fall back upon the proof of the presumption upon which it rests, he will feel himself obliged to investigate the ultimate foundation of all the cognition of pure reason with me more thoroughly.

these my thoughts, it exists in space and in time; for in that case I should contradict myself; because space and time, together with the appearances in them, are nothing existing in themselves and outside of my representations, but are themselves only modes of representation, and it is palpably contradictory to say, that a mere mode of representation exists without our representation. Objects of the senses therefore exist only in experience; whereas to give them a self-subsisting existence apart from experience or before it, is merely to represent to ourselves that experience actually exists apart from experience or before it.

Now if I inquire after the quantity of the world, as to space and time, it is equally impossible, as regards all my notions, to declare it infinite or to declare it finite. For neither assertion can be contained in experience, because experience either of an infinite space, or of an infinite time elapsed, or again, of the boundary of the world by a void space, or by an antecedent void time, is impossible; these are mere ideas. This quantity of the world, which is determined in either way, should therefore exist in the world itself apart from all experience. This contradicts the notion of a world of sense, which is merely a complex of the appearances whose existence and connexion occur only in our representations, that is, in experience, since this latter is not an object in itself, but a mere mode of representation. Hence it follows, that as the concept of an absolutely existing world of sense is self-contradictory, the solution of the problem concerning its quantity, whether attempted affirmatively or negatively, is always false.

The same holds good of the second antinomy, which relates to the division of phenomena. For these are mere representations, and the parts exist merely in their representation, consequently in the division, or in a possible experience where they are given, and the division reaches only as far as this latter reaches. To assume that an appearance, e. g., that of body, contains in itself before all experience all the parts, which any possible experience can ever reach, is to impute to a mere appearance, which can exist only in experience, an existence previous to experience. In other words, it would mean that mere representations exist before they can be found in our faculty of representation. Such an assertion is self-contradictory, as also every solution of our misunderstood problem, whether we maintain, that bodies in themselves consist of an infinite number of parts, or of a finite number of simple parts.

§ 53. In the first (the mathematical) class of antinomies the falsehood of the assumption consists in representing in one concept something self-contradictory as if it were compatible (i. e., an appearance as an object in itself). But, as to the second (the dynamical) class of antinomies, the falsehood of the representation consists in representing as contradictory what is compatible; so that, as in the former case, the opposed assertions are both false, in this case, on the other hand, where they are opposed to one another by mere misunderstanding, they may both be true.

Any mathematical connexion necessarily presupposes homogeneity of what is connected (in the concept of magnitude), while the dynamical one by no means requires the same. When we have to deal with extended magnitudes, all the parts must be homogeneous with one another and with the whole; whereas, in the connexion of cause and effect, homogeneity may indeed likewise be found, but is not necessary; for the concept of causality (by means of which something is posited through something else quite different from it), at all events, does not require it.

If the objects of the world of sense are taken for things in themselves, and the above laws of nature for the laws of things in themselves, the contradiction would be unavoidable. So also, if the subject of freedom were, like other objects, represented as mere appearance, the contradiction would be just as unavoidable, for the same predicate would at once be affirmed and denied of the same kind of object in the same sense. But if natural necessity is referred merely to appearances, and freedom merely to things in themselves, no contradiction arises, if we at once assume, or admit both kinds of causality, however difficult or impossible it may be to make the latter kind conceivable.

As appearance every effect is an event, or something that happens in time; it must, according to the universal law of nature, be preceded by a determination of the causality of its cause (a state), which follows according to a constant law. But this determination of the cause as causality must likewise be something that takes place or happens; the cause must have begun to act, otherwise no succession between it and the effect could be conceived. Otherwise the effect, as well as the causality of the cause, would have always existed. Therefore the determination of the cause to act must also have originated among appearances, and must consequently, as well as its effect, be an event, which must again have its cause, and so on; hence natural necessity must be

the condition, on which effective causes are determined. Whereas if freedom is to be a property of
certain causes of appearances, it must, as regards
these, which are events, be a faculty of starting them
spontaneously, that is, without the causality of the
cause itself, and hence without requiring any other
ground to determine its start. But then the cause,
as to its causality, must not rank under time-determi-
nations of its state, that is, it cannot be an appearance, and must be considered a thing in itself, while
its effects would be only appearances.[1] If without
contradiction we can think of the beings of understanding [*Verstandeswesen*] as exercising such an influence on appearances, then natural necessity will
attach to all connexions of cause and effect in the
sensuous world, though on the other hand, freedom
can be granted to such cause, as is itself not an appearance (but the foundation of appearance). Nature
therefore and freedom can without contradiction be
attributed to the very same thing, but in different relations—on one side as a phenomenon, on the other
as a thing in itself.

We have in us a faculty, which not only stands in

[1] The idea of freedom occurs only in the relation of the intellectual, as
cause, to the appearance, as effect. Hence we cannot attribute freedom to
matter in regard to the incessant action by which it fills its space, though
this action takes place from an internal principle. We can likewise find no
notion of freedom suitable to purely rational beings, for instance, to God, so
far as his action is immanent. For his action, though independent of external determining causes, is determined in his eternal reason, that is, in the
divine *nature*. It is only, if *something is to start* by an action, and so the
effect occurs in the sequence of time, or in the world of sense (e. g., the beginning of the world), that we can put the question, whether the causality of
the cause must in its turn have been started, or whether the cause can originate an effect without its causality itself beginning. In the former case the
concept of this causality is a concept of natural necessity, in the latter, that
of freedom. From this the reader will see, that, as I explained freedom to
be the faculty of starting an event spontaneously, I have exactly hit the notion which is the problem of metaphysics.

connexion with its subjective determining grounds that are the natural causes of its actions, and is so far the faculty of a being that itself belongs to appearances, but is also referred to objective grounds, that are only ideas, so far as they can determine this faculty, a connexion which is expressed by the word *ought*. This faculty is called *reason*, and, so far as we consider a being (man) entirely according to this objectively determinable reason, he cannot be considered as a being of sense, but this property is that of a thing in itself, of which we cannot comprehend the possibility—I mean how the *ought* (which however has never yet taken place) should determine its activity, and can become the cause of actions, whose effect is an appearance in the sensible world. Yet the causality of reason would be freedom with regard to the effects in the sensuous world, so far as we can consider objective grounds, which are themselves ideas, as their determinants. For its action in that case would not depend upon subjective conditions, consequently not upon those of time, and of course not upon the law of nature, which serves to determine them, because grounds of reason give to actions the rule universally, according to principles, without the influence of the circumstances of either time or place.

What I adduce here is merely meant as an example to make the thing intelligible, and does not necessarily belong to our problem, which must be decided from mere concepts, independently of the properties which we meet in the actual world.

Now I may say without contradiction : that all the actions of rational beings, so far as they are appearances (occurring in any experience), are subject to the necessity of nature ; but the same actions, as re-

gards merely the rational subject and its faculty of
acting according to mere reason, are free.   For what
is required for the necessity of nature? Nothing more
than the determinability of every event in the world
of sense according to constant laws, that is, a reference to cause in the appearance; in this process the
thing in itself at its foundation and its causality remain unknown.   But I say, that the law of nature
remains, whether the rational being is the cause of
the effects in the sensuous world from reason, that is,
through freedom, or whether it does not determine
them on grounds of reason.   For, if the former is the
case, the action is performed according to maxims,
the effect of which as appearance is always conformable to constant laws; if the latter is the case, and
the action not performed on principles of reason, it
is subjected to the empirical laws of the sensibility,
and in both cases the effects are connected according
to constant laws; more than this we do not require
or know concerning natural necessity.   But in the
former case reason is the cause of these laws of nature, and therefore free; in the latter the effects follow according to mere natural laws of sensibility, because reason does not influence it; but reason itself
is not determined on that account by the sensibility,
and is therefore free in this case too.   Freedom is
therefore no hindrance to natural law in appearance,
neither does this law abrogate the freedom of the
practical use of reason, which is connected with
things in themselves, as determining grounds.

Thus practical freedom, viz., the freedom in which
reason possesses causality according to objectively
determining grounds, is rescued and yet natural necessity is not in the least curtailed with regard to the

very same effects, as appearances. The same remarks
will serve to explain what we had to say concerning
transcendental freedom and its compatibility with
natural necessity (in the same subject, but not taken
in the same reference). For, as to this, every beginning of the action of a being from objective causes
regarded as determining grounds, is always a first
start, though the same action is in the series of appearances only a subordinate start, which must be
preceded by a state of the cause, which determines it,
and is itself determined in the same manner by another immediately preceding. Thus we are able, in
rational beings, or in beings generally, so far as their
causality is determined in them as things in themselves, to imagine a faculty of beginning from itself
a series of states, without falling into contradiction
with the laws of nature. For the relation of the action to objective grounds of reason is not a time-rela-
tion ; in this case that which determines the causality
does not precede in time the action, because such determining grounds represent not a reference to objects
of sense, e. g., to causes in the appearances, but to
determining causes, as things in themselves, which do
not rank under conditions of time. And in this way
the action, with regard to the causality of reason, can
be considered as a first start in respect to the series of
appearances, and yet also as a merely subordinate beginning. We may therefore without contradiction
consider it in the former aspect as free, but in the
latter (in so far as it is merely appearance) as subject
to natural necessity.

As to the fourth Antinomy, it is solved in the same
way as the conflict of reason with itself in the third.
For, provided the cause *in* the appearance is distin-

guished from the cause *of* the appearance (so far as it can be thought as a thing in itself), both propositions are perfectly reconcilable: the one, that there is no-where in the sensuous world a cause (according to similar laws of causality), whose existence is abso-lutely necessary; the other, that this world is never-theless connected with a Necessary Being as its cause (but of another kind and according to another law). The incompatibility of these propositions entirely rests upon the mistake of extending what is valid merely of appearances to things in themselves, and in gen-eral confusing both in one concept.

§ 54. This then is the proposition and this the so-lution of the whole antinomy, in which reason finds itself involved in the application of its principles to the sensible world. The former alone (the mere prop-osition) would be a considerable service in the cause of our knowledge of human reason, even though the solution might fail to fully satisfy the reader, who has here to combat a natural illusion, which has been but recently exposed to him, and which he had hitherto always regarded as genuine. For one result at least is unavoidable. As it is quite impossible to prevent this conflict of reason with itself—so long as the ob-jects of the sensible world are taken for things in themselves, and not for mere appearances, which they are in fact—the reader is thereby compelled to ex-amine over again the deduction of all our *a priori* cog-nition and the proof which I have given of my deduc-tion in order to come to a decision on the question. This is all I require at present; for when in this oc-cupation he shall have thought himself deep enough into the nature of pure reason, those concepts by which alone the solution of the conflict of reason is possible, will become sufficiently familiar to him. Without this preparation I cannot expect an unreserved assent even from the most attentive reader.

III. *The Theological Idea.*[1]

§ 55. The third transcendental Idea, which affords matter for the most important, but, if pursued only speculatively, transcendent and thereby dialectical use of reason, is the ideal of pure reason. Reason in this case does not, as with the psychological and the cosmological Ideas, begin from experience, and err by exaggerating its grounds, in striving to attain, if possible, the absolute completeness of their series. It rather totally breaks with experience, and from mere concepts of what constitutes the absolute completeness of a thing in general, consequently by means of the idea of a most perfect primal Being, it proceeds to determine the possibility and therefore the actuality of all other things. And so the mere presupposition of a Being, who is conceived not in the series of experience, yet for the purposes of experience—for the sake of comprehending its connexion, order, and unity —i. e., the idea [the notion of it], is more easily distinguished from the concept of the understanding here, than in the former cases. Hence we can easily expose the dialectical illusion which arises from our making the subjective conditions of our thinking objective conditions of objects themselves, and an hypothesis necessary for the satisfaction of our reason, a dogma. As the observations of the *Critique* on the pretensions of transcendental theology are intelligible, clear, and decisive, I have nothing more to add on the subject.

1 Cf. *Critique*, the chapter on " Transcendental Ideals."

General Remark on the Transcendental Ideas.

§ 56. The objects, which are given us by experience, are in many respects incomprehensible, and many questions, to which the law of nature leads us, when carried beyond a certain point (though quite conformably to the laws of nature), admit of no answer; as for example the question: why substances attract one another? But if we entirely quit nature, or in pursuing its combinations, exceed all possible experience, and so enter the realm of mere ideas, we cannot then say that the object is incomprehensible, and that the nature of things proposes to us insoluble problems. For we are not then concerned with nature or in general with given objects, but with concepts, which have their origin merely in our reason, and with mere creations of thought; and all the problems that arise from our notions of them must be solved, because of course reason can and must give a full account of its own procedure.[1] As the psychological, cosmological, and theological Ideas are nothing but pure concepts of reason, which cannot be given in any experience, the questions which reason asks us about them are put to us not by the objects, but by mere maxims of our reason for the sake of its

---

[1] Herr Platner in his Aphorisms acutely says (§§ 728, 729), "If reason be a criterion, no concept, which is incomprehensible to human reason, can be possible. Incomprehensibility has place in what is actual only. Here incomprehensibility arises from the insufficiency of the acquired ideas." It sounds paradoxical, but is otherwise not strange to say, that in nature there is much incomprehensible (e. g., the faculty of generation) but if we mount still higher, and even go beyond nature, everything again becomes comprehensible; for we then quit entirely the objects, which can be given us, and occupy ourselves merely about ideas, in which occupation we can easily comprehend the law that reason prescribes by them to the understanding for its use in experience, because the law is the reason's own production.

own satisfaction. They must all be capable of satisfactory answers, which is done by showing that they
are principles which bring our use of the understanding into thorough agreement, completeness, and
synthetical unity, and that they so far hold good of
experience only, but of experience as a whole.

Although an absolute whole of experience is impossible, the idea of a whole of cognition according
to principles must impart to our knowledge a peculiar
kind of unity, that of a system, without which it is
nothing but piecework, and cannot be used for proving the existence of a highest purpose (which can
only be the general system of all purposes), I do not
here refer only to the practical, but also to the highest purpose of the speculative use of reason.

The transcendental Ideas therefore express the
peculiar application of reason as a principle of systematic unity in the use of the understanding. Yet if
we assume this unity of the mode of cognition to be
attached to the object of cognition, if we regard that
which is merely regulative to be constitutive, and if
we persuade ourselves that we can by means of these
Ideas enlarge our cognition transcendently, or far beyond all possible experience, while it only serves to
render experience within itself as nearly complete as
possible, i. e., to limit its progress by nothing that
cannot belong to experience: we suffer from a mere
misunderstanding in our estimate of the proper application of our reason and of its principles, and from a
Dialectic, which both confuses the empirical use of
reason, and also sets reason at variance with itself.

Conclusion.

On the Determination of the Bounds of Pure Reason.

§ 57. Having adduced the clearest arguments, it would be absurd for us to hope that we can know more of any object, than belongs to the possible experience of it, or lay claim to the least atom of knowledge about anything not assumed to be an object of possible experience, which would determine it according to the constitution it has in itself. For how could we determine anything in this way, since time, space, and the categories, and still more all the concepts formed by empirical experience or perception in the sensible world (*Anschauung*), have and can have no other use, than to make experience possible. And if this condition is omitted from the pure concepts of the understanding, they do not determine any object, and have no meaning whatever.

But it would be on the other hand a still greater absurdity if we conceded no things in themselves, or set up our experience for the only possible mode of knowing things, our way of beholding (*Anschauung*) them in space and in time for the only possible way, and our discursive understanding for the archetype of every possible understanding; in fact if we wished to have the principles of the possibility of experience considered universal conditions of things in themselves.

Our principles, which limit the use of reason to possible experience, might in this way become transcendent, and the limits of our reason be set up as limits of the possibility of things in themselves (as

Hume's dialogues may illustrate), if a careful critique did not guard the bounds of our reason with respect to its empirical use, and set a limit to its pretensions. Scepticism originally arose from metaphysics and its licentious dialectics. At first it might, merely to favor the empirical use of reason, announce everything that transcends this use as worthless and deceitful; but by and by, when it was perceived that the very same principles that are used in experience, insensibly, and apparently with the same right, led still further than experience extends, then men began to doubt even the propositions of experience. But here there is no danger; for common sense will doubtless always assert its rights. A certain confusion, however, arose in science which cannot determine how far reason is to be trusted, and why only so far and no further, and this confusion can only be cleared up and all future relapses obviated by a formal determination, on principle, of the boundary of the use of our reason.

We cannot indeed, beyond all possible experience, form a definite notion of what things in themselves may be. Yet we are not at liberty to abstain entirely from inquiring into them; for experience never satisfies reason fully, but in answering questions, refers us further and further back, and leaves us dissatisfied with regard to their complete solution. This any one may gather from the Dialectics of pure reason, which therefore has its good subjective grounds. Having acquired, as regards the nature of our soul, a clear conception of the subject, and having come to the conviction, that its manifestations cannot be explained materialistically, who can refrain from asking what the soul really is, and, if no concept of experience suffices for the purpose, from accounting for it by a concept of **reason** (that of a simple immaterial being), though we cannot by any means prove its objective reality? Who can satisfy himself with mere empirical knowledge in all the cosmological questions of the duration and of the quantity of the world, of freedom or of natural necessity, since every answer given on principles of experience begets a fresh question, which likewise requires its answer and thereby clearly shows the insufficiency of all physical modes of explanation to satisfy reason? Finally, who does not see in the thorough-going contingency and dependence of all his thoughts and assumptions on mere principles of experience, the impossibility of stopping there? And who does not feel himself compelled, notwithstanding all interdictions against losing himself in transcendent ideas, to seek rest and contentment beyond all the concepts which he can vindicate by experience, in the concept of a Being, the possibility of which we cannot conceive, but at the same time cannot be refuted, because it relates to a mere being of the understanding, and without it reason must needs remain forever dissatisfied?

Bounds (in extended beings) always presuppose a space existing outside a certain definite place, and inclosing it; limits do not require this, but are mere negations, which affect a quantity, so far as it is not absolutely complete. But our reason, as it were, sees in its surroundings a space for the cognition of things in themselves, though we can never have definite notions of them, and are limited to appearances only.

As long as the cognition of reason is homogeneous, definite bounds to it are inconceivable. In mathematics and in natural philosophy human reason admits of limits, but not of bounds, viz., that something indeed lies without it, at which it can never arrive, but not that it will at any point find completion in its internal progress. The enlarging of our views in mathematics, and the possibility of new discoveries, are infinite; and the same is the case with the discovery of new properties of nature, of new powers and laws, by continued experience and its rational combination. But limits cannot be mistaken here, for mathematics refers to appearances only, and what cannot be an object of sensuous contemplation, such as the concepts of metaphysics and of morals, lies entirely without its sphere, and it can never lead to them; neither does it require them. It is therefore not a continual progress and an approximation towards these sciences, and there is not, as it were, any point or line of contact. Natural science will never reveal to us the internal constitution of things, which though not appearance, yet can serve as the ultimate ground of explaining appearance. Nor does that science require this for its physical explanations. Nay even if such grounds should be offered from other sources (for instance, the influence of immaterial beings), they must be rejected and not used in the progress of its explanations. For these explanations must only be grounded upon that which as an object of sense can belong to experience, and be brought into connexion with our actual perceptions and empirical laws.

But metaphysics leads us towards bounds in the dialectical attempts of pure reason (not undertaken arbitrarily or wantonly, but stimulated thereto by the nature of reason itself). And the transcendental Ideas, as they do not admit of evasion, and are never capable of realisation, serve to point out to us actually not only the bounds of the pure use of reason, but also the way to determine them. Such is the end and the use of this natural predisposition of our reason, which has brought forth metaphysics as its favorite child, whose generation, like every other in the world, is not to be ascribed to blind chance, but to an original germ, wisely organised for great ends. For metaphysics, in its fundamental features, perhaps more than any other science, is placed in us by nature itself, and cannot be considered the production of an arbitrary choice or a casual enlargement in the progress of experience from which it is quite disparate.

Reason with all its concepts and laws of the understanding, which suffice for empirical use, i. e., within the sensible world, finds in itself no satisfaction because ever-recurring questions deprive us of all hope of their complete solution. The transcendental ideas, which have that completion in view, are such problems of reason. But it sees clearly, that the sensuous world cannot contain this completion, neither consequently can all the concepts, which serve merely for understanding the world of sense, such as space and time, and whatever we have adduced under the name of pure concepts of the understanding. The sensuous world is nothing but a chain of appearances connected according to universal laws; it has therefore no subsistence by itself; it is not the thing in itself, and consequently must point to that which contains the basis of this experience, to beings which cannot be cognised merely as phenomena, but as things in themselves. In the cognition of them alone reason can hope to satisfy its desire of completeness in proceeding from the conditioned to its conditions.

We have above (§§ 33, 34) indicated the limits of reason with regard to all cognition of mere creations of thought. Now, since the transcendental ideas have urged us to approach them, and thus have led us, as it were, to the spot where the occupied space (viz., experience) touches the void (that of which we can know nothing, viz., noumena), we can determine the bounds of pure reason. For in all bounds there is something positive (e. g., a surface is the boundary of corporeal space, and is therefore itself a space, a line is a space, which is the boundary of the surface, a point the boundary of the line, but yet always a place in space), whereas limits contain mere negations. The limits pointed out in those paragraphs are not enough after we have discovered that beyond them there still lies something (though we can never cognise what it is in itself). For the question now is, What is the attitude of our reason in this connexion of what we know with what we do not, and never shall, know? This is an actual connexion of a known thing with one quite unknown (and which will always remain so), and though what is unknown should not become the least more known—which we cannot even hope—yet the notion of this connexion must be definite, and capable of being rendered distinct.

We must therefore accept an immaterial being, a world of understanding, and a Supreme Being (all mere noumena), because in them only, as things in themselves, reason finds that completion and satisfaction, which it can never hope for in the derivation of appearances from their homogeneous grounds, and because these actually have reference to something distinct from them (and totally heterogeneous), as appearances always presuppose an object in itself, and therefore suggest its existence whether we can know more of it or not.

But as we can never cognise these beings of understanding as they are in themselves, that is, definitely, yet must assume them as regards the sensible world, and connect them with it by reason, we are at least able to think this connexion by means of such concepts as express their relation to the world of sense. Yet if we represent to ourselves a being of the understanding by nothing but pure concepts of the understanding, we then indeed represent nothing definite to ourselves, consequently our concept has no significance ; but if we think it by properties borrowed from the sensuous world, it is no longer a being of understanding, but is conceived as an appearance, and belongs to the sensible world. Let us take an instance from the notion of the Supreme Being.

Our deistic conception is quite a pure concept of reason, but represents only a thing containing all realities, without being able to determine any one of them ; because for that purpose an example must be taken from the world of sense, in which case we should have an object of sense only, not something quite heterogeneous, which can never be an object of sense. Suppose I attribute to the Supreme Being understanding, for instance ; I have no concept of an understanding other than my own, one that must receive its perceptions (*Anschauung*) by the senses, and which is occupied in bringing them under rules of the unity of consciousness. Then the elements of my concept would always lie in the appearance ; I should however by the insufficiency of the appearance be necessitated to go beyond them to the concept of a being which neither depends upon appearance, nor is bound up with them as conditions of its determination. But if I separate understanding from sensibility to obtain a pure understanding, then nothing remains but the mere form of thinking without perception (*Anschauung*), by which form alone I can cognise nothing definite, and consequently no object. For that purpose I should conceive another understanding, such as would directly perceive its objects,[1] but of which I have not the least notion ; because the human understanding is discursive, and can [not directly perceive, it can] only cognise by means of general concepts. And the very same difficulties arise if we attribute a will to the Supreme Being ; for we have this concept only by drawing it from our internal experience, and therefore from our dependence for satisfaction upon objects whose existence we require ; and so the notion rests upon sensibility, which is absolutely incompatible with the pure concept of the Supreme Being.

Hume's objections to deism are weak, and affect only the proofs, and not the deistic assertion itself. But as regards theism, which depends on a stricter determination of the concept of the Supreme Being which in deism is merely transcendent, they are very strong, and as this concept is formed, in certain (in fact in all common) cases irrefutable. Hume always insists, that by the mere concept of an original being, to which we apply only ontological predicates (eternity, omnipresence, omnipotence), we think nothing definite, and that properties which can yield a concept *in concreto* must be superadded ; that it is not enough to say, it is Cause, but we must explain the nature of its causality, for example, that of an understanding and of a will. He then begins his attacks

[1] *Der die Gegenstände anschaute.*

on the essential point itself, i. e., theism, as he had previously directed his battery only against the proofs of deism, an attack which is not very dangerous to it in its consequences. All his dangerous arguments refer to anthropomorphism, which he holds to be inseparable from theism, and to make it absurd in itself; but if the former be abandoned, the latter must vanish with it, and nothing remain but deism, of which nothing can come, which is of no value, and which cannot serve as any foundation to religion or morals. If this anthropomorphism were really unavoidable, no proofs whatever of the existence of a Supreme Being, even were they all granted, could determine for us the concept of this Being without involving us in contradictions.

If we connect with the command to avoid all transcendent judgments of pure reason, the command (which apparently conflicts with it) to proceed to concepts that lie beyond the field of its immanent (empirical) use, we discover that both can subsist together, but only at the boundary of all lawful use of reason. For this boundary belongs as well to the field of experience, as to that of the creations of thought, and we are thereby taught, as well, how these so remarkable ideas serve merely for marking the bounds of human reason. On the one hand they give warning not boundlessly to extend cognition of experience, as if nothing but world[1] remained for us to cognise, and yet, on the other hand, not to transgress the bounds of experience, and to think of judging about things beyond them, as things in themselves.

But we stop at this boundary if we limit our judg-

---

[1] The use of the word "world" without article, though odd, seems to be the correct reading, but it may be a mere misprint.—*Ed.*

ment merely to the relation which the world may have to a Being whose very concept lies beyond all the knowledge which we can attain within the world. For we then do not attribute to the Supreme Being any of the properties in themselves, by which we represent objects of experience, and thereby avoid dogmatic anthropomorphism; but we attribute them to his relation to the world, and allow ourselves a symbolical anthropomorphism, which in fact concerns language only, and not the object itself.

If I say that we are compelled to consider the world, as if it were the work of a Supreme Understanding and Will, I really say nothing more, than that a watch, a ship, a regiment, bears the same relation to the watchmaker, the shipbuilder, the commanding officer, as the world of sense (or whatever constitutes the substratum of this complex of appearances) does to the Unknown, which I do not hereby cognise as it is in itself, but as it is for me or in relation to the world, of which I am a part.

§ 58. Such a cognition is one of analogy, and does not signify (as is commonly understood) an imperfect similarity of two things, but a perfect similarity of relations between two quite dissimilar things.[1] By means

---

[1] There is, e g., an analogy between the juridical relation of human actions and the mechanical relation of motive powers. I never can do anything to another man without giving him a right to do the same to me on the same conditions; just as no mass can act with its motive power on another mass without thereby occasioning the other to react equally against it. Here right and motive power are quite dissimilar things, but in their relation there is complete similarity. By means of such an analogy I can obtain a notion of the relation of things which absolutely are unknown to me. For instance, as the promotion of the welfare of children (= a) is to the love of parents (= b), so the welfare of the human species (= c) is to that unknown [quantity which is] in God (= x), which we call love; not as if it had the least similarity to any human inclination, but because we can suppose its relation to the world to be similar to that which things of the world bear one another. But the con-

of this analogy, however, there remains a concept of
the Supreme Being sufficiently determined *for us*,
though we have left out everything that could determine it absolutely or in itself; for we determine it as
regards the world and as regards ourselves, and more
do we not require.   The attacks which Hume makes
upon those who would determine this concept absolutely, by taking the materials for so doing from
themselves and the world, do not affect us; and he
cannot object to us, that we have nothing left if we
give up the objective anthropomorphism of the concept of the Supreme Being.

For let us assume at the outset (as Hume in his
dialogues makes Philo grant Cleanthes), as a necessary hypothesis, the deistical concept of the First Being, in which this Being is thought by the mere ontological predicates of substance, of cause, etc.   This
must be done, because reason, actuated in the sensible world by mere conditions, which are themselves
always conditional, cannot otherwise have any satisfaction, and it therefore can be done without falling
into anthropomorphism (which transfers predicates
from the world of sense to a Being quite distinct from
the world), because those predicates are mere categories, which, though they do not give a determinate
concept of God, yet give a concept not limited to any
conditions of sensibility.   Thus nothing can prevent
our predicating of this Being a causality through reason with regard to the world, and thus passing to theism, without being obliged to attribute to God in
himself this kind of reason, as a property inhering in
him.   For as to the former, the only possible way of

cept of relation in this case is a mere category, viz., the concept of cause,
which has nothing to do with sensibility.

prosecuting the use of reason (as regards all possible experience, in complete harmony with itself) in the world of sense to the highest point, is to assume a supreme reason as a cause of all the connexions in the world. Such a principle must be quite advantageous to reason and can hurt it nowhere in its application to nature. As to the latter, reason is thereby not transferred as a property to the First Being in himself, but only to his relation to the world of sense, and so anthropomorphism is entirely avoided. For nothing is considered here but the cause of the form of reason which is perceived everywhere in the world, and reason is attributed to the Supreme Being, so far as it contains the ground of this form of reason in the world, but according to analogy only, that is, so far as this expression shows merely the relation, which the Supreme Cause unknown to us has to the world, in order to determine everything in it conformably to reason in the highest degree. We are thereby kept from using reason as an attribute for the purpose of conceiving God, but instead of conceiving the world in such a manner as is necessary to have the greatest possible use of reason according to principle. We thereby acknowledge that the Supreme Being is quite inscrutable and even unthinkable in any definite way as to what he is in himself. We are thereby kept, on the one hand, from making a transcendent use of the concepts which we have of reason as an efficient cause (by means of the will), in order to determine the Divine Nature by properties, which are only borrowed from human nature, and from losing ourselves in gross and extravagant notions, and on the other hand from deluging the contemplation of the world with hyperphysical modes of explanation according to our notions of human reason, which we transfer to God, and so losing for this contemplation its proper application, according to which it should be a rational study of mere nature, and not a presumptuous derivation of its appearances from a Supreme Reason. The expression suited to our feeble notions is, that we conceive the world as if it came, as to its existence and internal plan, from a Supreme Reason, by which notion we both cognise the constitution, which belongs to the world itself, yet without pretending to determine the nature of its cause in itself, and on the other hand, we transfer the ground of this constitution (of the form of reason in the world) upon the relation of the Supreme Cause to the world, without finding the world sufficient by itself for that purpose.[1]

Thus the difficulties which seem to oppose theism disappear by combining with Hume's principle—"not to carry the use of reason dogmatically beyond the field of all possible experience"—this other principle, which he quite overlooked: "not to consider the field of experience as one which bounds itself in the eye of our reason." The *Critique of Pure Reason* here points out the true mean between dogmatism, which Hume combats, and skepticism, which he would substitute for it—a mean which is not like other means that we find advisable to determine for ourselves as it were mechanically (by adopting something from one side and something from the other), and by which nobody

---

[1] I may say, that the causality of the Supreme Cause holds the same place with regard to the world that human reason does with regard to its works of art. Here the nature of the Supreme Cause itself remains unknown to me: I only compare its effects (the order of the world) which I know, and their conformity to reason, to the effects of human reason which I also know; and hence I term the former reason, without attributing to it on that account what I understand in man by this term, or attaching to it anything else known to me, as its property.

is taught a better way, but such a one as can be accurately determined on principles.

§ 59. At the beginning of this annotation I made use of the metaphor of a boundary, in order to establish the limits of reason in regard to its suitable use. The world of sense contains merely appearances, which are not things in themselves, but the understanding must assume these latter ones, viz., noumena. In our reason both are comprised, and the question is, How does reason proceed to set boundaries to the understanding as regards both these fields? Experience, which contains all that belongs to the sensuous world, does not bound itself; it only proceeds in every case from the conditioned to some other equally conditioned object. Its boundary must lie quite without it, and this field is that of the pure beings of the understanding. But this field, so far as the determination of the nature of these beings is concerned, is an empty space for us, and if dogmatically-determined concepts alone are in question, we cannot pass out of the field of possible experience. But as a boundary itself is something positive, which belongs as well to that which lies within, as to the space that lies without the given complex, it is still an actual positive cognition, which reason only acquires by enlarging itself to this boundary, yet without attempting to pass it; because it there finds itself in the presence of an empty space, in which it can conceive forms of things, but not things themselves. But the setting of a boundary to the field of the understanding by something, which is otherwise unknown to it, is still a cognition which belongs to reason even at this standpoint, and by which it is neither confined within the sensible, nor straying without it, but only refers, as befits the knowledge of a boundary, to the relation between that which lies without it, and that which is contained within it.

Natural theology is such a concept at the boundary of human reason, being constrained to look beyond this boundary to the Idea of a Supreme Being (and, for practical purposes to that of an intelligible world also), not in order to determine anything relatively to this pure creation of the understanding, which lies beyond the world of sense, but in order to guide the use of reason within it according to principles of the greatest possible (theoretical as well as practical) unity. For this purpose we make use of the reference of the world of sense to an independent reason, as the cause of all its connexions. Thereby we do not purely invent a being, but, as beyond the sensible world there must be something that can only be thought by the pure understanding, we determine that something in this particular way, though only of course according to analogy.

And thus there remains our original proposition, which is the *résumé* of the whole *Critique:* "that reason by all its *a priori* principles never teaches us anything more than objects of possible experience, and even of these nothing more than can be cognised in experience." But this limitation does not prevent reason leading us to the objective boundary of experience, viz., to the reference to something which is not itself an object of experience, but is the ground of all experience. Reason does not however teach us anything concerning the thing in itself: it only instructs us as regards its own complete and highest use in the field of possible experience. But this is all that can be reasonably desired in the present case, and with which we have cause to be satisfied.

§ 60. Thus we have fully exhibited metaphysics as it is actually given in the natural predisposition of human reason, and in that which constitutes the essential end of its pursuit, according to its subjective possibility. Though we have found, that this merely natural use of such a predisposition of our reason, if no discipline arising only from a scientific critique bridles and sets limits to it, involves us in transcendent, either apparently or really conflicting, dialectical syllogisms; and this fallacious metaphysics is not only unnecessary as regards the promotion of our knowledge of nature, but even disadvantageous to it: there yet remains a problem worthy of solution, which is to find out the natural ends intended by this disposition to transcendent concepts in our reason, because everything that lies in nature must be originally intended for some useful purpose.

Such an inquiry is of a doubtful nature; and I acknowledge, that what I can say about it is conjecture only, like every speculation about the first ends of nature. The question does not concern the objective validity of metaphysical judgments, but our natural predisposition to them, and therefore does not belong to the system of metaphysics but to anthropology.

When I compare all the transcendental Ideas, the totality of which constitutes the particular problem of natural pure reason, compelling it to quit the mere contemplation of nature, to transcend all possible experience, and in this endeavor to produce the thing (be it knowledge or fiction) called metaphysics, I think I perceive that the aim of this natural tendency is, to free our notions from the fetters of experience and from the limits of the mere contemplation of nature so far as at least to open to us a field containing mere objects for the pure understanding, which no sensibility can reach, not indeed for the purpose of speculatively occupying ourselves with them (for there we can find no ground to stand on), but because practical principles, which, without finding some such scope for their necessary expectation and hope, could not expand to the universality which reason unavoidably requires from a moral point of view.

So I find that the Psychological Idea (however little it may reveal to me the nature of the human soul, which is higher than all concepts of experience), shows the insufficiency of these concepts plainly enough, and thereby deters me from materialism, the psychological notion of which is unfit for any explanation of nature, and besides confines reason in practical respects. The Cosmological Ideas, by the obvious insufficiency of all possible cognition of nature to satisfy reason in its lawful inquiry, serve in the same manner to keep us from naturalism, which asserts nature to be sufficient for itself. Finally, all natural necessity in the sensible world is conditional, as it always presupposes the dependence of things upon others, and unconditional necessity must be sought only in the unity of a cause different from the world of sense. But as the causality of this cause, in its turn, were it merely nature, could never render the existence of the contingent (as its consequent) comprehensible, reason frees itself by means of the Theological Idea from fatalism, (both as a blind natural necessity in the coherence of nature itself, without a first principle, and as a blind causality of this principle itself), and leads to the concept of a cause possessing freedom, or of a Supreme Intelligence. Thus the transcendental Ideas serve, if not to instruct us positively, at least to destroy the rash assertions of Materialism, of Naturalism, and of Fatalism, and thus to afford scope for the moral Ideas beyond the field of speculation. These considerations, I should think, explain in some measure the natural predisposition of which I spoke.

The practical value, which a merely speculative science may have, lies without the bounds of this science, and can therefore be considered as a scholion merely, and like all scholia does not form part of the science itself. This application however surely lies within the bounds of philosophy, especially of philosophy drawn from the pure sources of reason, where its speculative use in metaphysics must necessarily be at unity with its practical use in morals. Hence the unavoidable dialectics of pure reason, considered in metaphysics, as a natural tendency, deserves to be explained not as an illusion merely, which is to be removed, but also, if possible, as a natural provision as regards its end, though this duty, a work of supererogation, cannot justly be assigned to metaphysics proper.

The solutions of these questions which are treated in the chapter on the Regulative Use of the Ideas of Pure Reason [1] should be considered a second scholion which however has a greater affinity with the subject of metaphysics. For there certain rational principles are expounded which determine *a priori* the order of nature or rather of the understanding, which seeks nature's laws through experience. They seem to be

1 *Critique of Pure Reason*, II., chap. III., section 7.

constitutive and legislative with regard to experience, though they spring from pure reason, which cannot be considered, like the understanding, as a principle of possible experience. Now whether or not this harmony rests upon the fact, that just as nature does not inhere in appearances or in their source (the sensibility) itself, but only in so far as the latter is in relation to the understanding, as also a systematic unity in applying the understanding to bring about an entirety of all possible experience can only belong to the understanding when in relation to reason ; and whether or not experience is in this way mediately subordinate to the legislation of reason : may be discussed by those who desire to trace the nature of reason even beyond its use in metaphysics, into the general principles of a history of nature; I have represented this task as important, but not attempted its solution, in the book itself.[1]

And thus I conclude the analytical solution of the main question which I had proposed : How is metaphysics in general possible? by ascending from the data of its actual use in its consequences, to the grounds of its possibility.

[1]Throughout in the *Critique* I never lost sight of the plan not to neglect anything, were it ever so recondite, that could render the inquiry into the nature of pure reason complete. Everybody may afterwards carry his researches as far as he pleases, when he has been merely shown what yet remains to be done. It is this a duty which must reasonably be expected of him who has made it his business to survey the whole field, in order to consign it to others for future cultivation and allotment. And to this branch both the scholia belong, which will hardly recommend themselves by their dryness to amateurs, and hence are added here for connoisseurs only.

SCHOLIA.

SOLUTION OF THE GENERAL QUESTION OF THE PROLEGOMENA, "HOW IS METAPHYSICS POSSIBLE AS A SCIENCE?"

METAPHYSICS, as a natural disposition of reason, is actual, but if considered by itself alone (as the analytical solution of the third principal question showed), dialectical and illusory. If we think of taking principles from it, and in using them follow the natural, but on that account not less false, illusion, we can never produce science, but only a vain dialectical art, in which one school may outdo another, but none can ever acquire a just and lasting approbation.

In order that as a science metaphysics may be entitled to claim not mere fallacious plausibility, but insight and conviction, a *Critique of Reason* must itself exhibit the whole stock of *a priori* concepts, their division according to their various sources (Sensibility, Understanding, and Reason), together with a complete table of them, the analysis of all these concepts, with all their consequences, especially by means of the deduction of these concepts, the possibility of synthetical cognition *a priori*, the principles of its application and finally its bounds, all in a complete system. Critique, therefore, and critique alone, contains in itself the whole well-proved and well-tested plan,

and even all the means required to accomplish metaphysics, as a science ; by other ways and means it is
impossible.   The question here therefore is not so
much how this performance is possible, as how to set
it going, and induce men of clear heads to quit their
hitherto perverted and fruitless cultivation for one
that will not deceive, and how such a union for the
common end may best be directed.

This much is certain, that whoever has once tasted
Critique will be ever after disgusted with all dogmatical twaddle which he formerly put up with, because
his reason must have something, and could find nothing better for its support.

Critique stands in the same relation to the common metaphysics of the schools, as chemistry does to
alchemy, or as astronomy to the astrology of the for-
tune-teller.   I pledge myself that nobody who has
read through and through, and grasped the principles
of, the Critique even in these Prolegomena only, will
ever return to that old and sophistical pseudo-science;
but will rather with a certain delight look forward to
metaphysics which is now indeed in his power, requiring no more preparatory discoveries, and now at
last affording permanent satisfaction to reason.   For
here is an advantage upon which, of all possible sciences, metaphysics alone can with certainty reckon :
that it can be brought to such completion and fixity
as to be incapable of further change, or of any aug-
mentation by new discoveries ; because here reason
has the sources of its knowledge in itself, not in objects and their observation (*Anschauung*), by which
latter its stock of knowledge cannot be further increased.   When therefore it has exhibited the fundamental laws of its faculty completely and so definitely

as to avoid all misunderstanding, there remains nothing for pure reason to cognise *a priori*, nay, there is even no ground to raise further questions. The sure prospect of knowledge so definite and so compact has a peculiar charm, even though we should set aside all its advantages, of which I shall hereafter speak.

All false art, all vain wisdom, lasts its time, but finally destroys itself, and its highest culture is also the epoch of its decay. That this time is come for metaphysics appears from the state into which it has fallen among all learned nations, despite of all the zeal with which other sciences of every kind are prosecuted. The old arrangement of our university studies still preserves its shadow; now and then an Academy of Science tempts men by offering prizes to write essays on it, but it is no longer numbered among thorough sciences; and let any one judge for himself how a man of genius, if he were called a great metaphysician, would receive the compliment, which may be well-meant, but is scarce envied by anybody.

Yet, though the period of the downfall of all dogmatical metaphysics has undoubtedly arrived, we are yet far from being able to say that the period of its regeneration is come by means of a thorough and complete *Critique of Reason*. All transitions from a tendency to its contrary pass through the stage of indifference, and this moment is the most dangerous for an author, but, in my opinion, the most favorable for the science. For, when party spirit has died out by a total dissolution of former connexions, minds are in the best state to listen to several proposals for an organisation according to a new plan.

When I say, that I hope these *Prolegomena* will excite investigation in the field of critique and afford a new and promising object to sustain the general spirit of philosophy, which seems on its speculative side to want sustenance, I can imagine beforehand, that every one, whom the thorny paths of my *Critique* have tired and put out of humor, will ask me, upon what I found this hope. My answer is, upon the irresistible law of necessity.

That the human mind will ever give up metaphysical researches is as little to be expected as that we should prefer to give up breathing altogether, to avoid inhaling impure air. There will therefore always be metaphysics in the world ; nay, every one, especially every man of reflexion, will have it, and for want of a recognised standard, will shape it for himself after his own pattern. What has hitherto been called metaphysics, cannot satisfy any critical mind, but to forego it entirely is impossible ; therefore a *Critique of Pure Reason* itself must now be attempted or, if one exists, investigated, and brought to the full test, because there is no other means of supplying this pressing want, which is something more than mere thirst for knowledge.

Ever since I have come to know critique, whenever I finish reading a book of metaphysical contents, which, by the preciseness of its notions, by variety, order, and an easy style, was not only entertaining but also helpful, I cannot help asking, " Has this author indeed advanced metaphysics a single step?" The learned men, whose works have been useful to me in other respects and always contributed to the culture of my mental powers, will, I hope, forgive me for saying, that I have never been able to find either their essays or my own less important ones (though self-love may recommend them to me) to have advanced the science of metaphysics in the least, and why?

Here is the very obvious reason: metaphysics did not then exist as a science, nor can it be gathered piecemeal, but its germ must be fully preformed in the *Critique*. But in order to prevent all misconception, we must remember what has been already said, that by the analytical treatment of our concepts the understanding gains indeed a great deal, but the science (of metaphysics) is thereby not in the least advanced, because these dissections of concepts are nothing but the materials from which the intention is to carpenter our science. Let the concepts of substance and of accident be ever so well dissected and determined, all this is very well as a preparation for some future use. But if we cannot prove, that in all which exists the substance endures, and only the accidents vary, our science is not the least advanced by all our analyses.

Metaphysics has hitherto never been able to prove *a priori* either this proposition, or that of sufficient reason, still less any more complex theorem, such as belongs to psychology or cosmology, or indeed any synthetical proposition. By all its analysing therefore nothing is affected, nothing obtained or forwarded, and the science, after all this bustle and noise, still remains as it was in the days of Aristotle, though far better preparations were made for it than of old, if the clue to synthetical cognitions had only been discovered.

If any one thinks himself offended, he is at liberty to refute my charge by producing a single synthetical proposition belonging to metaphysics, which he would prove dogmatically *a priori*, for until he has actually performed this feat, I shall not grant that he has truly advanced the science; even should this proposition be sufficiently confirmed by common experience. No demand can be more moderate or more equitable, and in the (inevitably certain) event of its non-performance, no assertion more just, than that hitherto metaphysics has never existed as a science.

But there are two things which, in case the challenge be accepted, I must deprecate: first, trifling about probability and conjecture, which are suited as little to metaphysics, as to geometry; and secondly, a decision by means of the magic wand of common sense, which does not convince every one, but which accommodates itself to personal peculiarities.

For as to the former, nothing can be more absurd, than in metaphysics, a philosophy from pure reason to think of grounding our judgments upon probability and conjecture. Everything that is to be cognised *a priori*, is thereby announced as apodeictically certain, and must therefore be proved in this way. We might as well think of grounding geometry or arithmetic upon conjectures. As to the doctrine of chances in the latter, it does not contain probable, but perfectly certain, judgments concerning the degree of the probability of certain cases, under given uniform conditions, which, in the sum of all possible cases, infallibly happen according to the rule, though it is not sufficiently determined in respect to every single chance. Conjectures (by means of induction and of analogy) can be suffered in an empirical science of nature only, yet even there the possibility at least of what we assume must be quite certain.

The appeal to common sense is even more absurd, when concept and principles are announced as valid, not in so far as they hold with regard to experience, but even beyond the conditions of experience. For what is common sense? It is normal good sense, so far it judges right. But what is normal good sense? It is the faculty of the knowledge and use of rules *in concreto*, as distinguished from the speculative understanding, which is a faculty of knowing rules *in abstracto*. Common sense can hardly understand the rule, " that every event is determined by means of its cause," and can never comprehend it thus generally. It therefore demands an example from experience, and when it hears that this rule means nothing but what it always thought when a pane was broken or a kitchen-utensil missing, it then understands the principle and grants it. Common sense therefore is only of use so far as it can see its rules (though they actually are *a priori*) confirmed by experience; consequently to comprehend them *a priori*, or independently of experience, belongs to the speculative understanding, and lies quite beyond the horizon of common sense. But the province of metaphysics is entirely confined to the latter kind of knowledge, and it is certainly a bad index of common sense to appeal to it as a witness, for it cannot here form any opinion whatever, and men look down upon it with contempt until they are in difficulties, and can find in their speculation neither in nor out.

It is a common subterfuge of those false friends of common sense (who occasionally prize it highly, but usually despise it) to say, that there must surely be at all events some propositions which are immediately certain, and of which there is no occasion to give any proof, or even any account at all, because we otherwise could never stop inquiring into the grounds of our judgments. But if we except the principle of contradiction, which is not sufficient to show the truth of synthetical judgments, they can never adduce, in proof of this privilege, anything else indubitable, which they can immediately ascribe to common sense, except mathematical propositions, such as twice two make four, between two points there is but one straight line, etc. But these judgments are radically different from those of metaphysics. For in mathematics I myself can by thinking construct whatever I represent to myself as possible by a concept: I add to the first two the other two, one by one, and myself make the number four, or I draw in thought from one point to another all manner of lines, equal as well as unequal; yet I can draw one only, which is like itself in all its parts. But I cannot, by all my power of thinking, extract from the concept of a thing the concept of something else, whose existence is necessarily connected with the former, but I must call in experience. And though my understanding furnishes me *a priori* (yet only in reference to possible experience) with the concept of such a connexion (i. e., causation), I cannot exhibit it, like the concepts of mathematics, by (*Anschauung*) visualising them, *a priori*, and so show its possibility *a priori*. This concept, together with the principles of its application, always requires, if it shall hold *a priori*—as is requisite in metaphysics —a justification and deduction of its possibility, because we cannot otherwise know how far it holds good, and whether it can be used in experience only or beyond it also.

Therefore in metaphysics, as a speculative science of pure reason, we can never appeal to common sense, but may do so only when we are forced to surrender it, and to renounce all purely speculative cognition, which must always be knowledge, and consequently when we forego metaphysics itself and its instruction, for the sake of adopting a rational faith which alone may be possible for us, and sufficient to our wants, perhaps even more salutary than knowledge itself. For in this case the attitude of the question is quite altered. Metaphysics must be science, not only as a whole, but in all its parts, otherwise it is nothing; because, as a speculation of pure reason, it finds a hold only on general opinions. Beyond its field, however, probability and common sense may be used with advantage and justly, but on quite special principles, of which the importance always depends on the reference to practical life.

This is what I hold myself justified in requiring for the possibility of metaphysics as a science.

APPENDIX.

ON WHAT CAN BE DONE TO MAKE METAPHYSICS ACTUAL AS A SCIENCE.

SINCE all the ways heretofore taken have failed to attain the goal, and since without a preceding critique of pure reason it is not likely ever to be attained, the present essay now before the public has a fair title to an accurate and careful investigation, except it be thought more advisable to give up all pretensions to metaphysics, to which, if men but would consistently adhere to their purpose, no objection can be made.

If we take the course of things as it is, not as it ought to be, there are two sorts of judgments: (1) one a judgment which precedes investigation (in our case one in which the reader from his own metaphysics pronounces judgment on the *Critique of Pure Reason* which was intended to discuss the very possibility of metaphysics); (2) the other a judgment subsequent to investigation. In the latter the reader is enabled to waive for awhile the consequences of the critical researches that may be repugnant to his formerly adopted metaphysics, and first examines the grounds whence those consequences are derived. If what common metaphysics propounds were demonstrably certain, as for instance the theorems of geometry, the former way of judging would hold good. For if the consequences of certain principles are repugnant to established truths, these principles are false and without further inquiry to be repudiated. But if metaphysics does not possess a stock of indisputably certain (synthetical) propositions, and should it even be the case that there are a number of them, which, though among the most specious, are by their consequences in mutual collision, and if no sure criterion of the truth of peculiarly metaphysical (synthetical) propositions is to be met with in it, then the former way of judging is not admissible, but the investigation of the principles of the critique must precede all judgments as to its value.

ON A SPECIMEN OF A JUDGMENT OF THE CRITIQUE PRIOR TO ITS EXAMINATION.

This judgment is to be found in the *Göttingischen gelehrten Anzeigen*, in the supplement to the third division, of January 19, 1782, pages 40 et seq.

When an author who is familiar with the subject of his work and endeavors to present his independent reflexions in its elaboration, falls into the hands of a reviewer who, in his turn, is keen enough to discern the points on which the worth or worthlessness of the book rests, who does not cling to words, but goes to the heart of the subject, sifting and testing more than the mere principles which the author takes as his point of departure, the severity of the judgment may indeed displease the latter, but the public does not care, as it gains thereby; and the author himself may be contented, as an opportunity of correcting or explaining his positions is afforded to him at an early date by the examination of a competent judge, in such a manner, that if he believes himself fundamentally right, he can remove in time any stone of offence that might hurt the success of his work.

I find myself, with my reviewer, in quite another position. He seems not to see at all the real matter of the investigation with which (successfully or unsuccessfully) I have been occupied. It is either impatience at thinking out a lengthy work, or vexation at a threatened reform of a science in which he believed he had brought everything to perfection long ago, or, what I am unwilling to imagine, real narrowmindedness, that prevents him from ever carrying his thoughts beyond his school-metaphysics. In short, he passes impatiently in review a long series of propositions, by which, without knowing their premises, we can think nothing, intersperses here and there his censure, the reason of which the reader understands just as little as the propositions against which it is directed; and hence [his report] can neither serve the public nor damage me, in the judgment of experts. I should, for these reasons, have passed over this judgment altogether, were it not that it may afford me occasion for some explanations which may in some cases save the readers of these *Prolegomena* from a misconception.

In order to take a position from which my reviewer could most easily set the whole work in a most unfavorable light, without venturing to trouble himself with any special investigation, he begins and ends by saying:

"This work is a system of transcendent (or, as he translates it, of higher) Idealism."[1]

___

[1] By no means "*higher*." High towers, and metaphysically-great men resembling them, round both of which there is commonly much wind, are not for me. My place is the fruitful *bathos*, the bottom-land, of experience; and the word transcendental, the meaning of which is so often explained by me,

A glance at this line soon showed me the sort of criticism that I had to expect, much as though the reviewer were one who had never seen or heard of geometry, having found a Euclid, and coming upon various figures in turning over its leaves, were to say, on being asked his opinion of it: "The work is a text-book of drawing; the author introduces a peculiar terminology, in order to give dark, incomprehensible directions, which in the end teach nothing more than what every one can effect by a fair natural accuracy of eye, etc."

Let us see, in the meantime, what sort of an idealism it is that goes through my whole work, although it does not by a long way constitute the soul of the system.

The dictum of all genuine idealists from the Eleatic school to Bishop Berkeley, is contained in this formula: "All cognition through the senses and experience is nothing but sheer illusion, and only, in the ideas of the pure understanding and reason there is truth."

The principle that throughout dominates and determines my Idealism, is on the contrary: "All cognition of things merely from pure understanding or pure reason is nothing but sheer illusion, and only in experience is there truth."

But this is directly contrary to idealism proper.

but not once grasped by my reviewer (so carelessly has he regarded everything), does not signify something passing beyond all experience, but something that indeed precedes it *a priori*, but that is intended simply to make cognition of experience possible. If these conceptions overstep experience, their employment is termed transcendent, a word which must be distinguished from transcendental, the latter being limited to the immanent use, that is, to experience. All misunderstandings of this kind have been sufficiently guarded against in the work itself, but my reviewer found his advantage in misunderstanding me.

How came I then to use this expression for quite an opposite purpose, and how came my reviewer to see it everywhere?

The solution of this difficulty rests on something that could have been very easily understood from the general bearing of the work, if the reader had only desired to do so. Space and time, together with all that they contain, are not things nor qualities in themselves, but belong merely to the appearances of the latter: up to this point I am one in confession with the above idealists. But these, and amongst them more particularly Berkeley, regarded space as a mere empirical presentation that, like the phenomenon it contains, is only known to us by means of experience or perception, together with its determinations. I, on the contrary, prove in the first place, that space (and also time, which Berkeley did not consider) and all its determinations *a priori*, can be cognised by us, because, no less than time, it inheres in our sensibility as a pure form before all perception or experience and makes all intuition of the same, and therefore all its phenomena, possible. It follows from this, that as truth rests on universal and necessary laws as its criteria, experience, according to Berkeley, can have no criteria of truth, because its phenomena (according to him) have nothing *a priori* at their foundation; whence it follows, that they are nothing but sheer illusion; whereas with us, space and time (in conjunction with the pure conceptions of the understanding) prescribe their law to all possible experience *a priori*, and at the same time afford the certain criterion for distinguishing truth from illusion therein.[1]

[1] Idealism proper always has a mystical tendency, and can have no other, but mine is solely designed for the purpose of comprehending the possibility

My so-called (properly critical) Idealism is of quite a special character, in that it subverts the ordinary idealism, and that through it all cognition *a priori*, even that of geometry, first receives objective reality, which, without my demonstrated ideality of space and time, could not be maintained by the most zealous realists. This being the state of the case, I could have wished, in order to avoid all misunderstanding, to have named this conception of mine otherwise, but to alter it altogether was impossible. It may be permitted me however, in future, as has been above intimated, to term it the formal, or better still, the critical Idealism, to distinguish it from the dogmatic Idealism of Berkeley, and from the sceptical Idealism of Descartes.

Beyond this, I find nothing further remarkable in the judgment of my book. The reviewer criticises here and there, makes sweeping criticisms, a mode prudently chosen, since it does not betray one's own knowledge or ignorance ; a single thorough criticism in detail, had it touched the main question, as is only fair, would have exposed, it may be my error, or it may be my reviewer's measure of insight into this species of research. It was, moreover, not a badly conceived plan, in order at once to take from readers (who are accustomed to form their conceptions of books from newspaper reports) the desire to read the book itself, to pour out in one breath a number of passages in succession, torn from their connexion, and

---

of our cognition *a priori* as to objects of experience, which is a problem never hitherto solved or even suggested. In this way all mystical idealism falls to the ground, for (as may be seen already in Plato) it inferred from our cognitions *a priori* (even from those of geometry) another intuition different from that of the senses (namely, an intellectual intuition), because it never occurred to any one that the senses themselves might intuite *a priori*.

their grounds of proof and explanations, and which
must necessarily sound senseless, especially considering how antipathetic they are to all school-metaphysics ; to exhaust the reader's patience *ad nauseam*, and
then, after having made me acquainted with the sensible proposition that persistent illusion is truth, to
conclude with the crude paternal moralisation: to
what end, then, the quarrel with accepted language,
to what end, and whence, the idealistic distinction?
A judgment which seeks all that is characteristic of
my book, first supposed to be metaphysically hetero-
dox, in a mere innovation of the nomenclature, proves
clearly that my would-be judge has understood nothing of the subject, and in addition, has not understood himself.[1]

My reviewer speaks like a man who is conscious
of important and superior insight which he keeps hidden ; for I am aware of nothing recent with respect to
metaphysics that could justify his tone. But he should
not withhold his discoveries from the world, for there
are doubtless many who, like myself, have not been
able to find in all the fine things that have for long
past been written in this department, anything that
has advanced the science by so much as a finger-
breadth ; we find indeed the giving a new point to
definitions, the supplying of lame proofs with new
crutches, the adding to the crazy-quilt of metaphysics

[1] The reviewer often fights with his own shadow. When I oppose the
truth of experience to dream, he never thinks that I am here speaking simply
of the well-known *somnio objective sumto* of the Wolffian philosophy, which is
merely formal, and with which the distinction between sleeping and waking
is in no way concerned, and in a transcendental philosophy indeed can have
no place. For the rest, he calls my deduction of the categories and table of
the principles of the understanding, "common well-known axioms of logic
and ontology, expressed in an idealistic manner." The reader need only
consult these *Prolegomena* upon this point, to convince himself that a more
miserable and historically incorrect, judgment, could hardly be made.

fresh patches or changing its pattern; but all this is not what the world requires. The world is tired of metaphysical assertions; it wants the possibility of the science, the sources from which certainty therein can be derived, and certain criteria by which it may distinguish the dialectical illusion of pure reason from truth. To this the critic seems to possess a key, otherwise he would never have spoken out in such a high tone.

But I am inclined to suspect that no such requirement of the science has ever entered his thoughts, for in that case he would have directed his judgment to this point, and even a mistaken attempt in such an important matter, would have won his respect. If that be the case, we are once more good friends. He may penetrate as deeply as he likes into metaphysics, without any one hindering him; only as concerns that which lies outside metaphysics, its sources, which are to be found in reason, he cannot form a judgment. That my suspicion is not without foundation, is proved by the fact that he does not mention a word about the possibility of synthetic knowledge *a priori*, the special problem upon the solution of which the fate of metaphysics wholly rests, and upon which my *Critique* (as well as the present *Prolegomena*) entirely hinges. The Idealism he encountered, and which he hung upon, was only taken up in the doctrine as the sole means of solving the above problem (although it received its confirmation on other grounds), and hence he must have shown either that the above problem does not possess the importance I attribute to it (even in these *Prolegomena*), or that by my conception of appearances, it is either not solved at all, or can be better solved in another way; but I do not find a word of this in the criticism. The reviewer, then, understands nothing of my work, and possibly also nothing of the spirit and essential nature of metaphysics itself; and it is not, what I would rather assume, the hurry of a man incensed at the labor of plodding through so many obstacles, that threw an unfavorable shadow over the work lying before him, and made its fundamental features unrecognisable.

There is a good deal to be done before a learned journal, it matters not with what care its writers may be selected, can maintain its otherwise well-merited reputation, in the field of metaphysics as elsewhere. Other sciences and branches of knowledge have their standard. Mathematics has it, in itself; history and theology, in profane or sacred books; natural science and the art of medicine, in mathematics and experience; jurisprudence, in law books; and even matters of taste in the examples of the ancients. But for the judgment of the thing called metaphysics, the standard has yet to be found. I have made an attempt to determine it, as well as its use. What is to be done, then, until it be found, when works of this kind have to be judged of? If they are of a dogmatic character, one may do what one likes; no one will play the master over others here for long, before some one else appears to deal with him in the same manner. If, however, they are critical in their character, not indeed with reference to other works, but to reason itself, so that the standard of judgment cannot be assumed but has first of all to be sought for, then, though objection and blame may indeed be permitted, yet a certain degree of leniency is indispensable, since the need is common to us all, and the lack of the necessary insight makes the high-handed attitude of judge unwarranted.

In order, however, to connect my defence with the interest of the philosophical commonwealth, I propose a test, which must be decisive as to the mode, whereby all metaphysical investigations may be directed to their common purpose. This is nothing more than what formerly mathematicians have done, in establishing the advantage of their methods by competition. I challenge my critic to demonstrate, as is only just, on *a priori* grounds, in his way, a single really metaphysical principle asserted by him. Being metaphysical it must be synthetic and cognised *a priori* from conceptions, but it may also be any one of the most indispensable principles, as for instance, the principle of the persistence of substance, or of the necessary determination of events in the world by their causes. If he cannot do this (silence however is confession), he must admit, that as metaphysics without apodeictic certainty of propositions of this kind is nothing at all, its possibility or impossibility must before all things be established in a critique of the pure reason. Thus he is bound either to confess that my principles in the *Critique* are correct, or he must prove their invalidity. But as I can already foresee, that, confidently as he has hitherto relied on the certainty of his principles, when it comes to a strict test he will not find a single one in the whole range of metaphysics he can bring forward, I will concede to him an advantageous condition, which can only be expected in such a competition, and will relieve him of the *onus probandi* by laying it on myself.

He finds in these *Prolegomena* and in my *Critique* (chapter on the "Theses and Antitheses of the Four

Antinomies") eight propositions, of which two and two contradict one another, but each of which necessarily belongs to metaphysics, by which it must either be accepted or rejected (although there is not one that has not in this time been held by some philosopher). Now he has the liberty of selecting any one of these eight propositions at his pleasure, and accepting it without any proof, of which I shall make him a present, but only one (for waste of time will be just as little serviceable to him as to me), and then of attacking my proof of the opposite proposition. If I can save this one, and at the same time show, that according to principles which every dogmatic metaphysics must necessarily recognise, the opposite of the proposition adopted by him can be just as clearly proved, it is thereby established that metaphysics has an hereditary failing, not to be explained, much less set aside, until we ascend to its birth-place, pure reason itself, and thus my *Critique* must either be accepted or a better one take its place; it must at least be studied, which is the only thing I now require. If, on the other hand, I cannot save my demonstration, then a synthetic proposition *a priori* from dogmatic principles is to be reckoned to the score of my opponent, then also I will deem my impeachment of ordinary metaphysicsas unjust, and pledge myself to recognise his stricture on my *Critique* as justified (although this would not be the consequence by a long way). To this end it would be necessary, it seems to me, that he should step out of his incognito. Otherwise I do not see how it could be avoided, that instead of dealing with one, I should be honored by several problems coming from anonymous and unqualified opponents.

PROPOSALS AS TO AN INVESTIGATION OF THE CRI-
TIQUE UPON WHICH A JUDGMENT MAY FOLLOW.

I feel obliged to the honored public even for the silence with which it for a long time favored my *Critique*, for this proves at least a postponement of judgment, and some supposition that in a work, leaving all beaten tracks and striking out on a new path, in which one cannot at once perhaps so easily find one's way, something may perchance lie, from which an important but at present dead branch of human knowledge may derive new life and productiveness. Hence may have originated a solicitude for the as yet tender shoot, lest it be destroyed by a hasty judgment. A test of a judgment, delayed for the above reasons, is now before my eye in the *Gothaischen gelehrten Zeitung*, the thoroughness of which every reader will himself perceive, from the clear and unperverted presentation of a fragment of one of the first principles of my work, without taking into consideration my own suspicious praise.

And now I propose, since an extensive structure cannot be judged of as a whole from a hurried glance, to test it piece by piece from its foundations, so thereby the present *Prolegomena* may fitly be used as a general outline with which the work itself may occasionally be compared. This notion, if it were founded on nothing more than my conceit of importance, such as vanity commonly attributes to one's own productions, would be immodest and would deserve to be repudiated with disgust. But now, the interests of speculative philosophy have arrived at the point of total extinction, while human reason hangs upon them with inextinguishable affection, and only after having been ceaselessly deceived does it vainly attempt to change this into indifference.

In our thinking age it is not to be supposed but that many deserving men would use any good opportunity of working for the common interest of the more and more enlightened reason, if there were only some hope of attaining the goal. Mathematics, natural science, laws, arts, even morality, etc., do not completely fill the soul; there is always a space left over, reserved for pure and speculative reason, the vacuity of which prompts us to seek in vagaries, buffooneries, and myticism for what seems to be employment and entertainment, but what actually is mere pastime; in order to deaden the troublesome voice of reason, which in accordance with its nature requires something that can satisfy it, and not merely subserve other ends or the interests of our inclinations. A consideration, therefore, which is concerned only with reason as it exists for it itself, has as I may reasonably suppose a great fascination for every one who has attempted thus to extend his conceptions, and I may even say a greater than any other theoretical branch of knowledge, for which he would not willingly exchange it, because here all other cognitions, and even purposes, must meet and unite themselves in a whole.

I offer, therefore, these *Prolegomena* as a sketch and text-book for this investigation, and not the work itself. Although I am even now perfectly satisfied with the latter as far as contents, order, and mode of presentation, and the care that I have expended in weighing and testing every sentence before writing it down, are concerned (for it has taken me years to satisfy myself fully, not only as regards the whole, but in some cases even as to the sources of one particular proposition); yet I am not quite satisfied with my exposition in some sections of the doctrine of elements, as for instance in the deduction of the conceptions of the Understanding, or in that on the paralogisms of pure reason, because a certain diffuseness takes away from their clearness, and in place of them, what is here said in the *Prolegomena* respecting these sections, may be made the basis of the test.

It is the boast of the Germans that where steady and continuous industry are requisite, they can carry things farther than other nations. If this opinion be well founded, an opportunity, a business, presents itself, the successful issue of which we can scarcely doubt, and in which all thinking men can equally take part, though they have hitherto been unsuccessful in accomplishing it and in thus confirming the above good opinion. But this is chiefly because the science in question is of so peculiar a kind, that it can be at once brought to completion and to that enduring state that it will never be able to be brought in the least degree farther or increased by later discoveries, or even changed (leaving here out of account adornment by greater clearness in some places, or additional uses), and this is an advantage no other science has or can have, because there is none so fully isolated and independent of others, and which is concerned with the faculty of cognition pure and simple. And the present moment seems, moreover, not to be unfavorable to my expectation, for just now, in Germany, no one seems to know wherewith to occupy himself, apart from the so-called useful sciences, so

as to pursue not mere play, but a business possessing
an enduring purpose.

To discover the means how the endeavors of the
learned may be united in such a purpose, I must leave
to others. In the meantime, it is my intention to persuade any one merely to follow my propositions, or
even to flatter me with the hope that he will do so;
but attacks, repetitions, limitations, or confirmation,
completion, and extension, as the case may be, should
be appended. If the matter be but investigated from
its foundation, it cannot fail that a system, albeit not
my own, shall be erected, that shall be a possession
for future generations for which they may have reason
to be grateful.

It would lead us too far here to show what kind of
metaphysics may be expected, when only the principles of criticism have been perfected, and how, because the old false feathers have been pulled out, she
need by no means appear poor and reduced to an insignificant figure, but may be in other respects richly
and respectably adorned. But other and great uses
which would result from such a reform, strike one immediately. The ordinary metaphysics had its uses,
in that it sought out the elementary conceptions of
the pure understanding in order to make them clear
through analysis, and definite by explanation. In this
way it was a training for reason, in whatever direction
it might be turned; but this was all the good it did;
service was subsequently effaced when it favored conceit by venturesome assertions, sophistry by subtle
distinctions and adornment, and shallowness by the
ease with which it decided the most difficult problems
by means of a little school-wisdom, which is only the
more seductive the more it has the choice, on the one

hand, of taking something from the language of science, and on the other from that of popular discourse, thus being everything to everybody, but in reality nothing at all. By criticism, however, a standard is given to our judgment, whereby knowledge may be with certainty distinguished from pseudo-science, and firmly founded, being brought into full operation in metaphysics; a mode of thought extending by degrees its beneficial influence over every other use of reason, at once infusing into it the true philosophical spirit. But the service also that metaphysics performs for theology, by making it independent of the judgment of dogmatic speculation, thereby assuring it completely against the attacks of all such opponents, is certainly not to be valued lightly. For ordinary metaphysics, although it promised the latter much advantage, could not keep this promise, and moreover, by summoning speculative dogmatics to its assistance, did nothing but arm enemies against itself. Mysticism, which can prosper in a rationalistic age only when it hides itself behind a system of school-metaphysics, under the protection of which it may venture to rave with a semblance of rationality, is driven from this, its last hiding-place, by critical philosophy. Last, but not least, it cannot be otherwise than important to a teacher of metaphysics, to be able to say with universal assent, that what he expounds is Science, and that thereby genuine services will be rendered to the commonweal.

KANT'S PHILOSOPHY.

By DR. PAUL CARUS.

KANT'S PHILOSOPHY.

PHILOSOPHY is frequently regarded as idle ver-
biage; and the great mass of the average productions of this branch of human endeavor would seem
to justify the statement. Nevertheless, philosophy
has exercised a paramount influence upon the history
of mankind, for philosophy is the quintessence of
man's conception of the world and the view he takes
of the significance of life. While philosophical books,
essays, lectures, and lessons may be intricate and long-
winded, there is at the core of all the questions under
discussion a public interest of a practical nature. The
problems that have reference to it are, as a rule, much
simpler and of more common application than is apparent to an outsider, and all of them closely considered will be found to be of a religious nature.

KANT'S SIGNIFICANCE IN THE HISTORY OF
PHILOSOPHY.

When we try to trace the erratic lines of the history of philosophy, the advance seems slow, but the
results, meagre though they sometimes may be, can
be summarised in brief statements. Thus the sophistic
movement in Greece in contradistinction to the old
naïve naturalists, Thales, Anaximander, and Anaxi-
menes, is characterised by the maxim: πάντων μέτρον
ἄνθρωπος, [Man is the measure of all things], which is
the simple solution of a series of intricate problems.

In spite of its truth, it was misused by unscrupulous rhetoricians, who disgraced the profession of sophists and degraded the noble name of their science, called sophia, i. e., wisdom, to such an extent that the term "sophist" became an epithet of opprobrium. Socrates opposed the sophists, but in all theoretical points he was one of them. There was only this difference, that he insisted on the moral nature of man and thus became the noblest exponent of the sophistic principle. It indicates a new departure that he changed the name sophia to philosophia or *philosophy*, i. e., love of wisdom, which was universally accepted as more modest and better becoming to the teachers and spiritual guides of mankind. While he granted that man is the measure of all things, he pointed out the duty of investigating the nature of man, and he selected the Delphic maxim: γνῶθι σεαυτόν, "know thyself," as a motto for his life. It would lead us too far to show how Plato worked out the Socratic problem of the human soul, which led him to a recognition of the significance of forms, as expressed in his doctrine of ideas, and how Aristotle applied it to natural science. The Neo-Platonists developed Plato's mystical and supernatural tendencies and prepared thereby for the rise of a dualistic religion.

When Christianity became a dominating power in the world, philosophy disappeared for a while, being replaced by the belief in a divine revelation as the sole source of all wisdom; but in the Middle Ages philosophy was revived as scholasticism, the impulse to the movement being due to the revival of Aristotelianism, through an acquaintance with the writings of cultured Arabian sages.

In the era of scholasticism we have two authorities, Revelation and Science, the former conceived to be identical with the verdicts of the Church, the latter being a blind acceptance of a second-hand and much distorted knowledge of the philosopher's works. The Platonic problem of the eternal types of things was revived, and Nominalists and Realists contended with one another on the question of the reality of ideas. In their methods, however, these two conflicting schools were on the same level, for both were in the habit of appealing to certain authorities. With them proof consisted in quotations either of church doctrines or of passages from Aristotle. There was no genuine science, no true philosophy, the efforts of the age consisting in vain attempts at reconciling the two conflicting sources of their opinions.

Modern philosophy is a product of the awakening spirit of science, beginning with Descartes who proposed to introduce method into philosophy, as expressed in his *Discourse on Method*. He abolished the implicit belief in book authority. Falling back upon the facts of life, he bethought himself of the significance of Man's thinking faculty, and so, starting again from the subjective position of the sophists, he defined his solution of the basic problem with great terseness in the sentence: *Cogito ergo sum*, [I think, therefore I am].

The latest phase in philosophy begins with Kant, and it is his immortal merit to have gone to the bottom of the philosophical problem by reducing its difficulties to a system. In the Cartesian syllogism he saw a fallacy if it was interpreted to mean *"Cogito ergo ego sum."*

The subject *ego*, implied in *"sum,"* is implicitly contained in *"cogito,"* and thus if the sentence is

meant to prove the existence of a metaphysical ego,
the argument is a fallacy, being merely a deduction
derived from the assumption that the ego does the
thinking.

In spite of its syllogistic form the sentence was
not meant as a syllogism but as a statement of fact.
Kant's objection, however, holds good in either case,
for though the thinking be a fact, it is an assumption
to take for granted that the thinker is an ego, i. e., a
soul-entity that exists independently of its thinking.
Lichtenberg therefore said that we ought to replace
the sentence "*I think*" by "*it thinks*." Yet even if
we allow the statement "*I think*" to pass, the question arises: What do we understand by "*I*"? Is it a
collective term for all the thought-processes that take
place in one and the same personality, or is there a
separate soul-being which does the thinking and constitutes the personality? In other words, the existence of the thinking subject, called the *I*, does not
imply that it is a spiritual thing in itself, nor even
that it constitutes a unity.

Mystic tendencies of a religious nature such as
found a classical exposition in Kant's contemporary
and namesake, Emanuel Swedenborg, rendered some
of the problems of philosophy more complicated by
laying special stress upon the difference between matter and spirit, and discussing the possibility and probable nature of purely spiritual beings; but all philosophising on the subject consisted in declamations and
unproved propositions.

Wolf, a clear-headed thinker, though void of origi-
nality, reduced the metaphysical notions from Aristotle down to the eighteenth century into an elaborate

system, and thus became to Kant the typical exponent of dogmatism.

In contrast to the metaphysical school, the sensualists had risen. They are best represented by Locke who denied the existence of innate ideas (except the idea of causation) and tried to prove that all abstract thought had its origin in sensation. Hume, taking offence even at the claims of causation as a necessary connexion, declared that, accustomed to the invariable sequence of cause and effect, we mistake our subjective necessity of thinking them together for an objective necessity, which remains unproved. Thus he turned skeptic and gave by his doubts regarding the objective validity of causation as a universal principle and a metaphysical truth the suggestion to Kant to investigate the claims of all metaphysics, of which the notion of causality is only a part.

Here Kant's philosophical reform set in, which consists in rejecting both the skepticism of Hume and the dogmatism of Wolf and in offering a new solution which he called criticism.

Kant took the next step in seeking for the principle that determined all thinking, and discovered it in the purely formal laws of thought, which in their complete unity constitute pure reason. The investigation of the conditions of thought, he called "criticism." He insisted that the dogmatical declamations of all the various systems of metaphysics were idle and useless talk. He said they were vain attempts at building a mighty tower that would reach to Heaven. But at the same time he claimed to prove that the supply of building materials was after all sufficient for a dwelling-house spacious enough for the needs of life and high enough to survey the field of experience.[1]

In place of the old metaphysics which used to derive from pure concepts a considerable amount of pretended knowledge concerning God, the world, and man, concerning substance, as the substratum of existence, the soul, the future state of things, and immortality, Kant drew up an inventory of the possessions of Pure Reason and came to the conclusion that all knowledge of purely formal thought is in itself empty and that sense-experience in itself is blind; the two combined form the warp and woof of experience, which alone can afford positive information concerning the nature of objects. Empirical knowledge of the senses furnishes the material, while formal thought supplies the method by which perceptions can be organised and systematised into knowledge. Kant's aim was not to produce glittering generalities, but to offer critique, that is to say, a method of, and norm for, scientific thought; and he said, conscious of the significance of his philosophy:

"This much is certain, that whoever has once tasted critique will be ever after disgusted with all dogmatical twaddle."

Dogmatism in metaphysics is the dragon which Kant slew. But Kant's criticism was not purely negative. He recognised in the world as an undeniable fact the demand of the moral "ought" which he called "the categorical imperative," and while he insisted upon the determinism of natural law he would not deny the freedom of the will establishing it upon

1 See *Critique of Pure Reason* in the chapter "Transcendental Doctrine of Method," Max Müller's translation, p. 567, Meicklejohn's, p. 431, original edition, p. 707.

man's moral responsibility. He declared: "I shall, therefore I can."

PERSONAL TRAITS.

Kant, the son of simple but rigorously pious parents of Scotch extraction, lived at Königsberg in Prussia under the rule of Frederick the Great.[1] His moral sense was stern and unalloyed with sentimentality. He never married, and his relation to his relatives was regulated strictly according to his views of duty.[2] In his philosophy as well as in his private life he was duty incarnate. While he had imbibed the sense of duty that characterises the system of education in Prussia, he was also swayed by the ideals of liberty and fraternity so vigorously brought to the front by the French revolution.[3] His influence on the German nation, on science, religion, and even politics cannot be underrated, although his ideas did not reach the people directly in the form he uttered them, but only indirectly through his disciples, the preachers, teachers, and poets of the age. His main works which embody the gist of his peculiar doctrines are the *Critique of Pure Reason*, the *Critique of Practical Reason*, and the *Critique of Judgment*. Among them the *Critique*

[1] For a good condensed statement of Kant's life see page 245 of this volume, where Professor Windelband's account is reproduced. For a convenient chronological table of the data of Kant's life and publications see pages 287–291 of the present volume.

[2] We have had reproduced at p. 285 of this volume a specimen of Kant's handwriting, a letter of his to his brother, plainly characterising his business-like conception of duty which regulated his life with machine-like precision.

[3] Heinrich Heine described Kant to the French most drastically in an essay on German philosophy, of which an English translation has been reprinted in this volume at page 264.

of Pure Reason is by far the most important one.[1] It
is a pity that the *Critique of Pure Reason*, from the
appearance of which the historian dates the beginning
of the latest period in the evolution of philosophy, is
a ponderous and almost unintelligible work,—a book
with seven seals to the average reader; and it might
have remained ineffectual had not Kant been necessitated to rectify this defect by giving to the public a
popular explanation concerning his intentions.

The *Critique of Pure Reason* was published in 1781.
In the *Göttingenschen Gelehrten Anzeigen* of January
19, 1782, there appeared a review of the book, written
by Garve and modified by Feder, which irritated Kant
considerably, because the review treated his criticism
as a revival of Berkeley's idealism, which was commonly regarded as pure subjectivism.[2] There is no
need here of protesting in Berkeley's name against
this interpretation of his philosophy, for we are concerned here with Kant, not with Berkeley. But even
Kant misunderstood Berkeley,[3] and for our present

[1] A splendid analysis of the three *Critiques* is given by Prof. A. Weber in
his *History of Philosophy*, translated from the fifth French edition by Prof.
Frank Tilly, pp. 436–472. We have reprinted part of this analysis at p. 250.

The compilation of Kant's philosophy in a *Kantlexikon* by Gustav Wegner
(Berlin, 1893) is not very serviceable. The book is unhandy and lacks the
main requisite of a lexicon, a good index.

The exposition of Kant's philosophy by G. H. Lewes in his *Biographical
History of Philosophy* is an excellent sketch and worth a careful perusal. But
Lewes leaves the problem where Kant left it, saying : "There is, in truth, no
necessity in causation, except the necessity of our belief in it." But whence
does this necessity come, and what is its authority ?

[2] Garve's letter to Kant and Kant's answer contain the whole material of
the history of this garbled review. They are interesting reading but mainly
of a personal nature, consisting of explanations, excuses, and polite words.
For a reproduction of this correspondence see Reclam's text edition of Kant's
Prolegomena, Appendix, pp. 214–230.

[3] For a condensed statement of Berkeley's idealism see Thomas J. Mc-
Cormack's preface to Berkeley's *Treatise Concerning the Principles of Human
Knowledge*, Chicago, The Open Court Pub. Co., 1901, especially pp. xii–xiv.

purpose it is sufficient to say that Berkeley's idealism meant to Kant and his contemporaries pure subjectivism.

Kant was irritated because his philosophy was dis-

C. Garve.

posed of as an old error, a method which (as Paulsen says) has been developed into a regular system among a certain class of Roman Catholic critics who regard the possibilities of philosophising as exhausted in the history of philosophy. Claiming to be in possession of the whole truth, they are naturally disinclined to believe that new truths can be brought to light. Thus they have developed the habit of associating every new idea with some one of the systems of the past which to them are nothing but a *catalogus errorum*, and serve them as so many coffins in which to bury any doctrine that does not receive their approbation.

Kant's indignation was perhaps exaggerated, for he ought to have considered the difficulty of understanding a doctrine that was at the same time utterly new and presented in a most unattractive, pedantical form; but the result was happy, for he felt urged to write a popular explanation of his work, to offset Garve's misconception, which would serve the reader as *Prolegomena*, i. e , as prefatory remarks to the *Critique of Pure Reason*.

These *Prolegomena* insist on the newness of Kant's proposition and emphasise his adhesion to realism (or the doctrine that the objective world is actual) in contrast to the subjectivism of Berkeley, or what was supposed to be Berkeley. At the same time they possess the charm of wonderful vigor and directness. Here Kant does not write in the pedantic, dignified style of a professor, but with the boldness of a resentful author who, conscious of his title to careful consideration and believing himself to be wrongly criticised, is anxious to be properly understood by the public.

While the *Critique of Pure Reason* is synthetic, the *Prolegomena* are (as says Kant himself) analytic. In the *Critique of Pure Reason* Kant discourses as one who speaks *ex cathedra*, sitting in the professorial chair; he propounds his doctrine deductively, and I

---

1 See Friedrich Paulsen's *Kant*, p. 229.

for one can very well understand that his expositions appear to an uninitiated reader bewilderingly oracular. In the *Prolegomena* his style is not stilted but rather careless and though his periods are long they are fluent and easily understood.

KANT'S TERMS.

The main difficulty of understanding Kant, to later generations, and also to foreigners not to the manner born as regards the German vernacular, lies in his terminology. Simple though his terms are when once understood, they afford unsurmountable difficulties to those who are not familiar with their significance.

Familiarity with the following terms is indispensable for a comprehension of Kant: "metaphysics"; "understanding" and "reason"; "empirical" and "experience"; "noumenon" and "phenomenon"; *a priori* and *a posteriori*; "transcendental" and "transcendent"; and "intuition" or *Anschauung*.

First, above all, there is the term "metaphysics," which is the science of first principles. Aristotle, who discusses the subject of ἀρχαί, or first principles, in books placed after the physical treatises (hence the name τὰ μετὰ τὰ φυσικά, *sc.* βίβλια, corrupted into metaphysics), calls it First Philosophy, i. e., the Essence or basis of Philosophy, and identifies it with Theology, because he finds in God the ultimate *raison d'être* of all metaphysical concepts such as being and becoming, space and time, multiplicity and unity, things and the world, cause and effect, substance and quality, God and soul and immortality.

Kant defines metaphysics as:

"A system of all the principles of pure theoretical reason-cognition (*Vernunfterkenntniss*) in concepts,—briefly the system of pure theoretical philosophy." [1]

In another place Kant (IV., p. 236) speaks of metaphysics simply as "pure philosophy limited to the objects of the understanding," a definition which almost identifies it with Logic. [2] He insists that metaphysics is based upon man's faculty of thinking and not pure imagination. Being *a priori*, it deals with the acts of pure thought, which reduce the manifold sense-impressions to unity by law. (Vol. IV., p. 362.)

The sources of metaphysics are limited by Kant to the *a priori* (Vol. IV., p. 13); its possibility stands and falls with the possibility of synthetical judgments *a priori* (Vol. IV., p. 14); pre-Kantian metaphysics is declared to be uncritical and unscientific (IV., p. 23); as a science metaphysics must be a systematic presentation of all *a priori* concepts, including above all the synthetical propositions of man's philosophical cognition; and its final purpose (IV., p. 19) consists in the cognition of the Supreme Being as well as of the life to come (*die zukünftige Welt*). The latter expression had perhaps better be replaced by the broader idea of the *mundus intelligibilis*, the intelligible world, constituting the purely formal in contrast to the material, the Platonic ideas or types of things as distinguished from their accidental relations in space and time, exhibiting the abiding in the transcient and thus making it possible to view the world (as Spinoza has it) under the aspect of eternity,—*sub specie æterni*.

Kant started a new line of investigation and kept in view his main aim. So it was natural that he did

[1] Ed. Hartenstein, Vol. VIII., p. 521.

[2] Logic is defined by Kant (IV., p. 236) as "the pure philosophy which is purely formal."

not feel the need of certain discriminations before his work was pretty well advanced. This accounts for a few inaccuracies in the use of his terminology, covering the terms "understanding," "reason," and "experience." He distinguishes in his *Prolegomena* between reason and understanding, but the discrimination is by no means thoroughly carried out. The understanding is defined as the use of the categories, and reason the faculty of forming ideas. The understanding accordingly represents the logical functions, and reason the domain of abstractions and generalisations. The understanding draws conclusions and attends to the machinery of thinking, reason seeks oneness in plurality, aims at a systematical comprehension of things apparently different and establishes laws to explain the variety of phenomena by one common rule.

By "empirical" Kant understood all those judgments that contain sensory elements. They were either mere perceptions, i. e., a taking cognisance of sense-impressions, or experience, i. e., the product of thought and perceptions, resulting in empirical statements that are universally valid.[1]

The contrast of perceptions, as the sense-woven pictures of things, and ideas or the mind-begotten concepts of them, is expressed in the two terms "phenomenon" or appearance, and "noumenon" or thought. Kant translates the former by the word *Sinneswesen*, i. e., creature of the senses, and the latter by the word *Gedankenwesen*, i. e., creature of thought.[2]

---

[1] That Kant's use of the term "experience" was not always consistent I have endeavored to explain elsewhere. See *Primer of Philosophy*, pp. 30 ff.

[2] Pronounce *no-oomenon*, not *noomenon*. The original Greek reads νοού-μενον. The *ou* in the German transcription, "*No-umenon*" was misinterpreted as a French *ou;* hence the erroneous pronunciation of some English lexicographers as "noomenon."

Noumenon should not mean "thing in itself," as which it is actually used by Kant contrary to his own definition, but man's subjective conception of the thing in itself. If the phenomenon is subjective appearance, the noumenon, far from being objective, is, according to Kant, still more subjective, being a mere subjective digest of the materials furnished by the subjective phenomenon. The term "noumenon," however, is not limited to its original meaning. Kant understands by it, not only the subjective concept of things, but also the objective "thing in itself."

The terms *a priori* and *a posteriori* are of special significance. They mean "before" and "afterwards," but we must bear in mind that they should be understood, not as a temporal succession, but in a logical sense. *A priori* cognitions are the principles which the naturalist uses in his investigations; but his investigations themselves, consisting of sense-experience, are *a posteriori*. Before he begins his investigation, the naturalist must know that $2 \times 2 = 4$, that there can be no effect without a cause, that he can rely on the rule of three and on the syllogisms of logic. The knowledge of these truths is the condition of science, and all these truths are universal, i. e., they apply to all possible cases. *A priori* knowledge has developed through the practice of sense-experience. Indeed, sense-experience came first in temporal order; but sense-impressions would forever remain a mass of isolated things were they not systematised with the assistance of *a priori* principles.

A priori does not mean innate, for neither mathematics, nor arithmetic, nor logic is innate; but the theorems of these sciences can be deduced in our thoughts without calling upon sense-experience to aid us. Innate ideas would mean inherited notions, like the instincts of animals. The characteristic feature of *a priori* conceptions is not that we know them well nor that we find them ready-made in our minds, but that they have a universal application and are therefore necessary truths.

The contrast between *a priori* and *a posteriori* truths is easily explained when we consider that the former are purely formal, the latter sensory. The former therefore cannot give us any information concerning the substance, the matter, the thingish nature of things (as Kant expresses it, "they are empty"), but they can be used for determining the relations and forms of things, and this renders them uniquely valuable, for science is nothing but a tracing of the changes of form, an application of the laws of form, a measuring, a weighing, a counting; and their paramount importance appears in this that our knowledge of the laws of form will in consideration of their universal validity, result in the possibility of predetermining future modifications under given conditions.

There are two synonyms of *a priori*, the word "pure" and the term "transcendental."

Reason unalloyed with notions derived from sense-experience, and therefore limited to conceptions *a priori*, is called pure reason. "Transcendental" means practically the same as pure and *a priori*. By transcendental discourses Kant understands those which transcend experience and consider its *a priori* conditions. Thus, transcendental logic is pure logic in so far as pure logic is the condition of applied logic. Transcendental psychology is the doubtful domain of abstract notions concerning the unity of the ego, its substantiality and permanence, etc. Transcendental cosmology consists of the ideas of existence in general and the universe in particular. Then the questions arise as to the world's infinitude or limitedness, its eternity or beginning and end. Further, whether or not causality is absolute, viz., is there contingency only, or is an uncaused will possible? Here the oracle of pure reason fails and Kant formulates the result in his strange doctrine of contradictions, or, as he calls it, antinomies of pure reason.

Transcendental cosmology, transcendental psychology, transcendental theology, are not sciences, but the dreams of metaphysics. As such they transcend experience to the extent of becoming hazy. They cease to be accessible to comprehension and are then in Kant's terminology called "transcendent."

Mark the difference between the two terms: the word "transcendental" denotes the subjective conditions of all experience, consisting in the recognition of such truisms as logical, arithmetical, and geometrical theorems, which are the clearest, most indisputable, and most unequivocal notions we have. Transcendent, however, means that which lies beyond the ken of all possible knowledge within the nebulous domain in which we can as well affirm as deny the possibility of assumptions. Consider at the same time that in the English language "transcendental" is a synonym of "transcendent," and the difference made by Kant has been slurred over by many of his expositors. What a heap of confusion resulted from this carelessness! We need not wonder that his radical system of transcendental criticism was transformed into that uncritical metaphysicism, or dabbling in unwarranted transcendental notions which Kant so vigorously and effectually combated.

The confusion which English interpreters produced by their neglect of distinguishing between "transcendent" and "transcendental" was increased by their misconception of the term *Anschauung*, which, being properly but not adequately translated by its Latin equivalent "intuition," became tinged with all the mysticism and metaphysicism of intuitionalism. "Intuition," according to the commonly accepted use of the word, means in the English as well as in German "the power of the mind by which it immediately perceives the truth of things without reasoning or analysis." As such intuitions signify not only the images of sense-perception, but also, and indeed mainly, ecstatic visions in which the soul is face to face with presences spiritual, supernal, or divine; and thus it happened that under the guarantee of Kant's criticism the most extravagant speculations could gain admission to the philosophical world as genuine philosophical ideas.

Anschauung, like the Latin *intuitio*, signifies the act of *looking at* an object; it denotes the sensation of sight. However, its use is not restricted to sight, but extends to all sense-perception. The peculiar feature of sense-perception consists in its directness and immediate appearance in our organs of sense as sensation. When we look at a tree we do not argue; we simply see the tree. We need not know anything about the physical processes that take place both outside in the domain of ether-waves which are reflected on the sighted object, and within our eye where the lens produces an image that is thrown upon the surface of the retina, in the same way in which the photographer's camera produces a picture on the sensitive plate. The picture seen is the result of the process, and all epistemological considerations are after-thoughts. The same is true of all sensations. Sensations, though the result of complicated processes, are given facts; they are the data of experience and there is no argument in them, no reasoning, no deliberation, no hesitation, as to their truth; they are the realities of life, and from them we construct our notions of the world in which we live.

It is a pity that we have not a Saxon equivalent for the German *Anschauung*. We might coin the word "atsight," which (in contrast to insight) would denote the act of perceiving a sighted object; but the word, in order to make the same impression, ought to be current, which the term atsight is not. The translation "intuition" is admissible only on the condition that we exclude from it all mystical notions of subjective visions and define it as visualised perception. There are passages where *Anschauung* is an exact synonym for "sense-experience" or "perception," and we might translate it thus were it not for the extended use Kant makes of the term by speaking of *reine Anschauung*, meaning thereby the pure forms of sense-experience which are as much immediate data of perception as are the sense-elements of sensation.

If we had to recast the exposition of Kant's philosophy we could avoid the term "pure intuition" and replace it by the pure forms of sense-experience, but if we would render Kant in his own words we cannot do so. The translator must reproduce Kant in his own language, and thus must either invent a new word such as *atsight*, or must cling to the traditional term *intuition*.[1]

---

[1] Mr. Kroeger's proposition, made in the *Journal of Speculative Philosophy*, II., p. 191, to translate *Anschauung* by *contemplation* seems inadmis-

KANT'S IDEALISM.

The contrasts in Kant's terminology, *a priori* and *a posteriori*, formal and material, pure reason and experience, etc., do not yet imply the conclusion at which he arrives, the main result being the ideality of space and time and of all pure forms of thought. Kant was led to it by a strange fallacy, the error of which we intend to trace in the subsequent pages.

First let us try to understand the point of view which Kant took.

The pure form of our sense-perception is the relational in the domain of sensory elements, viz., their juxtaposition, or space, and their succession, or time, their shape, their causal intercatenation, etc.

In his discourse on the pure forms of sense-perception (called "Transcendental Æsthetics"), Kant points out first of space, then of time, that they are notions which are:

1. Insuppressible (viz., we can think or assume in thought the non-existence of all objects, but not of space or time).

2. Necessary *a priori* (viz., they are of universal application and transcendental, i. e., the condition of all sense-perceptions.)

3. Unique (viz., there is but one space and one time; all spaces, so called, are parts only of, or rooms in, that one space; and different times are periods of that one time).

4. Infinite (viz., all concrete objects are finite;

sible. Compare for further details of the use of the word the author's pamphlet *Kant and Spencer*, pp. 76 ff. In the present translation of Kant's *Prolegomena* we have rendered it a few times by *sense-perception* and *visualisation*, but mostly by *intuition*, and have (wherever it is not translated by "intuition") alway added in parenthesis the German original.

but time and space, not being concrete entities, are
limitless).

He concludes that space and time are not properties of objects as things-in-themselves, but the forms
of their phenomenal existence.

It is obviously a mistake to regard space and time
as concrete objects. Infinite objects would be mon-
ster-existences the reality of which cannot but pass
our comprehension. They are the forms of things,
indispensable not only for their existence in general
but also for determining their several individual and
characteristic types; for that which constitutes the
difference of things, so far as science has been able to
penetrate into the mysteries of being, is always due
to a difference of form. Kant guardedly grants empirical reality to space and time; he ascribes space
and time to things as phenomena, and denies only
their being properties of things as things-in-themselves. But he adds the explicit statement that space
as well as time are "the *subjective* conditions of the
sensibility under which alone external intuition (*Anschauung*, i. e., sense-perception) becomes possible."
Thus, Kant concludes space and time are *a priori* intuitions; they do not belong to the external domain
of reality or objectivity, but to the sphere of subjectivity; and being forms of the sensibility of the intuitive mind they are (says Kant) ideal.

Kant does not deny the reality of things, but having established the ideality of space and time he believes that,

"If we regarded space and time as properties which must be
found in objects as things-in-themselves, as *sine quibus non* of
the possibility of their existence, and reflect on the absurdities in
which we then find our~~-~~elves involved, inasmuch as we are com-

pelled to admit the existence of two infinite things, which are nevertheless not substances, nor anything really inhering in substances, nay, to admit that they are the necessary conditions of the existence of all things, and moreover, that they must continue to exist, although all existing things were annihilated,—we cannot blame the good Berkeley for degrading bodies to mere illusory appearances. Nay, even our own existence which would in this case depend upon the self-existent reality of such a mere nonentity as time, would necessarily be changed with it into mere appearance— an absurdity which no one has as yet been guilty of." [1]

Thus, Kant believes that if space and time were objective they would impart their ideality to the objective world and change it to mere appearance; by conceiving space and time (and in addition to the forms of our sensibility also the forms of our thinking) as purely ideal, viz., as subjective properties of the mind, he assures us that the world, our own existence included, will be saved from the general collapse which it otherwise in his opinion must suffer.

KANT AND SWEDENBORG.

The development of Kant's theory of the ideality of space and time coincides with his investigation of Swedenborg's philosophy, if that word be applicable to a world-conception which afterwards was denominated by Kant himself as "dreams of a visionary." Swedenborgians claim that Kant was influenced by Swedenborg in the formulation of his critical idealism; and Mr. Albert J. Edmunds discusses the subject in an article which appeared in the *New Church Review*, Vol. IV., No. 2, under the title: *Time and Space: Hints Given by Swedenborg to Kant.* While it appears that there is less borrowing on the part of Kant than can be made out by Swedenborg's adher-

1 *Critique of Pure Reason*, Supplement VI. of 2nd edition.

ents, there is more justice in the claim of Swedenborg's influence over Kant than seems to be palatable to such Kant scholars as is Professor Vaihinger. Frank Sewall, the editor of the *New Church Review*, goes over the field in an article entitled: *Kant ana Swedenborg on Cognition*, in which he makes out a good case scarcely less favorable for Swedenborg than does Edmunds. The fact is that the mystical ideas on space and time which permeate religious thought had their effect on Swedenborg as much as on other thinkers, mystics as well as philosophers, and among the latter, on Kant; and certain formulations of the problem which can be found in Swedenborg, did not strike Kant as much as may appear by a mere comparison of the passages.

Mr. Edmunds quotes the following passages from Leibnitz, on space and time:

"Since space in itself is an ideal thing like time, it must necessarily follow that space outside the world is imaginary, as even the schoolmen have acknowledged it to be. The same is the case with empty space in the world—which I still believe to be imaginary, for the reasons which I have set forth." (V. 33.)

"There is no space at all where there is no matter." (V. 62.)

"Space . . . is something ideal." (V. 104.)

"The immensity of God is independent of space, as the eternity of God is independent of time." (V. 1c6.)

"Had there been no creatures, space and time would only have existed in the ideas of God." (Paper IV. 41.)

Here Leibnitz uses the very word "ideal," of both space and time. Incidentally we must add that naturalists of to-day will no longer countenance Leibnitz's view of the non-existence of empty space.

There is even the religious mysticism displayed by Leibnitz which makes God independent of space and time. Swedenborg says the same about the angels:

"The angels have no idea of time. Such is the case in the world of spirits and still more perfectly in heaven: how much more before the Lord." (*Arcana Cœlestia*, 1274.)

It is a fact that Kant had read Swedenborg, but the coincidences as to the ideality of space and time and the theory of cognition are trivial as compared with the coincidences with former philosophers, such as Leibnitz. The truth is, we have in Swedenborg the type of a religious thinker who formulates his conception of space and time and other metaphysical doctrines in the shape of mystical allegories, after the fashion of Jacob Boehme and other religious vision- aries. It is wrong on the one side to overestimate his mystical expressions, which are commonplace among authors of his ilk, and, on the other hand, to ridicule them as purely visionary, devoid of philosophical value. It is characteristic of the human mind at a certain stage of its development to formulate in mys- tical language philosophical conceptions which lie beyond the grasp of the intellect of that peculiar stage of growth. It is the religious attitude of approaching philosophical problems in mystical expressions. While it is natural for a scientist to ridicule the mystic for claiming to have solved the world-problem though producing nothing but air-bubbles, it is at the same time a one-sidedness to see in mysticism nothing but wild and worthless hallucinations. Mysticism is a solution of the world-problem by sentiment, and it affords the great advantage of determining and estab- lishing the moral attitude of its devotees. Considered as science it is absolutely worthless, considered as a guide in life its worth is determined by the spirit of which it is born. Where the religious sentiment is serious, deep, and noble, mysticism will find a poeti-

cal expression full of significance, depth, and aspira-
tion.   Kant as a religious man was attracted by Swedenborg, but when he weighed his revelations as philosophy he was so disappointed that he felt ashamed
of having been caught among the credulous investi-
gators of occult phenomena.

Swedenborg is one of the most representative mystics, and while his books may be worthless as philosophical treatises, they are not only interesting to the
scientist because typical of a certain phase in the religious development of human nature, but also classical as mystical literature.   The appreciation which he
has found among a number of adherents proves too
well how deeply his way of presenting metaphysical
problems in the shape of allegorical dreams is founded
in the peculiar constitution of man's spiritual system.
Those who took the trouble to investigate his miracles
and prophecies found that, however much might be
surmised, nothing could be definitely proved, except
the fact that there are people of fair and sometimes
even extraordinary intelligence who have a decided
inclination to believe in occult phenomena, that they,
though subjectively honest, can easily become convinced of things which they are anxious to believe,
and finally that in minds where a vivid imagination
checks the development of critical acumen, the poetical conceptions of religious faith grow so definite and
concrete as to become indistinguishable from actual
life and reality.

Now, what are the lessons of the relation of mysticism to science?

We ought to consider that certain metaphysical
truths (as to the nature of space, time, our mode of
cognition, causation, infinity, eternity, etc.), when

stated in abstract formulas, seem dry and unmeaning
to unscientific minds, yet they possess a deep religious
significance which finds allegorical expression in the
various religious systems in myths, ceremonial institutions, and dogmas.   By sensual natures who cling
to the allegorical feature of the allegory, they can be
appreciated only if they are expressed in a sensual
way, if spiritual truths are told in parables of concrete
instances as if they were material facts of the material
world.   It is characteristic of mystical minds to live
in an atmosphere of sensual symbolism in such a way
that they believe their own dreams, and their assurance makes their statement so convincing that they
easily find followers among those who are kin to them
in their mental constitution.   As soon as a critical
reader tries to verify the statements of such men, he
finds himself irritated by a heap of worthless evidence,
and the result is an indignation such as Kant showed
after his perusal of Swedenborg's *Arcana*.

The following summarised statement of Swedenborg's world-conception is given by Kant in his *Essay
on Swedenborg,* which appeared in 1766 :[1]

"Each human soul has in this life its place in the spirit-world,
and belongs to a certain society, which in every case is in harmony
with its internal condition of truth and good, that is, of understanding and will.   But the location of spirits among themselves
has nothing in common with space in the material world.   The
soul of one man, therefore, in India can be next-door neighbor to
that of another in Europe, so far as spiritual position is concerned; while those who, as to the body, live in one house, may
be quite far enough distant from one another as to those [that is,
spiritual] conditions.   When man dies his soul does not change its
place, but only perceives itself in the same wherein, with regard
to other spirits, it already was in this life.   Besides, although the

1 We quote from Mr. Albert J Edmunds's essay in the *New Church Review*,
Vol. IV., p. 261.

mutual relation of spirits is not in real space, yet it has to them the appearance of space, and their relations are represented, with their accompanying conditions, as nearnesses; their differences as distances, even as the spirits themselves have not really extension, yet present to one another the appearance of a human form. In this imaginary space there is a plenary community of spiritual natures. Swedenborg speaks with departed souls whenever he pleases, etc."

Now, if we comprehend that besides the causal connexion of things in space and time there is a logical interrelation which appertains to pure reason, we shall come to the conclusion that Swedenborg's ideas are quite legitimate, if they are but understood to be poetical and if we are permitted to conceive them in a strictly scientific sense. We read:

"The soul of one man in India can be next-door neighbor to that of another in Europe so far as spiritual position is concerned; while those who as to the body live in one house may be quite far enough distant from one another as to those (that is, spiritual) conditions."

Now, it is obvious that this sympathy of souls, which is not according to space and time, but according to spiritual kinship, is quite legitimate and very important to those who understand it. The sensual man will find difficulty in grasping its significance, except that it be stated to him in a sensual way. Obviously, it is true that "spirits themselves have not really extension." Their interrelation is of a different kind. But if we imagine them, as Swedenborg does, "to present to one another the appearance of a human form," we conceive of their existence as though it were in space, another kind of space than that filled by matter, and "in this imaginary space there is a plenary community of spiritual natures." Thus logicians represent the interrelation between genus and species by geometrical figure, the one including the other.

Swedenborg is simply a man whose imagination is so vivid and whose scientific criticism is so little developed that the imaginary space invented to represent the interrelations of spiritual realities which are in neither space nor time, becomes an actual space to him; his spirits become materialised shapes, and thus it happens that he can speak "with departed souls whenever he pleases." A scientist too, a historian or a naturalist, can consult the wisdom of the departed spirits. He can make himself acquainted with the views of Newton, of Goethe, of Kant; he can incorporate their souls in his own being, but being of a critical nature, he will not see them as bodily shapes. It is characteristic of mystics that their imagination outruns their sobriety, and thus the flights of their fancy become real to them.

While it is not impossible that Swedenborg became the fulcrum on which Kant elaborated his metaphysics, we may at the same time justify the opposite statement that Kant's relation to Swedenborg is purely incidental and without significance. The elaboration of his theories as to space and time and cognition, Kant made at the time when he read Swedenborg's works, but we must be aware of the fact that Kant was familiar with mystic views in general, and Swedenborg's expressions did not strike him as much as it might appear to those who compare Swedenborg and Kant only, but have no reference to Leibnitz and other thinkers. Certainly, Kant would have come to the same conclusion if he had dealt with any other thinker of a similar type, Jacob Boehme, or even spirits on a lower level in the line of mysticism.

While Kant's statements show a certain resemblance to those of Swedenborg, we find that their agreement with Leibnitz (a philosopher whom both Immanuels, the great mystic as well as the great critic, had studied carefully) is much closer. We shall at the same time understand why Kant exhibited a decided contempt and scorn for the dreamy haziness of these visionaries, which, when dealing with scientific problems, is sterile and unprofitable. In contrasting the philosophical study of metaphysics with those vague fancies of religio-philosophical dreams, Kant compared the latter to the intangible shade of a departed spirit, quoting Virgil's well-known verses where Æneas in the under-world tries to embrace the soul of his departed father, Anchises.[1] Kant says:

"Metaphysics, with whom it is my destiny to be in love, offers two advantages, although I have but seldom been favored by her: the first is, to solve the problems which the investigating mind raises when it is on the track of the more hidden properties of things through reason. But here the result very frequently deceives hope, and has also in this case escaped our longing hands.

"Ter frustra comprensa manus effugit imago,
Par levibus ventis volucrique simillima somno."—(VIRGIL.)

[Thrice I tried to embrace and thrice it escaped me, the image, Airy and light as the wind, and to volatile dreams to be likened.]

KANT'S ANTINOMIES.

After this digression we revert to Kant's idealism and will now point out the result to which it leads.

Kant, as we have seen, protests against being an idealist in the sense that the reality of the external world of objects or things be denied. His idealism insists only on the ideality of space and time; and by ideality he understands subjectivity. But together

---

⁎ Æneas, Book VI., Verses 701-702.

with time and space all our forms of thought are assumed to be purely ideal. Hence there is a rift rending asunder form and substance, thought and reality, representative image or phenomenon and the represented objects. We know phenomena, not noumena. Things in themselves are unknowable, for the laws of pure form have reference to appearances only.

If purely formal thought has no objective value, it can be used merely to decide problems that lie within the range of experience—the domain of appearance; but things in themselves, the domain of transcendent existence, lies without the pale of any possible knowledge.

Kant's method of dealing with these subjects is peculiar. He neither leaves them alone nor solves them, but formulates the affirmations as well as the negations of a series of contradictory statements in what he calls "the antinomies." Here the weakness of Kant's philosophy comes out, indicating that there must be a flaw in it somewhere.

It is interesting to notice that as to Kant's Antinomies of Pure Reason the great Königsberg philosopher has been anticipated by Buddhism in which (according to Neumann's *Reden Gautamo's*, Vol. II., Nos. 60 and 72) the antinomies are taught in a similar, partly literally in the same, form. But there, too, the contradiction belongs to the formulation of the statement of facts, not to the facts themselves.

In a certain sense we can say, the world must have had a beginning, and must come to an end; and the world had no beginning and can have no end. If we speak of this definite nebular system of stars comprising the entire milky way we are compelled to admit that it began and will at some definite though distant future be dissolved again; but if we mean by world the totality of existence in all its shapes, prior forms and causes of origin, we must own that it has existed and ever will exist. We could go back in thought to the time before the present cosmos started, when other worlds were evolving or dissolving and a different kind of universe or condition of things prevailed and so on without coming to an end. But these conditions being the causes of the present world are included in our concept of the universe. The antinomies are due to the equivocal significance of our words, not to a fault of reason; nor do they indicate that existence itself is self-contradictory. The contradiction is not in the things but in our conception of things.[1]

Schopenhauer has vigorously attacked Kant on account of his antinomies, insinuating weakness and hypocrisy. But it seems to us, while by no means agreeing with Kant on this particular point, that granting his premises his conclusion was justified. The four points of the antinomies, viz., the eternity and infinite divisibility of the world, the contrast of freedom to causation and the existence of God, are no longer of a purely formal nature; some notions of experience are inevitably mixed up in them, and thus

[1] That the antinomies cannot be regarded as true antinomies or contradictions of reason, but as the result of a misconception and lack of clearness in our formulation of the several problems, becomes apparent in the antinomy of freedom *versus* necessity. Kant's definition of freedom (§ 53) as a faculty of starting a chain of events spontaneously without antecedent causes and his way of reconciling freedom and nature (or as we would say "determinism") is subject to serious criticism. Compare the author's solution of the problem in *Fundamental Problems*, pp. 191–196; *Ethical Problems*, pp. 45–50, 152–156; *Primer of Philosophy*, pp. 159–164; *Soul of Man*, pp. 389–397. See also *The Monist*, Vol. III., pp. 611 ff., "The Future in Mental Causation." Concerning the *ought* and its assumed mysterious nature compare the chapters "The *Is* and the *Ought*," and "An Analysis of the Moral *Ought*," in *The Ethical Problem*, pp. 279–295.

pure reason is unable to decide either way. We might as well try to determine by *a priori* considerations as to whether or not electricity can be produced by friction, or whether or not by rubbing an old metal lamp the genii of the lamp will appear. Hence, before the tribunal of pure reason either side, the affirmative as well as the negative, is defensible, and thus we should be obliged to settle the question with other methods; other methods, however, according to Kant's notions concerning the nature of metaphysical questions, would not be admissible, because he insists that all metaphysical notions must be derived from pure concepts alone.

KANT'S PROBLEM.

Kant's philosophy has become the beginning of a new epoch in the evolution of human thought through a formulation of its basic problem and by starting out in the right direction for its solution; but Kant has not spoken the final word.

Kant was awakened from his dogmatic slumber by Hume's scepticism, and it was Hume's problem as to the nature of causation which prompted him to strike a new path in the conception of philosophical problems.

Kant threw light on Hume's problem by generalising it and recognising the kinship of the conception of causation to mathematics and logic, all of them being purely formal knowledge. The significance of formal thought and its power of affording *a priori* cognition is Kant's peculiar problem.

It is generally conceded that Kant solved Hume's problem, but he failed to solve his own.

By a strange misapprehension of the nature of form and its non-objectivity, he has switched off into an idealism (so called by himself) which it will be hard to distinguish from that subjectivism which he assumed Berkeley's philosophy to be. The difference between the two (in Kant's opinion) consists in this, that according to Kant, the world itself is real but in the form in which it represents itself in space and time it is phenomenal, while he declares that according to Berkeley the world itself is "illusory appearance." Further Kant insists that the world as appearance, though purely phenomenal, is not an arbitrary illusion, but governed by laws which render it necessary in all its details.

The great merit of Kant is his wonderfully keen discrimination between the purely formal and the sensory, showing that the former is throughout universal and necessary in its principles, while the latter is incidental and concrete or particular; but he fails to apply the same discrimination to his conception of experience and to the objects of experience, and thus he limits the formal to the subject, while it is obviously the universal feature of all existence, objective as well as subjective, constituting between them the connecting link that makes science, i. e., objective cognition, possible.

Before we examine Kant's position, we must first discuss, at least briefly, Hume's problem and offer the solution in the form which Kant, in our opinion, ought to have given it. It will then be easy to point out the error that led him astray and prevented him from offering a definite and final doctrine as to the nature of form which should become the basis of all scientific inquiry, and enable philosophy to become a science as definite, or nearly so, as are mathematics and logic, or even physics.

HUME'S PROBLEM.

Locke objected to the doctrine of innate ideas, claiming that all ideas were the products of sense-impressions, and he excepted only one idea, viz., the principle of necessary connexion, i. e., causality. Hume accepted Locke's sensualism, but, endeavoring to be more consistent, drew its last consequence by denying even the idea of cause and effect as a necessary connexion. He argued that we meet with constant conjunctions in experience, but not with necessity. By habit we are compelled to expect that upon every cause its due effect will follow, but there is no reason to assume that causation is due to a universal and necessary law of objective validity. Hume saw in the relation between cause and effect a synthesis, calling it "the sequence of two objects"; and if it were a synthesis, or a mere sequence, he would be right that the connexion between cause and effect is accidental and our belief in its necessity a mere habit.

The truth is that causation is not a sequence of two objects following one another, but one process, a motion, or a change of place; and the simplest kind of motion implies that there are at least three phases or states of things in the system in which the motion takes place : first the original condition (which for simplicity's sake we may assume to be in a relative equilibrium); secondly, the motion disturbing the equilibrium so as to make one or several elements in the system seek new places; and thirdly, the new adjustment (which for simplicity's sake we will again regard as being in equilibrium). The first phase is called the conditions or circumstances, the second is the cause, and the third the effect. Cause and effect are not combined into a unity by the compulsion of a law of necessary connexion; they are two phases of one and the same process. The duality is a product of abstraction; the unity of the two is the original fact, and we know now that causality is but another expression for the law of the conservation of matter and energy. The naturalist assumes that matter and energy are indestructible, and thus every process that takes place in nature is only a transformation. Accordingly, our belief in causation is after all, although Hume denied it, finally based upon the logical principle of identity $A=A$. It is an extension of this principle to a state of motion.

Cause, accordingly, is never an object, but always an event, viz., a motion of some kind. We cannot call the bullet the cause and death the effect; or mercury the cause and paralysis the effect; or worse still (as says George Lewes) that whiskey, water, sugar, and lemon are the causes of punch.

We distinguish between cause and reason, reason being the law under which a single event is subsumed for the sake of explaining the effectiveness of the cause.[1]

[1] The instinct of language has here proved wiser than the scholarship of philosophers. All European languages (the Greek, the Latin, together with its derivatives the French, Italian, etc., the German, the English) distinguish between "αἰτία, *causa*, *Ursache* (from the same root as the English verb 'to seek') cause," and "ἀρχή (i. e., first principle) *ratio, Grund*, reason," the former being the particular incident that starts a process, the latter the *raison d'être*, the principle, or general rule, the natural law that explains it. When the two ideas are confounded as has been done frequently by philosophers, the greatest confusion results leading to such self-contradictory notions as "*causa sui*," "first cause," "ultimate cause," etc., which lead either to agnosticism or to mysticism. For further details see the author's *Primer of Philosophy*, the chapter on Causation, pp. 30-34, and *Fundamental Problems*, pp. 29-30.

Kant, following the suggestion of Hume, devoted special attention to the problem of causality, but he solved it by simply declaring that it was a concept *a priori*, and thus belonged to the same class of truths as mathematical, arithmetical, and logical theorems. He never attempted to explain its truth, let alone to prove it, or to demonstrate its universality and necessity. Mathematicians deem it necessary to prove their theorems, but Kant, strange to say, neglected to deduce the law of causation from simpler truths or analyse it into its elements. If Kant had made attempts to analyse causation for the sake of proving its validity after the fashion of logicians and mathematicians, he might, with his keen insight into the nature of physical laws and natural sciences, have anticipated the discovery of the law of the conservation of matter and energy, and might furthermore have been preserved from the error of his subjectivism which affected the whole system of his thought and twisted his philosophy out of shape.

KANT'S PROLEGOMENA.

In the *Critique of Pure Reason* Kant's position remains unintelligible; we understand his arguments and may even approve the several statements from which they proceed, but we are astonished at the boldness of the conclusion, and fail to be convinced. His objections to the belief in space and time as objective things hold good only if space and time are assumed to be things or objects; but not if they are thought to be mere forms of objects. They are thinkable as forms of thought not less than as forms of objects. When assumed to be solely forms of thought to the exclusion of the idea that there are any objective relations corresponding to them, they become mysterious and quite mystical, and here lies the reason why Kant's *Critique of Pure Reason* is actually mystifying. He bewilders the reader. We become acquainted with his argument but do not feel sure that we have rightly apprehended his meaning. In the *Prolegomena* Kant is, at least, not unintelligible. The *Prolegomena* are not deductive, but inductive. In them Kant leads us the way he travelled himself, and this is the reason of the importance of the *Prolegomena*. Kant embodied their contents in various places into the second edition of his *Critique of Pure Reason*. But the passages are scattered and lose the plainness and power which they possess in the context of the *Prolegomena*. Here we are face to face with Kant as a man; he gives us a personal reply, as if he were interviewed; and while we grant the significance of transcendentalism and the truth of many of his observations and deductions, we can at the same time understand how he arrived at errors. We can lay our finger on the very spot where he went astray, and I cannot but wonder at the courage of this undaunted thinker who abided by the consequences of an apparently trivial fallacy, due to the neglect to investigate one feature of the problem to which he devoted many years of his life in profound reflexion and close study.

Kant was puzzled that we could know anything *a priori* concerning the formal constitution of things. The celestial bodies obey laws which man develops out of his mind. That the highest (i. e., the most general or universal) laws of nature should happen to be the same as the highest (i. e., the formal) laws of the thinking mind, and yet should be of an independent origin, seemed absurd to Kant. He saw only two possibilities; either, he said, we have derived our formal knowledge from the things by experience, or we ourselves have put it into the things to which it really does not belong.   The former possibility is excluded, because, says Kant (*Prolegomena*, § 9), "The properties of a thing cannot migrate into my faculty of representation," while on the other hand the purely formal truths are not derived from experience, but produced by the mind as cognitions *a priori*.   Thus, Kant accepts the other horn of the dilemma, declaring (*Prolegomena*, § 36) that our faculty of cognition does not conform to the objects, but contrariwise, that the objects conform to cognition.   Objects, he claimed, do not in themselves possess form, but our mind is so constituted that it cannot help attributing form and everything formal to the object of our experience.

IDEALITY NOT SUBJECTIVITY.

Now, it is true that our purely formal notions of mathematical and logical truths are ideal (made of the stuff that ideas consist of), but being purely formal they are definitely determined, that is to say that, wherever the same constructions are made, either by the operations of other minds or of natural conditions in the facts of objective reality, they will be found to be the same.   Thus, our mental constructions can reconstruct the processes and formations of nature, and we can learn to predetermine the course of natural events.

Kant did not see that form might be a property of all existence and that, in that case, the purely formal in things would be of the same nature as the purely formal in man's mind.   It is true that the properties

of things do not migrate from the objects into the subject, but they make impressions upon the senses and
these several impressions possess analogies to the
qualities by which they are caused. The analogies
between matter and sensation seem much more arbitrary than those between the shapes of things and the
outlines of our sense-images. Nevertheless even here
we grant that the reduction of the latter to universal
laws is purely subjective, for there are no laws, *qua*
formulated laws, in the objective world, there are only
uniformities. But if we understand by the term law
a description of uniformities we must see at once that
there are objective realities (or rather features of reality) corresponding to our correct notions of the several formal laws.

If the uniformities of nature are not transferred
to the mind directly, but if the purely formal concepts are developed independently of sense-experience
a priori, how is it possible that the two present the
wonderful agreement that puzzled Kant?

Nature is throughout activity, and so is our existence. Nature is constantly combining and separating;
we observe transformations; things move about; and
their constituent parts change places. Similar operations are inalienable functions of the mind. The
subtlest analysis as well as the most complicated composition and every investigation, be it ever so intricate, are mere combinations and separations, activi-
ties given together with our existence.

The arguments of Kant by which he proves the
apriority of purely formal laws must be granted to be
true. The source of all purely formal thought is the
mind, and not sense-perceptions. They are ideal.
But the mind has been built up by experience, viz.,

by sense-impressions of different but definite forms, and the formal order of objective nature is the mould in which the mind has been formed. The brute cannot as yet analyse sensations into their forms and materials, i. e., into the purely relational and the purely sensory features; but man can; and when he has acquired the power of abstraction he can build models of forms, exhausting the entire scope of all possible cases, and these models serve him as examples of the several analogous formations of nature. Accordingly, our mental constitution, though a subjective construction, is built up with materials quarried from the formal uniformities of objective nature. Thus the spider undoubtedly weaves his web from his own bodily self, but the materials have first been deposited there by nature. Man's mind is not less than the spider's silken thread, produced by, and remaining a part and an expression of, that great All-Being in which all creatures live and move and have their being.

There is this difference between the spider's web and formal thought: the former consists of matter, the pure forms of mathematical, logical, and other ideas are immaterial; they are abstracts made of the purely relational features of sense-impressions. They are ideal, viz., mental pictures, and as such they are subjective. But they are not purely subjective. The sensory part of a retinal image is purely subjective, but the formal preserves in a reduced size the projection of the shape of the object. Form belongs to the object as well as to its subjective image, and thus the subjective conception of form possesses an objective value.

Everything ideal is subjective, but it need not be purely subjective. Because the rational is ideal, it by no means follows that it is not, and cannot be, objective.

When we construct some purely formal configuration with our nature-given mental operations, it will be the same as any other construction which has been made in the same way, be it in the domain either of things or of other minds. Nature performs the same operations which appear in man's mental activity. Man being a part of existence, what is more natural than that his bodily and mental constitution partakes of the same form as all the other parts of the world that surrounds him?

A great and important part of our knowledge consists of purely formal theorems; they are *a priori*. And these purely formal theorems contain actual information concerning the formal aspect of the real world. And why? Because they are systematic reconstructions of the formal features of reality by imitating operations of motion which take place throughout the universe.

All formal theorems have a general application, hence, whenever applicable, they afford *a priori* information and can be employed as a key to unlock the mysteries of the unknown.

By the rule of three we calculate the distance from the earth to the sun, and map out the paths of the several celestial bodies.

When Kant says: Our mind "dictates" certain laws to the objects of experience, he uses a wrong expression or takes a poetical license seriously. The mind "dictates" nothing to reality. Reality including its form is such as it is independently of what we think it to be. That which Kant calls dictating is a mere determining, a description, implying at the same

time a foretelling or predicting of natural events which
(as we saw) is done by constructing in our mind anal·
ogous models.   The agreement between our model
and reality proves only that the scheme on which the
model has been constructed is correct; it does not
prove that the model does any dictating.   The model
dictates as little to reality as a barometer dictates what
air-pressure there is to be in the atmosphere.

THE FORMAL AND THE SENSORY.

While we must object to Kant's doctrine that
everything ideal is subjective and that what is directly
derived from the mind cannot be objective, we must
not (with the Sensualists) place the formal and the
sensual on the same level.   Kant is right that space
and time are not objects or things or entities; they
are forms, and as forms they possess the quality of
being empty.   There is no particularity about them
anywhere.   Thus, space is space anywhere; it is not
like matter, denser here and looser there; nor like
energy, here intense, there weak.   Considered in itself, space is the mere potentiality of existence.   It is
a description of the condition of granting motion to
move in all directions.   Its very indifference and absence of anything particular implies uniformity; and
thus the laws of potentiality (i. e., the qualities of
possible forms) are mere schedules; they are empty
in themselves, but possess universal application.[1]

The formal aspect of reality is its suchness; the
material element is its thisness.   All suchness can be

[1] These truths have been felt by philosophers of all nations, and it is surprising to find them in the writings of Lao Tze and the Buddhist scriptures
in both of which the absence of materiality, the not-being, plays an important part and is endowed with religious sanctity.

formulated in general, and even in universal, descriptions; all thisness is individual and particular. Statements of a general nature, such as are formulated by employing the methods of formal thought, are not single and concrete facts, but omnipresent and eternal laws; they are true or untrue, correct or incorrect. Facts of thisness are always in a special time and in a special spot in space. They are definite *nunc* and *hic*, not a *semper* and *ubique*. They are not true or untrue, but real or unreal.

The essential feature of things is their form; for their form, which is their suchness, viz., their external shape as well as internal structure, constitutes their character, their soul, their spiritual significance, making them what they are. Their thisness is their concrete presence which actualises the thing as a stubborn fact of the material universe.

It is true that the sense-pictures in which the world is represented to us are subjective; they are appearances or phenomena; it is further true that these pictures are radically different from the things which they represent. The color-sensation red has no similarity (as Kant rightly observes) to the physical qualities of vermillion; and physicists have sufficiently penetrated into the constitution of matter of any kind (though most of the problems remain still unsolved) to convince us that matter as it is in itself is radically different from the subjective picture as which it presents itself to the senses. But the scientist assumes form to be objective, and all the theories as to the constitution of matter, in chemistry as well as in the several branches of physics, are based on the principle of eliminating the subjective element, that is to say, the properly sensory ingredients of our experience, by reducing them to statements in purely formal terms, which is done by measuring, by counting, by weighing, by defining their proportions, by describing their shape and structure, by determining their relations; and if we have succeeded in doing so, we claim to have understood the objective nature of things. How can Kant's statement be upheld, that the sensation red is not an objective quality of vermillion? Is it not because physics has taught us that difference of color depends upon a difference of wavelength in ether vibration? Kant's argument is based upon a tacit but indispensable recognition of the objectivity of form and formal qualities.

Therefore, while granting that the sense-begotten world-picture of our intuition is subjective appearance (cf. footnote on page 232), we claim in contrast to Kant that its formal elements represent a feature that inheres in existence as the form of existence.

In making form purely subjective, Kant changes —notwithstanding his protestations—all ideas, all thoughts, all science, into purely subjective conceits. He is more of an idealist than Berkeley. Science can be regarded as an objective method of cognition only if the laws of form are objective features of reality

THE MORAL ASPECT.

An incidental remark on the moral aspect of the contrast between the purely formal and the sensory would not seem out of place here. Man has risen from the sensual plane into the abstract realms of reason, and morality becomes possible only by man's ability to make general principles the basis of his actions. Thus it happens that at a certain period of man's development the sensory is regarded as the lower, and generalisations with what they imply, ideals, maxims, abstract thought, as the higher. The sensory is thus discriminated against and even denounced as the enemy of the spiritual. Hence the dualistic phase in the religious and philosophical evolution of mankind in which sensuality is branded as sin and salvation sought in asceticism, i. e., the mortification of the body.

We must consider, however, that the contrast between form and matter, general law and particular existence, the ideal and sensory, spirit and matter, does not imply a contradictory antithesis, let alone any hostility or exclusivity of the two. That the spiritual, viz., the conception of the purely formal with reason and its generalisations, develops only on a higher plane, cannot be used to incriminate the sensory and the bodily. On the contrary, the spiritual justifies the sensory and points out the higher aims which it can attain.

And how indispensable is the sensory in religion! Consider but love, so much insisted on by the preachers of almost all higher faiths. Is it not even in its present form a sentiment, i. e., a sensory emotion? The truth is that morality consists in the sanctification of the sensory, not in its eradication; and sanctification means setting aside and devoting to a special purpose, to the exclusion of a general use. Particularity is the nature of bodily existence and particularity demands exclusiveness. Any general use of bodily functions will prostitute them. Reason, on the contrary, is meant for general use and can never suffer from a general application.

Kant's conception of morality is based upon reason, to the exclusion of sentiment. Reason makes action according to principles or maxims possible, and all those maxims are moral which can become universally established. Thus the basis of ethics is the golden rule, pronounced by Confucius, Christ, and other religious leaders of mankind. Lao-Tze says of the sage: "His methods invite requital."[1]

FORM BOTH SUBJECTIVE AND OBJECTIVE.

We believe we have satisfactorily explained the problem of the *a priori*, of the purely formal, which puzzled Kant; we have further shown how and why the laws of purely formal thought agree with the highest laws of nature; why being devoid of particularity they are universal (implying necessity); and there remains only to be pointed out that the validity of science rests upon the assurance of the identity of the subjective and the objective laws of form. Form, being common to both domains, the objectivity of things and the subjectivity of the mind, serves as a bridge on which cognition can advance into the unknown realms of objective existence, and thus the formal sciences constitute our organ of cognition, the objective reliability of which depends upon form being an objective feature of things.

It goes without saying that all that Kant says concerning their infinity, uniqueness, universality, and necessity as being against the belief that space and time are objects or things holds good; it proves that they are forms. Yet though they must not be regarded as objects, they are objective; they are the forms of intuition but also of the objects intuited. Further, what Kant says (relying on symmetry as in

1 *Tao-Teh-King*, Chapter 30.

tuitively perceived) to prove that they are forms of intuitions and not concepts, holds as well to prove that they are sighted forms of existence, not internally hidden qualities of a stuffy, thingish nature to be distilled from sense-perception in the alembic of the observation before its existence can be known. It is true that the world as it appears to us is a sense-woven, subjective picture; things as we perceive them are phenomena. Further, our concepts, including the world-conception of science, which is built up with the help of the purely formal laws of thought, is a mental construction; they are noumena. Both worlds, that of sense and that of thought, are subjective; but they represent reality; the senses picture the world in the beauteous glow of sensations, and the mind describes it in the exact measures of formal determinations; but the latter, if true, offers an objectively valid model of the constitution of things, explaining their suchness without, however, giving any information as to the nature of reality in itself, i. e., what matter is in itself; whether it is eternal or not; why it exists; and if it came into being, or how it happened to originate. It is obvious that things are not matter, but matter of a definite form; the form is cognisable, while matter is simply the indication of their concrete reality as objects in the objective world.

SUBJECTIVE CONSTRUCTIONS OF OBJECTIVE VALIDITY.

Kant in discriminating between empirical perception (viz., the sense-impressions possessing only subjective validity) and experience (viz., the product of sense-impressions worked out by the *a priori* methods of pure reason imparting to our judgments universal·

ity and necessity)[1] goes far in refuting himself and his
pet theory. He speaks of universality and necessity
as the only means by which the subjective elements
can become objectively valid. He claims, e. g., to
"have amply shown that they (the concepts of the
pure understanding, causality, including also mathematics, etc.) and the theorems derived from them are
firmly established *a priori,* or before all experience,
and *have their undoubted objective value,* though only
with regard to experience."

If the concepts of the pure understanding have
objective value, why are they not objective? Why
must they be regarded as purely subjective? We
grant the strength of Kant's argument that, being un-
equivocally creations of the mind independent of
sense-experience, or, as Kant calls them, *a priori,*
they are subjective. But is not the question legitimate that they may be at once subjective and objective? Kant disposes of this question too quickly, and
here lies his mistake: instead of investigating how
certain uniformities of law may be at once indigen-
ously subjective, i. e., originated by purely mental
operations, and at the same time objective, i. e., actualised by the operations of material bodies in the
concrete world of real existence, he jumps at the conclusion that all things ideal are necessarily purely
subjective. The ideal, viz., all that belongs to the
realm of ideas, is subjective, but it has objective validity, and that which gives it objective validity is the
mind's power of forming universal and necessary
judgments. In fact, the terms universal and necessary would have no sense if they were limited to the
realm of subjectivity and if objective validity did not

1 *Prolegomena,* § 2 ff.

imply true objectivity. Hence our aim is to explain the correspondence between the subjective and the objective, and we come to the conclusion that the *a priori* judgments are based upon the conditions of pure form, and form is a quality of the object as well as of the subject.

Thus while Kant's doctrine implies that

the forms of intuition (space and time) and the formal laws are *a priori* in the mind; therefore they are purely subjective and the intuiting and thinking subject transfers them upon the objective world;

our position is the reverse.

What Kant calls *a priori* is purely formal; therefore the mind can produce its laws and theorems by purely mental operations, yet at the same time, being purely formal, they apply to objective reality as the formal conditions of all objects, and thus the operations of objects, as far as their formal conditions are concerned, bear a close analogy to the *a priori* theorems.

We construct the purely formal in our mind, but we do not create it. Nor are the propositions of mathematics a quality of space. We do not deduce the Pythagorean theorem from space, but we construct a right-angled triangle and investigate the results of our construction. Accordingly the theorems thus evolved are products of our mental operations executed on conditions given in our space conception. There are no mathematical theorems in the stellar universe, but there are conditions in the starry heavens which make it possible to calculate distances or other relations with the help of arithmetical computations and geometric constructions. And the conditions which make this possible can only be the objectivity of form implying that the *a priori* laws of subjective form as constructed in our mental models possess an objective validity.

THE OBJECTIVE ANALOGUES OF MENTAL CONSTRUCTIONS.

Zeno's paradox and the difficulties which Clifford found in the continuity conception of space, it seems to me, arise from a direct identification of the mental construction of space with the objective formal features of things that constitute what may be called objective space. Objective space is an inherent quality of things as the relational of their parts and is not, as in subjective space, a construction. The path of a body can be represented by a mathematical line, and a line is infinitely divisible; but for that reason it is not composed of infinite parts. Nor has a moving body to construct a line of an infinite number of infinitely minute parts by adding them piecemeal. The mental analysis and construction of a line is different from traversing it. For moving over a definite stretch of ground it is not necessary to go through the process of separately adding the imaginary infinitely small parts of which it is supposed to consist and into which it may be divided. It has not actually been divided, it is only infinitely divisible.

It is true that time (as time) is purely subjective, but there is a reality that corresponds to time. Time is the measure of motion. We count the running sand of the hour-glass, we divide the face of the sun-dial, we build a clock to determine the lapse of time. There is no time (as time) in the objective world, but there are motions, such as the revolutions of the earth round its axis, or round the sun, and these motions possess succession with definite duration, rendering time, viz., their determination, possible. Duration with succession of events in the world of things is the objective equivalent of time. The measurement of time is a subjective device.

The same is true of space as a conception of the extended world of things. There is no space conception in things, but bodies are extended; and their relation among themselves is an arrangement of innumerable juxtapositions. Extension, juxtaposition, direction of motion, is the objective quality of things that corresponds to the purely mental concept of space.

The untrained and philosophically crude man transfers subjective conceptions of things directly upon the objective world. He speaks of light and colors, of sounds, of time and numbers and things as existing outside of his mind; but a close inspection of the origin of mind will teach us to discriminate between sound and air waves, between colors and the cause of colors (produced by a commotion in the ether,—a reality whose existence is directly imperceptible and can only be deduced indirectly by argument). We shall learn by reflexion that geometrical lines are purely mental constructions, but that the paths of the stars possess qualities (viz., all those which depend upon purely formal conditions) that closely correspond to the conic sections of mathematics.

Further, it becomes obvious that our division of the world into separate things is artificial, for things are only clusters of predicates which impress us as being units. The truth is that the world is so consti-

tuted as to render a perfect separation impossible.
Things are in a perpetual flux, and the limits between
them are arbitrary. As the whole atmosphere and its
pressure belong to our lungs, so the gravity of the sun
is an integral part of the weight of the earth. Thus
we can truly say that there are no separate things except in our minds where they are artificial divisions
invented for the practical purpose of describing the
world, of mapping out its parts, of comprehending
its actions and having a means of adjusting ourselves
to our surroundings.

Logic is purely mental, but there is something in
the objective world that tallies with logic ; we call it
natural law, but the term law is misleading. There
are no laws in nature, but only uniformities resulting
from the condition that the purely formal is the same
everywhere and that the same formal conditions will
produce the same formal effects.

Purely formal laws are universally valid only as
purely formal laws. Twice two will be four in all
arithmetical systems of any possible rational being,
and the statement is universally valid so far as pure
forms are concerned. If we deal with actualities possessed of additional qualities where multiplication
ceases to have its strict mathematical sense, the statement will no longer be tenable. The accumulation of
power on a definite occasion may have results that
cannot be calculated by addition or multiplication.
The associated wealth of twice two millions may far
exceed four millions; and twice one half will never be
one when we deal with living organisms. All this is
conceded. Ideal operations are purely mental and as
such subjective, but for all that they possess objective validity which implies that there are objective

features exhibiting close analogies, by being products of a fundamental sameness of conditions. This fundamental sameness is the universality of form which is common to both the domain of the objective world and the ideal realm of the mind, the thinking subject

There are neither categories nor classes in the objective world, but the different modes of existence are classified by sentient beings and the scheme of the classification is the result. A reflexion upon our modes of thought objectifies them as modes of existence. The Platonic ideas, i. e., the eternal types of the various beings, do not possess a concrete existence as do, e. g., the moulds of a potter, but there are uniformities among the living forms which are obviously apparent. The doctrine of evolution proves that the lines of division between the types of beings are not so distinct in reality as they seem to be, and before a strictly scientific inspection they fade away as imaginary; yet they remain and are indispensable for our method of classification; and the unities which they represent justify us in speaking of objective features as corresponding to the mental conception of Platonic ideas.

THE ORIGIN OF GENERALISATIONS.

The sense-impressions of things are registered according to their difference of form. Every sense-impression runs along in the groove prepared for it by a former sense-impression. Thus the same is registered with the same, and similar ones are correlated. The result is a systematisation of sensory impressions, and the relations that obtain in this system which is built up in the natural course of growth, may appropriately be compared to the pigeon-holes of a methodically arranged cabinet. The difference between the cabinet with pigeon-holes and the human mind is this, that the former is artificial, the latter natural. The human mind with its rationality has been developed according to mechanical law and the classification of sense-impressions is done by it as automatically as the distribution of the different letters in a type-distributing machine.

Our ideas, our names of things, our system of classification is purely subjective, but there is an objective analogue of the eternal types, which consists in the uniformities of all possible formations. This is true of living creatures as well as of machines and other concepts of human fancy. In the domain of invention we know very well that the inventor sometimes creates a combination of parts never actualised before on earth; but the inventor is a finder: he is as much a discoverer as Columbus who found a new continent, or the scientist who succeeds in formulating an unknown law. America existed before Columbus, the law of gravitation held good before Newton, and the idea of a steam engine was a realisable combination before James Watts. It is a feature of objective existence that certain functions can be performed in perfectly definite interrelations. Such conditions which are actualised by a certain combination and disappear as soon as the combination is destroyed, are the objective features in things which justify the subjective idea of unities finding expression in concepts of things and beings.

THE IDEAS OF PURE REASON.

Kant grants the objective applicability of the categories but he denies the validity of the ideas of pure reason, especially the cosmological, the psychological, and the theological idea. We are unable to follow Kant and are inclined to consider his three ideas of Pure Reason in the same light as time and space and the categories. The concept of unity is not a mere assumption but it has its correspondent analogue in reality[1] and has its practical use; only we must beware of treating unities as concrete objectivities, as separate and discrete entities, as things in themselves which have an objective existence apart from and independently of their constituent parts. Thus the soul of man is as real on the assumption of an ego entity as on the theory of its denial. Life is as true whether or not vitalism can be established. The world is a great interrelated system, whether or not the uniformities of nature are called laws. There is a creation of the world, a formation of its life, a dispensation of its destinies, taking place, whether or not this ultimate norm of being be called God; the facts of the cosmic order remain the same on the assumptions of both theism and atheism. But obviously, this decision is not an endorsement of Kant's antinomies, but an explanation of his reasons for formulating them.

While we grant that there is a reality corresponding to Kant's three ideas of pure reason, we do not mean to say that there is a God such as the crude belief of an untrained mind represents him to be, nor further that there is a soul such as it is assumed to exist in the annals of superstition, nor finally that the crude notions of a cosmos, the limits of the world or its infinitude, its composition, its determinedness, and

---

[1] Thus not only all organisms are unities, but also steam-engines, dynamos, or any machinery that would not work unless it were constructed of interacting parts in a definite way.

its absolute existence should be such as abstract reason might arbitrarily construct: we only mean to say
that there are factors in life which caused man to construct such mental images or ideas as are called God,
soul, and world. The ideas may be wrong, but the
factors which produced them are real, and the duty
devolves upon theology, psychology, and cosmology
to eliminate error and bring out the truth.

My objection to Kant's doctrine is not an objection
to his terminology nor to idealism in general. We
may form our world-view in an idealistic as well as a
realistic nomenclature. Object may mean either the
sense-woven picture or the outside thing which it signifies. We may say that the objective world is ideal,
for such it is, meaning by objects the things as we see
them. We may say that the objective world is real,
meaning by objects the actual things represented in
our sense-images. The nomenclature of a philosophical system is important but it is arbitrary. We may
criticise it as impractical, but we cannot on its account
reject a philosophy as untrue.

REALISM OR IDEALISM.

We object to Kant's doctrine of limiting form to
the subject and thus denying the objective value of
the ideal. We may define terms as we please but we
must remain consistent. If the objects are ideal, I
gladly grant that the forms of the objects are ideal;
but for all that, being forms of the objects, they are
objective, as much as the objects themselves.

The sense-woven pictures of things, though subjective images, are the realities of life, and our concepts of things are symbols of them in terms of their
formal features expressed according to schedules

which we construct *a priori*. Time and space, the forms of our sense-world (of our *Anschauung*), accordingly are as real as these things, and I cannot say that the things themselves are real while the forms of things are purely ideal, i. e., not real.

Schopenhauer, a one-sided but nevertheless one of the most prominent and faithful disciples of Kant, defends Kantian idealism against the misinterpretations of the so-called realists in these sentences:

"In spite of all that one may say, nothing is so persistently and ever anew misunderstood as *Idealism*, because it is interpreted as meaning that one denies the *empirical* reality of the external world. Upon this rests the perpetual return to the appeal to common sense, which appears in many forms and guises; for example, as an 'irresistible conviction' in the Scotch school, or as Jacobi's *faith* in the reality of the external world. The external world by no means presents itself, as Jacobi declares, upon credit, and is accepted by us upon trust and faith. It presents itself as that which it is, and performs directly what it promises."[1]

THE SUBJECT AS ITS OWN OBJECT.

The quarrel between the idealists so called and the realists of Jacobi's stamp is purely a question of terminology. It is a vicious circle to ask whether the real is real; the question is, "What do we understand by real?" Now we agree with Kant in accepting *Anschauung* as real. Our perceptions are the data of experience, they are the facts of life about which there is no quibbling and the question of unreality originates only in the realm of abstract thought, viz., in the domain of interpretation. Perceptions are classified; perceptions of the same kind are subsumed under the general conception of their class and if a perception is misinterpreted, our notion concerning it is errone-

1 From Schopenhauer's *The World as Will and Idea*.

ous. An after-image is as real as the original pei ception, but it is called an illusion when it suggests the presence of an object; in other words when its cause is misinterpreted.

Perceptions accordingly are what we define as real, and space and time are, abstractly stated, the forms of perception. Time and space, accordingly, are as real as perceptions.

Now we may ask what are the objects of the perceptions, defining objects this time not as the sense-woven images of our perception inside our senses, but as the external presences which are supposed to cause them. Since it is impossible here to enter into a detailed epistemological discussion of the subject, we state the answer for brevity's sake dogmatically as follows: The objects (viz., the external presences which are supposed to cause perceptions) are, ultimately, i. e., in their inmost constitution, of the same nature as are the perceptions themselves. The perceptions in their totality are called the subject—which is a sentient body, an intricate organism consisting of different organs of sense and a superadded organ of thought for preserving the sense-images, collating them, classifying them, and interpreting them. We are a system of perceptions and impulses, guided by memories and thoughts, but we represent ourselves in our own perception as a body in time and space. Thus our representation of ourselves is our self-perception, i. e., a representation of the subject as its own object, and our self-perception is as real as are perceptions in general. Succession of sense-impressions and reactions thereupon, accordingly, form part and parcel of our subject as its own object; and in the same way, juxtaposition of organs is an attribute of our self, not as it is as a subject in itself, but of our self as it represents itself as its own object. Other objects are in the same predicament and partake of the same nature. If time and space are the forms of the objectified subject, viz., of our own bodily existence we have good reasons to ascribe objectivity to the facts from which the ideas of time and space are derived, viz., to extension and succession.

THE OBJECTIVE ORIGIN OF SPACE AND TIME.

It is true that the factors which generate in the mind our conceptions of time and space, together with the entire formal aspect of being, lie in the subject, in the sentient thinking being, but they lie not in the abstract subject in itself, not in the subjectivity of the subject, not in the quality of the subject which remains when all other qualities, i. e., the objective features of its own actualisation as a concrete being, are omitted by the process of abstraction, i. e., when they have been cancelled in thought. The subject in itself will be found to be an empty generalisation which contains nothing but a product of our analysis of perception, the bare idea of the perceiving in contrast to the perceived. It contains nothing either *a priori* or *a posteriori;* merely itself, the shadow of a thing. But the actual subject, which is an object in the objective world, exists somewhere in space and in a given time. It moves, i. e., it changes its position. It consists of juxtaposed organs and its experiences exhibit a definite succession, each act having its own definite duration. Therefore we do not hesitate, when drawing a line of demarcation between the subjective and the objective features of the thinking subject, to include its form together with its bodily objectivation in the realm of objectivity. In this way it happens that time and space may be called subjective, because the objectified subject finds them *a priori* in itself, but their ultimate root lies in the domain of objectivity, and we can therefore just as well call them objective, because they are the forms of the objective world and originate in the subject only because it is an object belonging to the objective world.

UNIVERSALITY DUE TO SYSTEMATISATION.

Kant was puzzled mainly by the subjective apriority of the laws of time and space and of all other formal relations, but this puzzling apriority is, closely considered, nothing but their general applicability to all possible experience, which is due to the fact that all formal relations admit of systematisation. Formal possibilities can be exhausted and purely formal statements apply to *all* pure forms. Hence they possess universality, and universality admits of no exception, hence it implies necessity, which involves *a priori* applicability.

It is true (as Kant says) that purely formal knowledge is empty; but we know at the same time that the purely formal knowledge gives system to the empirical, to the sense-given facts of our experience. If we could not classify sense-impressions, they would remain a useless chaos, and human reason would not have developed. Kant expresses this truth by saying that the sensory impressions without the guidance of the purely formal are blind.

But as the formative norms of the objective world shape things and make them such as they are, our formal cognition classifies sense-impression according to their forms and thus makes a knowledge of objects

possible. Our formal cognition is not the cause of
the objective uniformities (as Kant suggests) but one
of their applications only, being, as it were, their own
reflexion in the consciousness of a sentient being. By
being systematised in the shape of formulas, they apply *a priori* to experience and become in this way a
key, with the help of which we can unlock the closed
doors of the mysteries of nature and decipher the
riddles of the universe.

THE REAL AND THE SUPERREAL.

We may call the eternal norms of existence which
condition the formation of things "being" or "*Sein*"
and the concrete actualisation of the types of being
their "becoming," *Werden* or *Dasein*. We become
acquainted with the norms of existence, part of which
are formulated as natural laws, by abstraction and
generalisation, but for that reason they are not mere
glittering generalities, abstract nonentities, or unreal
inventions, but significant features of objective existence, depicting not accidental but necessary uniformities. While we concede that the world of becoming
is real, we must grant that the realm of being is superreal. Both *Sein* and *Werden*, Being and Becoming,
are real; but the reality of the two is different in kind.
The latter's reality is actualisation, the reality of the
former is eternality. Thus the former is immutable,
the latter a perpetual flux. The fleeting realities of
sense are definite objects in the objective world, but
the norms of eternal being are the formative factors
which shape them.

Obviously the eternal norms of existence, which
are identical with the purely formal laws constituting
the cosmic order, though not material facts, are the

most effective presences of the world. They are not only real, they are superreal. They remain the same whether realised or not in the actual world. They produce the cosmic order, render the rise of rational beings possible, they are the condition of the intelligibility of things, they are the prototype of mind and spirituality, they are the corner-stone of both science and ethics and constitute Kant's *mundus intelligibilis*— the realm of spiritual being; Swedenborg's sphere of spirits, of angels, and archangels; the kingdom of God, to be realised on earth; yea, God himself, for God is all these norms in their totality and systematic unity. In Lao-Tze's philosophy it is the eternal Tao, the world-reason or primordial Logos. In Buddhist metaphysics it corresponds to Açvaghosha's Tathâgatagarbha, i. e., the womb of Buddhahood and the origin of all things; to Amitâbha, the source of all light and wisdom, and also to the deathless, the uncreate, the non-corporeal existence (*arûpa*), the Nirvâna of the older Buddhists.

NOUMENA.

The data of experience are sensations, or sense-perceptions, which represent themselves as images of things in time and space. The sensory element of the images, which is conditioned by the material composition of the sentient subject, is purely subjective and need not be uniform. Thus we know that colors are perceived differently by different eyes; the color-blind see the world like a steel-engraving, or rather a wash-picture, gray in gray. To the red-blind red appears green, to the green-blind red appears dark yellow and green pale yellow. If all men were color-blind, the gray image would have to be regarded as normal. The forms of things, too, are conditioned to some extent by the material composition of our sense-organs, as much so as the picture on the sensitive plate of a photographer's camera depends upon the lens. Further, we see not things as they are, but as they are projected according to the laws of perspective. But we can from the given data of the projected images and additional considerations of other data of experience reconstruct the form and structure of things as they are in space and of the events as they and their accelerations take place in time. This construction of things is called in Kant's terminology things as creations of thought, or noumena, and the noumena are intended as models of the objects themselves, for they mean to depict things in their objective nature, as they are after the elimination of all subjective elements of cognition. Accordingly noumena (as noumena) are scientific notions, products of reasoning, and subjective in a higher degree even than sense-perceptions. They are the interpretations of the sense-perceptions and are as such ideal, i. e., representations not things. But they represent things as they are, independent of the senses of the sentient subject. Noumena would be unmeaning, if they did not represent objective realities, if they were purely fictitious, if they did not portray the things as objects in the objective world. We may fitly call the realities for whose designation noumena (i. e., scientific concepts) have been invented objects, or more definitely, objects in themselves.

They constitute the realm of experience, and time and space are the generalised modes of their existence by which we determine their formal qualities. Nothing is real in the sense of concrete existence, except

it be in time and space. Accordingly time and space
(though not objects but mere forms) are objective
qualities of things, and without time and space concrete things cease to be concretely real and become
either mere ideas or nonentities.

We may with Kant distinguish between thing and
thing in itself and may understand by the latter the
eternal foundation of the thing, its metaphysical *raison
d'être*, whatever that may mean (either its Platonic
idea, its eternal type, or the Schopenhauerian conception of its "will to be," or the general and abstract
idea of its existence), but under all conditions space
and time belong (as Kant says) to the things as appearances, viz., the things as objects in the objective
world which implies (the contrary to that which Kant
says) that they are not purely subjective, but objective.

THE OBJECTIVITY OF SPACE AND TIME.

Now we may call the perpetual flux of concrete
objects "appearance," and the domain of eternal being
"the real things": in that case the real things come to
appearance by becoming actual in time and space. In
this sense we agree with Kant, that time and space are
real for our experience, though not for our experience
alone, but for any experience. Every sentient subject, in so far as it is sentient, every individual man,
is not a subject pure and simple, but an actualised
subject, an objectified thing, for all acts of cognition
are acts of an objective significance, taking place in
the domain of objective existence, as an interrelation
between two or several objects. One party to this
interrelation (viz., my bodily organisation) happens
to be the sentient and thinking subject, but that alters

nothing in the case, for all its actions take place in time, and the concrete corporeality of its organs is somewhere in space. Again therefore we come to the conclusion that space and time appertain (as Kant says) to the appearances of things. They appertain to the subject, not in itself, but to the appearance of the subject, viz., to its objectivation; accordingly they are (as opposed to what Kant says) objective, not purely subjective, and may be called subjective only in a special sense, viz., in so far as they appertain to the objectified subject, which, however, is an object like any other object in the objective world. The subject does not transfer time and space into the objective world, but anything that becomes actual thereby makes its appearance in time and space. In other words, Time, Space, and all the norms of purely formal relations, are the forms of any possible concrete existence. Whatever the metaphysical *raison d'être* of things may be, the "why there is anything," reality, when actualised, represents itself objectively as being in time and space. The thinking subject does not represent things in time and space, but in so far as it is an actual object in the objective world, it represents itself (i. e., it appears) in time and space. So do all other things: hence the concurrence of the formal notions of the objectified subject with the formal conditions of the objectified things of our surroundings. Kant says (§ 52*c*):

> "Space and time together with the appearances in them are nothing existing in themselves and outside of my representations but are themselves only modes of representation."[1]

[1] It is very strange that the same Kant who says that space (viz., extension) is only a mode of representation declares (in § 2) that the sentence

He should have said (and here we use purposely Kant's own term "appearance" [1]):

Time and space are modes of appearance, viz., of self-representation.

Being modes of appearance they are inside every subject in so far as it has made its appearance in the objective world. They are in all objects as those relational features which determine the juxtaposition of things. It is the actualised appearance that needs extension (i. e., space) for the distribution of the several organs of the thinking subject. We feel our limbs as being in different places, as moving about, as touching, as separating, etc., and these feelings are parts of our soul : they are the inside of the subject which is objectified (or comes to appearance) in our bodily existence. Our body (viz., our self as appearance) is extended, and the space, needed for it, is limited by the skin. The remainder of extension which accomodates the other objects of the surrounding world is designated as the outside ; and if the extension within our skin is real, the outside must also be real. Both together constitute space.

"bodies are extended" is analytical; accordingly he regards extension or space as the essential feature of a thing, of an object. Why then does he not recognise space as the mark of objectivism, which might have led him to concede the objective nature of the operations of the thinking subject?

[1] Appearance or phenomenon means originally the picture of objects as it appears on the retina and generally all the data of sense-perception ; but the word is used in contrast to noumenon, or abstract thought, denoting the concrete object as it is given to the senses distinguished from its general and abstract idea. Thus, the world of appearances means the concrete world of objects that affect our senses, though the term might be interpreted to stand for the retinal picture as a mere subjective image in contrast to the material world of objective reality. Indeed, there are authors who do use the word in the latter sense, while in the minds of most readers the two conceptions are mixed and the former is imperceptibly affected by the latter. It would not be difficult to point out what an interminable confusion the use of this word has produced in philosophy.

When Kant denies that space and time are objec-
Jve, he becomes confused and self-contradictory. For
ne would either have to say that space and time are
limited within the boundary of the body of the thinking subject, which is nonsense, or he must attribute
them to the subject as a thing in itself, which contradicts his own theory according to which time and
space do not refer to things in themselves, but to appearances only. Thus even from Kant's own premises
and when employing his own terminology the theory
becomes untenable that space and time are purely
subjective attributes. Their very nature is objectivity,
and if objects are appearances, time and space as the
forms of all appearance must be regarded as features
of existence which in their very nature are objective.

It appears that Kant was not sufficiently careful to
distinguish between space-conception, which is subjective, and space itself, which, being the juxtaposition of things and their parts, is objective. Space-
conception originates from within sentient organisms,
viz., in the mind, by its adjustment to the surrounding world through the use of its organs. Its ultimate
sources are of a physiological nature consisting in the
motion of the limbs and especially the eyes. This is
what Ernst Mach calls physiological space.[1] Mathematical space is a higher abstraction than physiological space. In mathematical space all incidental features, the differences of right and left, of high and low,
etc., are dropped, and space is regarded as homa-
loidal, viz., as constituted alike throughout. The
homaloidality of space is the simplest way of depriv-
ing space of all positive attributes, of rendering it the

[1] See Ernst Mach's article "On Physiological, as Distinguished from
Geometrical Space," in *The Monist*, Vol. XI., No. 3., April, 1901.

"same" throughout. At any rate it is a mental construction as much as the idea of a straight line and all geometrical figures. The construction has been made without any concrete building material, with mere mental operations, simply by proceeding on the assumption of logical consistency, where the same procedure yields the same result. That other space constructions are possible need not concern us here. At any rate, our space-conception is built up in the thinking subject by operations of which it is possessed in its capacity as an object moving about in the objective world. Our space-conception is a noumenon (a product of thought), and like all noumena, it is intended to describe features of objective reality; and these features of objective reality intended to be delineated in our space-conception is objective space—viz., the extension of the world and of its parts, the juxtaposition of bodies, and the range of directions all around every moving point.

Our space-conception is subjective, but for that reason space itself remains as objective as any object in space. Moreover, the data from which our space-conception has been constructed are as objective as are all the acts and facts of our bodily organism.

THINGS IN THEMSELVES.

Where, then, are the things in themselves, which, according to Kant, remain unintelligible?

There is a truth in the idea that our mind is so constituted as to transfer to the phenomenal world its *a priori* notions of time and space and its thought-forms. The world of our senses which appears to us as the objective world that surrounds us, is truly a construction of our organs of sense; the construction is as necessary as is for example the reflexion of a picture in a mirror; things in themselves remain outside. In this sense Kant's doctrine of idealism is undeniably true.

But Kant goes further in saying that things in themselves, meaning things viewed independently of our sense-perception, do not partake of form and are therefore unknowable. But what is knowledge if not a correct description of things? Things are mirrored in our eyes, and abstract notions are formed to represent them in mental symbols. It would be absurd to expect that things should bodily migrate into our heads.

It is the ideal of science to eliminate the subjectivity of the thinking subject and construct a world-picture in terms of formal laws, by the guidance of the several sciences of formal thought; this is the noumenal world, the world of thought; but this noumenal world is nothing but a picture (more or less accurate) of the objective world as things are independently of sense-perception. Here everything changes into motion of a definite form; the rainbow with the warm beauty of its colors becomes the reflexion of ether waves of a definite angle with definite wave-lengths. Though the noumenon is a subjective construction, it is an analogue of the objects as they are in themselves, describing their suchness. Accordingly, this would be a cognition of things in themselves, for Kant defines things in themselves as the ground which determines our sensibility to have sense-perceptions, or briefly the causes of phenomena.

Cognition is nothing more nor less than the construction of analogous symbols of things by which we can know their nature for the sake of determining their action, thus enabling us to direct the course of events by adaptation partly of ourselves to conditions, partly of our surroundings to our wants. Unless we denounce science as a vagary of the human mind, we must grant that in spite of the shortcomings of the individual scientist, the ideal of science (which consists in describing things in their objective existence) is justified, and can be more and more realised.

And what becomes of things in themselves?

If things in themselves cannot be described with the assistance of formal thoughts, they degenerate into dim chimerical and contradictory notions, such as unextended bodies, or substances without qualities, or unmaterial entities, or causes which remain outside the pale of causation.

The conception of things in themselves is a vagary of pre-Kantian metaphysics, the empty shell of which, as an irrational quantity, transcendent and unknowable, was by some mishap suffered to remain in Kant's philosophy.

If things in themselves mean objective things, viz., things as they are, independently of our sensibility, we must deny that they are unknowable. If they mean that which constitutes the essential character of the things, making them what they are, they will be seen to be determined by their suchness; they are what Plato called the eternal types of being, or ideas; and we ought to call them not "things in themselves," but "forms in themselves."

Schopenhauer interprets the Kantian conception of things in themselves as the metaphysical *raison d'être* of their existence, but he denies that its nature cannot be known and discovers its manifestation in "the Will." According to him it is the Will that makes every one what he is, and Schopenhauer's Will is not the physiological process of willing, the conscious effort of causing an idea to pass into an act, but the tendency to motion such as it inheres in all existence, in the stone as gravity, in chemicals as affinity, in sentient beings as desire. He expressly excludes that feature which distinguishes will from unconscious motions, viz., intelligence, and speaks of the blind Will. The blind Will is practically deified by him, for it is supposed to be above time and space and credited with creative omnipotence. In reality it is nothing but the widest generalisation of motion.

Clifford offers another interpretation of the term "thing in itself," viz., the sentiency of organised beings, constituting their subjectivity and corresponding to what in man is called his "soul." But, again, this subjectivity, the spiritual inside, is always the sentient accompaniment of the organisation, the bodily outside; and its nature can be determined by studying the visible exponents of its objective expression in which it is realised. Thus Clifford's things in themselves are as little unknowable as Schopenhauer's.

Agnosticism, the egg-shell of metaphysicism, prevented Kant from taking the last step suggested by his doctrine of the necessity and universality of the laws of pure form. He lost himself in contradictions and became satisfied with his statement of the antinomies of pure reason, according to which we may prove with equal plausibility that God exists or that he does not.

THE GOD PROBLEM.

If Kant had followed the course which we here, under the guidance of the principles laid out by him, have briefly sketched out, his philosophy not only would have become less artificial and remained in close touch with the natural sciences, but it would also have helped theology to develop purer, truer, and nobler religious ideals. With the egg-shell of agnosticism on its back, Kantism was satisfied with the existing state of beliefs and things; not that Kant endorsed the various irrationalities of the Christianity of his day, the literalism of dogma, the implicit belief in the very text of the Bible, the Creation story, paternalism of the Prussian State Church, etc.; he criticised them occasionally in mild terms; but instead of going to work to purify religion (not in the narrow and prosaic spirit of his disciples, the Rationalists, but with due reverence for the poetry of dogma and legend, and at the same time with a consideration for the practical needs of the heart): he simply justified them in general terms on account of their moral usefulness in his *Critique of Practical Reason.*

As an instance, let us point out his unsatisfactory solution of the God problem.

Kant accepted in his conception of God the traditional views of the Church, and discussed it as one of the several metaphysical notions, the result being that the idea is pronounced to be transcendent, and we can with equally plausible reasons both affirm and deny his existence. It is one of Kant's four antinomies of Pure Reason. But God unknown to pure reason and not discoverable in the domain of experience and resuscitated only as a postulate of practical reason is a poor substitute even for the mythological conception of the god of the uneducated masses. An hypothetical god cannot help; he is sicklied over with the pale cast of thought; he is not real; he is paralysed. I am far from blaming Kant, who has done so much for philosophy, for not having done more and performed a reformer's work for religion; but I would suggest that he might as well from his own principles have investigated the nature of formal laws, which in the subjective sphere of reason appear as transcendental ideas, and have come to the conclusion that a truer God-conception could be derived therefrom, which then would commend itself as the higher ideal. The popular notions of the several religions and also of a primitive theology are dim foreshadowings of a scientific God-conception, the purity of which is increasing with the progress of scientific truth.

The world-order, that purely formal law in the objective world which forms and creates, shaping the stellar universe (as Kant set forth so forcibly in his *General Natural History and Theory of the Heavens*), and revealing itself in the social development of man as the power that makes for righteousness, must have made its influence felt in the life of mankind at the very beginning, and would naturally, according to the practical needs of the intelligence of the successive ages, assume the shape of a conception of God, more or less crude in the beginning, and more or less philosophical in the mind of the wise. The world-order, this superpersonal spirituality that acts as the divine dispensation in the world, is hyperphysical (I purposely avoid the much-abused term "supernatural," but I might as well say supernatural). It is intrinsically necessary, it is omnipresent, it is unerring in the truth of its various applications which form as it were a grand system, comparable to the articulated differe῾t ἀἰῃ of a spiritual organism,—a personality; it is as unfailingly just as the law of causation is rigid ; and every God-conception is but an attempt at comprehending its moral significance.

The fetishist's notion of a power to which he must conform is not absolutely wrong. It contains a truth, but is alloyed with superstitions. The idea of thinking of God as a king of kings, as a supreme judge, is more advanced, inasmuch as God henceforth represents a moral maxim, the principle of justice in the world. The God-father idea of Christianity surpasses the theology of the prophets of the Old Testament, but it, too, falls short of the truth in all its perfection. All we have to do is to be serious in scientifically thinking the divine attributes of omnipresence, of eternality, of infinitude, of omniscience, of all-justice, of the irrefragability of law in the physical, the psychical, and the social spheres of existence, which, reflected in the instructive growth of his conscience, become to man the moral norm of life, and the ultimate authority of conduct.

Kant cited the religious notions of the theology of his age before the tribunal of pure reason and dismissed the suit as offering no issue, leaving the question in the state in which he had found it. He would have served his age better had he worked out the philosophical significance of the idea of God, on the basis of the practical significance of his Transcendentalism; he would then, instead of leaving the problem unsolved, have boldly propounded the gospel of the superpersonal God as coming, not to destroy the old theology, but to fulfil its yearnings and hopes, without in the least doing violence to the demands of criticism and scientific exactness.

SUPPLEMENTARY MATERIALS FOR THE STUDY OF KANT'S LIFE AND PHILOSOPHY.

INTRODUCTORY NOTE.

THESE materials, culled from Kantian literature, are intended as specimens of the various opinions which prevail concerning Kant, and have been arranged and added to this book for the purpose of enabling the student to study Kant in the impressions which he made upon the philosophical public. The selection has at the same time been offered with the intention of giving a brief synopsis of Kant's work, at least so far as the systematic construction, or *Ausbau*, of his transcendental criticism is concerned. It is understood that Kant's merits as a thinker and inquirer are not limited to metaphysics, but it would have led us too far, and would have swelled the book to too bulky a size, without doing justice to the subject, if we had also attempted to consider here Kant's researches in physics, mechanics, astronomy, and the other natural sciences. That Kant had a clear idea, not only of evolution and of the descent of man from lower forms of life, but also of the difficulties of the evolution theory, is well attested by many remarkable passages, collected by Fritz Schultze[1].

We have only to add that we have selected Windelband as a representative historian of philosophy, in preference, say, to Erdmann and Ueberweg, solely because of the terseness of his statements. Schwegler is a Hegelian, Weber an Alsatian under French influence. Lange represents the large class of agnostics who grant that materialism is untenable as a philosophy but deem it to be the best working hypothesis in science. Schopenhauer is one of the most original disciples of Kant, and set up a philosophy of his own, conceiving the world under the double aspect of Will and Idea. He hates Hegel and all "school-philosophy," saying that he himself, the true philosopher, lives *for* philosophy, while the professors appointed to teach philosophy live *on* philosophy. **Heine**

---

[1] *Kant und Darwin, ein Beitrag zur Geschichte der Entwickelungslehre* Jena, 1875.

is peculiarly interesting, being brilliant and cynical at the same time. He speaks sometimes as if he were an atheist, and again advocates a theism verging on pantheism. Theodore F. Wright's digest of Stückenberg is cavilling and spiteful. His is the most unfavorable view of Kant, and we quote it on that account. Paulsen's chronological table will be welcome as a useful synopsis of the data of Kant's life.   P. C.

KANT'S LIFE AND WRITINGS.

(AFTER WINDELBAND.[1])

IMMANUEL KANT was born April 22, 1724, at Königsberg, Prussia, the son of a saddler. He was educated at the Pietistic Collegium Fridericianum, and attended in 1740 the University of his native city to study theology ; but subjects of natural science and philosophy gradually attracted him. After concluding his studies, he became a private teacher in various families in the vicinity of Königsberg from 1746 to 1755 ; in the autumn of 1755 he habilitated as *Privatdocent* in the philosophical faculty of Königsberg University, and was made full Professor there in 1770. The cheerful, brilliant animation, and versatility of his middle years gave place with time to an earnest, rigorous conception of life and to the control of a strict consciousness of duty, which manifested itself in his unremitting labour upon his great philosophical task, in his masterful fulfilment of the duties of his academic profession, and in the inflexible rectitude of his life, which was not without a shade of the pedantic. The uniform course of his solitary and modest scholar's life was not disturbed by the brilliancy of the fame that fell upon his life's evening, and only transiently by the dark shadow that the hatred of orthodoxy, which had obtained control under Frederick William II., threatened to cast upon his path by a prohibition of his philosophy. He died from the weakness of old age on the 12th of February, 1804.

Kant's middle and later life and personality has been drawn most completely by Kuno Fischer (*Geschichte der neueren Philosophie*, III. and IV., 3d ed., Munich, 1882); E. Arnoldt has treated of his youth and the first part of his activity as a teacher (Königsberg, 1882). See also J H. W. Stuckenberg, *Life of Kant* (London, 1882).

---

[1] *History of Philosophy*. Translated from the German by James H. Tufts, New York : Macmillan, 1893. Price $5.00. This work is especially valuable as a comparative treatment of the history of thought

The change which was taking place in the philosopher toward the end of the seventh decade of the eighteenth century appears especially in his activity as a writer. His earlier "pre-critical" works are distinguished by easy-flowing, graceful presentation, and present themselves as admirable occasional writings of a man of fine thought who is well versed in the world. His later works show the laboriousness of his thought and the pressure of the contending *motifs*, both in the form of the investigation, with its circumstantial heaviness and artificial architectonic structure, and in the formation of his sentences, which are highly involved, and frequently interrupted by restriction. Minerva frightened away the graces; but instead, the devout tone of deep thought and earnest conviction, which here and there rises to powerful pathos and weighty expression, hovers over his later writings.

For Kant's theoretical development, the antithesis between the Leibnizo-Wolffian metaphysics and the Newtonian natural philosophy was at the beginning of decisive importance. The former had been brought to his attention at the University by Knutzen, the latter by Teske, and in his growing alienation from the philosophical school-system, his interest for natural science, to which for the time he seemed to desire to devote himself entirely, cooperated strongly. His first treatise, 1747, was entitled *Thoughts upon the True Measure of Vis Viva*, a controverted question between Cartesian and Leibnizian physicists; his great work upon the *General Natural History and Theory of the Heavens* was a natural science production of the first rank, and besides small articles, his promotion-treatise, *De Igne* (1755), which propounded a hypothesis as to imponderables, belongs here. His activity as a teacher also showed, even on into his later period, a preference for the subjects of natural sciences, especially for physical geography and anthropology.

In theoretical philosophy Kant passed through many reversals (*mancherlei Umkippungen*) of his standpoint. At the beginning (in the *Physical Monadology*) he had sought to adjust the opposition between Leibniz and Newton, in their doctrine of space, by the ordinary distinction of things-in-themselves (which are to be known metaphysically), and phenomena, or things as they appear (which are to be investigated physically); he then (in the writings after 1760) attained to the insight that a metaphysics in the sense of rationalism is impossible, that philosophy and mathematics must have diametrically opposed methods, and that philosophy as the empirical knowledge of the given cannot step beyond the circle of experience. But while he allowed himself to be comforted by Voltaire and Rousseau for this falling away of metaphysical insight, through the instrumentality of the "natural feeling" for the right and holy, he was still working with Lambert at an improvement of the method of metaphysics, and when he found this, as he hoped, by the aid of Leibniz's *Nouveaux Essais*, he constructed in bold lines the mystico-dogmatic system of his *Inaugural Dissertation*.

The progress from this point to the *System of Criticism* is obscure and controverted. For this development, and for the time in which he was influenced by Hume, as well as for the direction which that influence took, consult the following works: Fr. Michelis, *Kant vor und nach 1770* (Braunsberg, 1871); Fr. Paulsen, *Versuch einer Entwicklungsgeschichte der Kantischen Erkenntnisstheorie* (Leipsic, 1875); A. Riehl, *Geschichte und Methode des philosophischen Kriticismus* (Leips. 1876); B. Erdmann, *Kant's Kriticismus* (Leips. 1878); W. Windelband, *Die verschiedenen Phasen der Kantischen Lehre vom Ding-an-sich* (*Vierteljahrsschrift für wissenschaftliche Philosophie*, 1876). Cf. also the writings by K. Dieterich on Kant's relation to Newton and Rousseau under the title *Die Kantische Philosophie in ihrer inneren Entwicklungsgeschichte*, Freiburg i. B. 1885; also A. Wreschner, *Ernst Platner und Kant's Kritik der reinen Vernunft* (Leipsic, 1893); E. Adickes, *Kant-Studien* (Kiel and Leipsic, 1895); F. Paulsen, *Immanuel Kant* (Stuttgart, 1898). For Kant on Evolution, see P. Carus, *Kant and Spencer* (Chicago, 1900).

From the adjustment of the various tendencies of Kant's thought proceeded the "Doomsday-book" of German philosophy, the *Critique of Pure Reason* (Riga, 1781). It received a series of changes in the second edition (1787), and these became the objec, of very vigorous controversies after attention had been called to them by Schelling (W., V. 196) and Jacobi (W., II. 291). Cf. concerning this, the writings cited above. H. Vaihinger, *Commentar zu Kant's Kritik der reinen Vernunft* (Vol. I., Stuttgart, 1887, Vol. II., 1892), has diligently collected the literature. Separate editions of the *Kritik*, by K. Kehrbach, upon the basis of the first edition, and by B. Erdmann and E. Adickes upon the basis of the second edition, have been published.

There is an English translation of the *Critique* (2d ed.), by Meiklejohn, in the Bohn Library, and also one by Max Müller (text of 1st ed. with supplements giving changes of 2d ed.), Lond. 1881. We have further a Paraphrase and Commentary by Mahaffy and Bernard, 2d ed., Lond. and N. Y. 1889; and partial translations in J. H. Stirling's *Text-book to Kant*, and in Watson's *Selections*, Lond. and N. Y. 1888. This last contains also extracts from the ethical writings and from the *Critique of Judgment*.

The additional main writings of Kant in his critical period are: *Prolegomena zu einer jeden künftigen Metaphysik*, 1783; *Grundlegung zur Metaphysik der Sitten*, 1785; *Metaphysische Anfangsgründe der Naturwissenschaft*, 1785; *Kritik der praktischen Vernunft*, 1788; *Kritik der Urtheilskraft*, 1790; *Die Religion innerhalb der Grenzen der blossen Vernunft*, 1793; *Zum ewigen Frieden*, 1795; *Metaphysische Anfangsgründe der Rechts- und Tugendlehre*, 1797; *Der Streit der Fakultäten*, 1798. There is an English translation of the *Prolegomena*, by Mahaffy and Bernard, Lond. and N. Y., 1889; of the *Prolegomena* and *Metaphysical Foundation of Natural Science*, by Bax, Bohn Library; of the ethical writings, including the first part of the *Religion within the Bounds of Pure Reason*, by T. K. Abbott, 4th ed., Lond. 1889; of the *Critique of Judgment*, by J. H. Bernard, Lond. and N. Y. 1892; of the *Philosophy of Law*, by W. Hastie, Edin. 1887; *Principles of Politics*, including the essay on *Perpetual Peace*, by W. Hastie, Edin. 1891; of Kant's *Inaugural Dissertation*, W. J. Eckoff, (New York, 1894). The contents of *Kant's Essays and Treatises*, 2 vols., Lond. 1798, is given in *Ueberweg*, II. 138 (Eng. tr.).

Complete editions of his works have been prepared by K. Rosenkranz and F. W. Schubert (12 vols., Leips. 1833 ff.); by G. Hartenstein (10 vols., Leips. 1838 f.; more recently 8 vols., Leips. 1867 ff.); and by J. v. Kirchmann (in the *Philos. Biblioth.*). They contain, besides his smaller articles, etc., his lectures upon logic, pedagogy, etc., and his letters. A survey of all that has been written by Kant (including also the manuscript of the *Transition from Metaphysics to Physics*, which is without value for the interpretation of his critical system) is found in *Ueberweg-Heinze*, III, § 24; there, too, the voluminous literature is cited with great completeness. Of this we can give here only a choice of the best and most instructive; a survey of the more valuable literature, arranged according to its material, is offered by the article *Kant*, by W. Windelband in *Ersch und Gruber's Enc.* The *Journal of Speculative Philosophy* contains numerous articles upon Kant.

We may mention also Adamson, *The Philosophy of Kant*, Edin, 1879; art. *Kant*, in *Enc. Brit.*, by the same author; arts. in *Mind*, Vol. VI., by J. Watson, and in *Philos. Review*, 1893, by J. G. Schurmann.—E. Adickes has published an exhaustive bibliography of the German literature in the *Philos. Review*, 1893 ff.

THE CRITIQUE OF PRACTICAL REASON,
AND THE CRITIQUE OF JUDGMENT.

(AFTER WEBER.[1])

I. THE CRITIQUE OF PRACTICAL REASON.[2]

ALTHOUGH the *Critique of Pure Reason* reduces us to a scepticism which is all the more absolute because it is reasoned, proved, cientifically established, and legitimised, it would be a grave mistake to consider the sage of Koenigsberg as a sceptic in the traditional sense, and to impute to him a weakness for the materialism of his age. Scepticism is the upshot of the *Critique of Pure Reason;* it is not, however, the ultimatum of Kantianism. To assert the contrary is completely to misunderstand the spirit of the philosophy of Kant and the final purpose of his critique. This is by no means hostile to the moral faith and its transcendent object, but wholly in its favor. It is, undoubtedly, not Kant's intention to "humiliate" reason, as Tertullian and Pascal had desired to do, but to assign to it its proper place among all our faculties, its true rôle in the complicated play of our spiritual life. Now, this place is, according to Kant, a subordinate one; this function is *regulative* and modifying, not *constitutive* and creative. *The* WILL, *and not reason, forms the basis of our faculties and of things,* that is the leading thought of Kantian philosophy. While reason becomes entangled in inevitable antinomies and involves us in doubts, the will is the ally of faith, the source, and therefore, the natural guardian of our moral and religious beliefs. Observe that

[1] From Weber's *History of Philosophy*. Translated by Frank Thilly. New York: Scribner's. Price, $2 50. Weber's book is one of the clearest, concisest, and most readable of the histories of philosophies.

[2] H. Cohen, *Kant's Begründung der Ethik*, Berlin, 1877; E. Zeller, *Ueber das Kantische Moralprincip*, Berlin, 1880; J. G. Schurman, *Kantian Ethics and the Ethics of Evolution*, London, 1881; N. Porter, *Kant's Ethics*, Chicago, 1886; F. W. Förster, *Der Entwickelungsgang der Kantischen Ethik*, etc., Berlin, 1894; Pünjer, *Die Religionslehre Kant's*, Jena, 1874.

Kant in no wise denies the existence of the thing-in-itself, of the soul, and of God, but only the possibility of proving the reality of these Ideas, by means of reasoning. True, he combats spiritualistic dogmatism, but the same blow that brings it down overthrows materialism; and though he attacks theism, he likewise demolishes the dogmatic pretensions of the atheists. What he combats to the utmost and pitilessly destroys is the dogmatism of *theoretical* reason, under whatever form it may present itself, whether as theism or atheism, spiritualism or materialism; is its assumption of authority in the system of our faculties; is the prejudice which attributes metaphysical capacity to the understanding, *isolated from the will and depending on its own resources.* By way of retaliation—and here he reveals the depth of his philosophic faith—he concedes a certain metaphysical capacity to *practical reason*, i. e., to *will.*

Like the understanding, the will has its own character, its original forms, its particular legislation, a legislation which Kant calls "practical reason." In this new domain, the problems raised by the *Critique of Pure Reason* change in aspect; doubts are dissipated, and uncertainties give way to practical certainty. The moral law differs essentially from physical law, as conceived by theoretical reason. Physical law is irresistible and inexorable; the moral law does not compel, but bind; *hence it implies freedom.* Though freedom cannot be proved theoretically, it is not in the least doubtful to the will: it is a *postulate* of practical reason, an immediate fact of the moral consciousness.[1]

Here arises one of the great difficulties with which philosophy is confronted: How can we reconcile the postulate of practical reason with the axiom of pure reason that every occurrence in the phenomenal order is a necessary effect, that the phenomenal world is governed by an absolute determinism? Kant, whose belief in free-will is no less ardent than his love of truth, cannot admit an absolute incompatibility between natural necessity and moral liberty. The conflict of reason and conscience, regarding freedom, can only be a seeming one; it must be possible to resolve the antinomy without violating the rights of the intelligence or those of the will.

The solution would, undoubtedly, be impossible, if the *Critique of Pure Reason* absolutely denied liberty, but the fact is, it

---

[1] *Grundlegung zur Metaphysik der Sitten*, p. 80 (Rosenkranz); *Kritik der praktischen Vernunft*, p. 274.

excludes freedom from the phenomenal sphere only, and not from the intelligible and transcendent world, which exists behind the phenomenon, though it is unknowable. Theoretical reason declares: Freedom, though impossible in the phenomenal world, is possible in the absolute order; it is conceived as a noumenon; it is intelligible; and practical reason adds: it is certain. Hence, there is no real contradiction between the faculty of knowledge and of will. Our acts are determined, in so far as they occur in time and in space, indetermined and free, in so far as the source whence they spring, *our intelligible character*, is independent of these two forms of sensibility.[1]

This would not be a solution if time and space were objective realities, as dogmatic philosophy conceives them. *From that point of view*, Spinoza is right in denying freedom. However, as soon as we agree with criticism, that space and, above all, time are modes of seeing things, and do not affect the things themselves, determinism is reduced to a mere theory or general conception of things, a theory or conception which reason cannot repudiate without abdicating, but which by no means expresses their real essence.

The Kantian solution of the problem of freedom at first sight provokes a very serious objection. If the soul, as intelligible character, does not exist *in time*, if it is not a phenomenon, we can no longer subsume it under the category of causality, since the categories apply only to phenomena and not to ''noumena.' Hence it ceases to be a cause and a free cause. Nor can we apply to it the category of unity. Hence it ceases to be an individual apart from other individuals: it is identified with the universal, the eternal, and the infinite. Fichte, therefore, consistently deduces his doctrine of the absolute ego from Kantian premises. Our philosopher, however, does not seem to have the slightest suspicion that this is the logical conclusion of this theory. Nay, he postulates, always in the name of practical reason, individual immortality[2] as a necessary condition of the solution of the moral problem, and the existence of a God[3] apart from the intelligible ego, as the highest guarantee of the moral order and the ultimate triumph of the good. It is true, Kant's theology is merely an appendix to his ethics, and is not to be taken very seriously. It is

[1] *Kritik der praktischen Vernunft*, pp. 225 ff.
[2] *Kritik der praktischen Vernunft*, p. 261.
[3] *Id.*, p. 264.

no longer, as in the Middle Ages, the queen of the sciences, but the humble servant of independent ethics. This personal God, afterwards postulated by the *Critique of Practical Reason*, forcibly reminds us of the celebrated epigram of a contemporary of our philosopher : " If there were no God, we should have to invent one."

The real God of Kant is Freedom in the service of the ideal, or the good Will *(der gute Wille)*.[1]

His conviction in this matter is most clearly expressed by the doctrine of the *primacy of practical reason*,[2] i. e., of the *will*.[3] Theoretical reason and practical reason, though not directly contradicting each other, are slightly at variance as the most important questions of ethics and religion, the former tending to conceive liberty, God, and the absolute as ideals having no demonstrable objective existence, the latter affirming the reality of the autonomous soul, responsibility, immortality, and the Supreme Being. The consequences of this dualism would be disastrous if theoretical reason and practical reason were of equal rank ; and they would be still more disastrous, were the latter subordinated to the former. But the authority of practical reason is superior to that of theoretical reason, and in real life the former predominates. Hence we should, in any case, act *as if it were proved* that we are free, that the soul is immortal, that there is a supreme judge and rewarder.

In certain respects, the dualism of understanding and will is a happy circumstance. If the realities of religion, God, freedom, and the immortality of the soul, were self-evident truths, or capable of theoretical proof, we should do the good for the sake of future reward, our will would cease to be autonomous, our acts would no longer be strictly moral ; for every other motive except the *categorical imperative* of conscience and the respect which it inspires, be it friendship or even the love of God, renders the will *heteronomous*, and deprives its acts of their ethical character. Moreover, religion is true only when completely identical with morality. Religion within the bounds of reason consists in morality, nothing more nor less. The essence of Christianity is eternal

[1] *Grundlegung zur Metaphysik der Sitten*, p. 11 : *Es ist überall nichts in der Welt, ja überhaupt auch ausser derselben zu denken möglich, was ohne Einschränkung für gut könnte gehalten werden, als allein ein* GUTER WILLE.

[2] *Kritik der praktischen Vernunft*, p. 258.

[3] *Id.*, pp. 105 ff.

morality ; the goal of the church is the triumph of right in human-
ity. When the church aims at a different goal, it loses its *raison
d'être*.[1]

II. CRITIQUE OF JUDGMENT.[2]

While the *Critique of Practical Reason*, with its categorical
imperative, its primacy of the conscience, and its absolute independence of morality, satisfies Kant's moral feeling and his great
love of liberty, which had been shaken by the conclusions of the
Critique of Pure Reason, the philosophical instinct reasserts itself in his æsthetics and teleology, which form the subject-matter
of his *Critique of Judgment*. We have seen how, in the *Critique
of Pure Reason*, he universally combines synthesis with analysis,
how he solders together the heterogeneous parts of the cognitive
apparatus : between the functions of sensibility and those of reason
he discovers the intermediate function of the idea of time, which
is half intuition, half category ; between *a priori* concepts which
are diametrically opposed, he inserts intermediary categories. The
same synthetic impulse leads him, in his *Critique of Judgment*,
to bridge over the chasm which separates theoretical reason and
the conscience.[3]

The æsthetical and teleological sense is an intermediate faculty,
a connecting link between the understanding and the will. Truth
is the object of the understanding, nature and natural necessity its
subject-matter. The will strives for the good ; it deals with freedom. The æsthetical and teleological sense (or judgment in the
narrow sense of the term) is concerned with what lies between the
true and the good, between nature and liberty : we mean the

1 *Die Religion innerhalb der Grenzen der blossen Vernunft*, pp. 130 ff.; 205
ff.—The *independent morality* of the socialist P. J. Proudhon (1809—1865) is
grounded on these principles. It is based on the following proposition:
"Morality must cease to lean on theology for support, it must free itself from
all so-called revealed dogmas, and base itself solely on conscience and the
innate principle of justice, without requiring the support of the belief in God
and the immortality of the soul." This doctrine of Proudhon has been reproduced and popularized by a weekly journal, the "*Morale indépendante*,'
edited by Massol, Morin and Coignet (1895 ff.).

2[A. Stadler, *Kant's Teleologie, etc.*, Berlin, 1874; H. Cohen, *Kant's Be-
gründung der Aesthetik*, Berlin, 1889; J. Goldfriedrich, *Kant's Aesthetik*,
Leipsic, 1895; J. H. Tufts, *The Sources and Development of Kant's Teleology*,
Chicago, 1892.]

3 *Kritik der Urtheilskraft*, p. 14.

beautiful and the purposive. Kant calls it judgment because of the analogy between its manifestations and what is called judgment in logic, like the judgment, the sense of the beautiful and the teleological establishes a relation between two things which as such have nothing in common : between what ought to be and what is, between freedom and natural necessity.

1. *Æsthetics.*—The æsthetical sense differs both from the understanding and the will. It is neither theoretical nor practical in character ; it is a phenomenon *sui generis.* But it has this in common with reason and will, that it rests on an essentially subjective basis. Just as reason constitutes the true, and will the good, so the æsthetical sense makes the beautiful. Beauty does not inhere in objects; it does not exist apart from the æsthetical sense ; it is the *product* of this sense, as time and space are the products of the theoretical sense. That is beautiful which pleases (quality), which pleases all (quantity), which pleases without interest and without a concept (relation), and pleases necessarily (modality).[1]

What characterizes the beautiful and distinguishes it from the sublime, is the feeling of peace, tranquillity, or harmony which it arouses in us, in consequence of the perfect agreement between the understanding and the imagination. The sublime, on the other hand, disturbs us, agitates us, transports us. Beauty dwells in the form ; the sublime, in the disproportion between the form and the content. The beautiful calms and pacifies us ; the sublime brings disorder into our faculties ; it produces discord between the reason, which conceives the infinite, and the imagination, which has its fixed limits. The emotion caused in us by the starry heavens, the storm, and the raging sea springs from the conflict aroused by these different phenomena between our reason, which can *measure* the forces of nature and the heavenly distances without being overwhelmed by the enormous figures, and our imagination, which cannot follow reason into the depths of infinity. Man has a feeling of grandeur, because he himself is grand through reason. The animal remains passive in the presence of the grand spectacles of nature, because its intelligence does not rise beyond the level of its imagination. Hence we aptly say, the sublime elevates the soul (*das Erhabene ist erhebend*). In the feeling of the sublime, man reveals himself as a being infinite in reason, finite in imagi-

[1] *Kritik der Urtheilskraft*, pp. 45 ff.

nation.   Both infinite and finite : how is that possible ?   Kant can-not fathom this mystery without surpassing the limits which he has prescribed to knowledge.[1]

2.   *Teleology*.[2]—There are two kinds of purposiveness.   The one arouses in us, immediately and without the aid of any con-cept, a feeling of pleasure, satisfaction, and inner harmony : this is subjective finality, which constitutes the beautiful.   The other also arouses pleasure, but mediately, in consequence of an experience or an intermediate process of reasoning : this is objective finality, which constitutes the suitable (*das Zweckmässige*).   Thus, a flower may be both the object of an æsthetical judgment in the artist, and of a teleological judgment in the naturalist, who has tested its value as a remedy.   Only, the judgment which stamps it as beautiful is immediate and spontaneous, while that of the naturalist depends on previous experience.

The *Critique of Pure Reason* regards every phenomenon as a necessary effect, and therefore excludes purposiveness from the phenomenal world.   Physics merely enumerates an infinite series of causes and effects.   Teleology introduces between the cause and the effect, considered as the end or goal, the means, the in-strumental cause.   Theoretically, teleology is valueless.   However, we cannot avoid it so long as we apply our teleological sense to the study of nature.   Unless we abandon one of our faculties, which is as real and inevitable as reason and will, we cannot help recognizing purposiveness in the structure of the eye, the ear, and the organism in general.   Though mechanism fully explains the inorganic world, the teleological view forces itself upon us when we come to consider anatomy, physiology, and biology.

The antinomy of mechanism, affirmed by the theoretical rea-son, and teleology, claimed by the teleological sense, is no more insoluble than that of necessity and freedom.[3]   Teleology is noth-ing but a theory concerning phenomena.   It no more expresses the essence of things than mechanism.   This essence is as unknowable for the *Critique of Judgment* as for the *Critique of Pure Reason.* Things-in-themselves are not in time ; they have no succession, no duration.   According to mechanism, the cause and its effect, ac-cording to teleology, the free cause, the means, and the goal at which it aims, follow each other, i. e., they are separated in time.

1 *Kritik der Urtheilskraft*, pp. 97 ff. ; 399 ff.

2 *Id* , pp. 239 ff.   3 *Kritik der Urtheilskraft*, pp. 302 ff.

But time is merely an *a priori* form of intuition, a mode of conceiving things; *as such* and apart from my thought or my theory, the cause and the effect of the mechanist, the creative agent, the means, and the goal of the teleologist, are in each other, inseparable, simultaneous. Imagine an understanding which is not bound to the *a priori* forms of space and time like ours, a free and absolute intellectual intuition : such an understanding would perceive the cause, the means, and the end at one glance; it would identify the end and the principle; the end would not follow the efficient cause, but would be immanent in it and identical with it. *Immanent teleology*, which identifies the ends of nature with the acting causes, is the natural solution of the antinomy of mechanism and purposiveness.

We see that the subjectivity of time and space is the most original and, on the whole, the most fruitful of Kant's teachings. There is no question so subtle, no problem so obscure, as not to be illuminated by it. Space and time are the eyes of the mind, the organs which reveal to it its inexhaustible content. These organs are at the same time the boundaries of its knowledge. But in spite of this insurmountable barrier, it feels free, immortal, and divine; and it declares its independence in the field of action. It is the mind which prescribes its laws to the phenomenal world; it is the mind from which the moral law proceeds ; it is the mind and its judgment which make the beautiful beautiful. In short, the three *Critiques* culminate in absolute spiritualism. Kant compared his work to that of Copernicus : just as the author of the *Celestial Revolutions* puts the sun in the place of the earth in our planetary system, so the author of the *Critique* places the mind in the centre of the phenomenal world and makes the latter dependent upon it. Kant's philosophy is, undoubtedly, the most remarkable and most fruitful product of modern thought. With a single exception, perhaps,[1] the greatest systems which our century has produced are continuations of Kantianism. Even those—and their number has grown during the last thirty years—who have again taken up the Anglo French philosophy of the eighteenth century, revere the illustrious name of Immanuel Kant.

[1] We mean the system of Comte, which is closely related to the French philosophy of the eighteenth century. Comte himself says, in a letter to Gustave d'Eichthal, dated December 10th, 1824 : " I have always considered Kant not only as a very powerful thinker, but also as the metaphysician who most closely approximates the positive philosophy."

KANT'S VIEWS ON RELIGION.

(AFTER SCHWEGLER.[1])

KANT'S views of religion appear in his treatise on *Religion within the Bounds of Pure Reason*. The fundamental idea of this treatise is the reduction of religion to morality. Between morality and religion there may be the twofold relation, that either morality is founded upon religion, or else religion upon morality. If the first relation were real, it would give us fear and hope as principles of moral action; but this cannot be; there remains, therefore, only the second. Morality leads necessarily to religion, because the highest good is a necessary ideal of the reason, and this can only be realized through a God; but in no way may religion first incite us to virtue, for the idea of God may never become a moral motive. Religion, according to Kant, is the recognition of all our duties as divine commands. It is revealed religion when I must first know that something is a divine command, in order to know that it is my duty: it is natural religion when I must first know that something is my duty, in order to know that it is a divine command. The Church is an ethical community, which has for its end the fulfilment and the most perfect exhibition of moral commands,—a union of those who with united energies purpose to resist evil and advance morality. The Church, in so far as it is no object of a possible experience, is called the invisible Church, which, as such, is merely the idea of the union of all the righteous under the divine moral government of the world. The visible Church, on the other hand, is that which represents the kingdom of God upon earth, so far as this can be attained through men. The requisites, and hence also the characteristics of the true visible Church (which are divided according to the table of the categories since this Church is given in experience) are the following:

---

[1] Schwegler's *History of Philosophy*. Translated by Seelye. New York Appleton Schwegler's compendium has enjoyed the greatest popularity both in Germany and abroad, for its accuracy and trustworthiness.

(*a*) In respect of *quantity* the Church must be total or *universal;* and though it may be divided in accidental opinions, yet must it be instituted upon such principles as will necessarily lead to a universal union in one single church. (*b*) The *quality* of the true visible Church is *purity*, as a union under no other than moral motives, since it is at the same time purified from the stupidness of superstition and the madness of fanaticism. (*c*) The *relation* of the members of the Church to each other rests upon the principle of freedom. The Church is, therefore, a *free state*, neither a hierarchy nor a democracy, but a voluntary, universal, and enduring spiritual union. (*d*) In respect of *modality* the Church demands that its constitution should be unchangeable. The laws themselves may not change, though one may reserve to himself the privilege of changing some accidental arrangements which relate simply to the administration —That alone which can establish a universal Church is the moral faith of the reason, for this alone can be shared by the convictions of every man. But, because of the peculiar weakness of human nature, we can never reckon enough on this pure faith to build a Church on it alone, for men are not easily convinced that the striving after virtue and an irreproachable life is every thing which God demands: they always suppose that they must offer to God a special service prescribed by tradition, which only amounts to this—that he is served.

To establish a Church, we must therefore have a statutory faith historically grounded upon facts. This is the so-called faith of the Church. In every Church there are therefore two elements—the purely moral, or the faith of reason, and the historico-statutory, or the faith of the Church It depends now upon the relation of these two elements whether a Church shall have any worth or not. The statutory element should ever be only the vehicle of the moral element. Just so soon as this element becomes in itself an independent end, claiming an independent validity, will the Church become corrupt and irrational, and whenever the Church passes over to the pure faith of reason, it approximates to the kingdom of God. Upon this principle we may distinguish the true from the spurious service of the kingdom of God, religion from priestcraft. A dogma has worth alone in so far as it has a moral content. The apostle Paul himself would scarcely have given credit to the dicta of the creed of the Church without this moral faith. From the doctrine of Trinity, *e. g.*, taken literally, nothing actually practical can be derived. Whether we have to reverence in the Godhead three persons or ten makes no difference, if in both cases we have the same rules for our conduct of life. The Bible also, with its interpretation, must be considered in a moral point of view. The records of revelation must be interpreted in a sense which will harmonize with the universal rules of the religion of reason. Reason is in religious things the highest interpreter of the Bible. This interpretation in reference to some texts may seem forced, yet it must be preferred to any such literal interpretation as would contain nothing for morality, or perhaps go against every moral feeling. That such a moral signification may always be found without ever entirely repudiating the literal sense, results from the fact that the foundation for an ethical religion lay originally in the human reason. We need only to divest the representations of the Bible of their mythical dress (an attempt which Kant has himself made, by an ethical interpretation of some of the weightiest doctrines), in order to attain for them a rational meaning which shall be universally valid. The historical element of the sacred books is in itself of no account. The maturer the reason becomes, the more it can hold fast for itself the moral sense, so much the more unnecessary will be the statutory institutions of the faith of the Church. The transition from the creed of the Church to the pure faith of reason is the approximation to the kingdom of God, to which however, we can only approach nearer and nearer in an infinite progress. The actual realization of the kingdom of God is the end of the world, the termination of history

KANT AND MATERIALISM.

(AFTER LANGE.[1])

AS a routed army looks around it for a firm point where it may hope to collect again into order, so recently there has been heard everywhere in philosophic circles the cry, "Retreat to Kant!" Only more recently, however, has this retreat to Kant become a reality, and it is found that at bottom the standpoint of the great Königsberg philosopher could never have been properly described as obsolete; nay, that we have every reason to plunge into the depths of the Kantian system with most serious efforts, such as have hitherto been spent upon scarcely any other philosopher save Aristotle.

Misapprehension and impetuous productiveness have combined in an intellectually active age to break through the strict barriers which Kant had imposed upon speculation. The reaction which succeeded the metaphysical intoxication contributed the more to the return to the prematurely abandoned position, as men sound themselves again confronted by the Materialism which at the appearance of Kant had disappeared and left scarcely a wrack behind. At present we have not only a young school of Kantians in the narrower and wider sense, but those also who wish to try other paths see themselves compelled first to reckon with Kant, and to offer a special justification for departing from his ways. Even the factitious and exaggerated enthusiam for Schopenhauer's philosophy partly owed its origin to a related tendency, while in many cases it formed for more logical minds a transition to Kant. But a special emphasis must here be laid on the friendly attitude of men of science, who, so far as Materialism failed to satisfy them, have inclined for the most part to a way of thinking which, in very essential points, agrees with that of Kant.

---

[1] *History of Materialism.* Trans. by Thomas. 3 vols. London: Trübne Co. 1880.

And it is, in fact, by no means strictly orthodox Kantianism upon which we must have laid distinctive stress; least of all that dogmatic turn with which Schleiden thought he could crush Materialism when he compared Kant, Fries, and Apelt with Keppler; Newton, and Laplace, and maintained that by their labors the ideas "Soul," "Freedom," "God," were as firmly established as the laws of the stellar world.   Such dogmatism is entirely foreign to the spirit of the critique of reason, although Kant personally attached great value to his having withdrawn these very ideas from the controversy of the schools, by relegating them, as utterly incapable as well of positive as negative proof, to the sphere of practical philosophy.   But the whole of the practical philosophy is the variable and perishable part of Kant's philosophy, powerful as were its effects upon his contemporaries.   Only its site is imperishable, not the edifice that the master has erected on this site. Even the demonstration of this site, as of a free ground for the building of ethical systems, can scarcely be numbered among the permanent elements of the system, and therefore, if we are speaking of the salvation of moral ideas, nothing is more unsuitable than to compare Kant with Keppler, to say nothing of Newton and Laplace.   Much rather must we seek for the whole importance of the great reform which Kant inaugurated in his criticism of the *theoretical* reason; here lies, in fact, even for ethics, the lasting importance of the critical philosophy, which not only aided the development of a particular system of ethical ideas, but, if properly carried on, is capable of affording similar aid to the changing requirements of various epochs of culture.

Kant himself was very far from comparing himself with Keppler; but he made another comparison, that is more significant and appropriate.   He compared his achievement to that of Copernicus.   But this achievement consisted in this, that he reversed the previous standpoint of metaphysics.   Copernicus dared, "by a paradoxical yet true method," to seek the observed motions, no, in the heavenly bodies, but in their observers.   Not less "paradoxical" must it appear to the sluggish mind of man when Kant lightly and certainly overturns our collective experience, with all the historical and exact sciences, by the simple assumption that our notions do not regulate themselves according to things, but things according to our notions.[1]   It follows immediately from

[1] Compare the preface to the second edition of the *Critique*. Kant indeed lets it here appear (note to p. xxii., Hartenst., iii. 20 ff.) that in thoroughgoing

tnis that the objects of experience altogether are only *our* objects;
that the whole objective world is, in a word, not absolute objectivity, but only objectivity for man and any similarly organised beings, while behind the phenomenal world, the absolute nature of
things, the "thing-in-itself" is veiled in impenetrable darkness.

criticism he claims the rôle of a Newton, by whose theory had been *proved*
what Copernicus in his opinion (comp. as to this vol. I., p. 230) had only proposed as "hypothesis." But for the purpose of gaining a first view of the
nature of the Kantian reform, the comparison with Copernicus made in the
preface is more important.

KANT AND DEISM.

(AFTER HEINRICH HEINE.[1])

LESSING died at Brunswick in 1781, misunderstood, hated, and decried. In the same year appeared at Königsberg Immanuel Kant's *Critique of Pure Reason*. With this book (which through a singular delay did not become generally known till the close of the decade) there begins in Germany an intellectual revolution which offers the most striking analogies to the material revolution in France, and which must to the deeper thinkers appear of at least as great importance as the latter. It developed itself in the same phases, and between both revolutions there exists the most remarkable parallelism. On each side of the Rhine we see the same breach with the past; all respect for tradition is withdrawn. As here, in France, every privilege, so there, in Germany, every thought, must justify itself; as here, the monarchy, the keystone of the old social edifice, so there, deism, the keystone of the old intellectual *régime*, falls from its place.

Of this catastrophe, the 21st of January, for deism, we shall speak in the concluding part of this volume. A peculiar awe, a mysterious piety, overcomes us. Our heart is full of shuddering compassion: it is the old Jehovah himself that is preparing for death. We have known him so well from his cradle in Egypt, where he was reared among the divine calves and crocodiles, the sacred onions, ibises, and cats. We have seen him bid farewell to these companions of his childhood and to the obelisks and sphinxes of his native Nile, to become in Palestine a little god-king amidst a poor shepherd people, and to inhabit a temple-palace of his own. We have seen him later coming into contact with Assyrian-Babylonian civilisation, renouncing his all-too-human passions, no

From *Religion and Philosophy in Germany*. Translated by John Snodgrass. Boston: Houghton, Mifflin & Co., 1882. This work by Heine is celebrated for its trenchant wit, and is the literary story of German philosophy *par excellence*.

Critik
der
reinen Vernunft

von

Immanuel Kant
Professor in Königsberg.

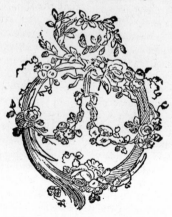

Riga,
verlegts Johann Friedrich Hartknoch
1781.

longer giving vent to fierce wrath and vengeance, at least no longer thundering at every trifle. We have seen him migrate to Rome, the capital, where he abjures all national prejudices and proclaims the celestial equality of all nations, and with such fine phrases establishes an opposition to the old Jupiter, and intrigues ceaselessly till he attains supreme authority, and from the Capitol rules the city and the world, *urbem et orbem*. We have seen how, growing still more spiritualised, he becomes a loving father, a universal friend of man, a benefactor of the world, a philanthropist; but all this could avail him nothing!

Hear ye not the bells resounding? Kneel down. They are bringing the sacraments to a dying god!

*   *   *

It is related that an English mechanician, who had already invented the most ingenious machines, at last took it into his head to construct a man; and that he succeeded. The work of his hands deported itself and acted quite like a human being; it even contained within its leathern breast a sort of apparatus of human sentiment, differing not greatly from the habitual sentiments of Englishmen; it could communicate its emotions by articulate sounds, and the noise of wheels in its interior, of springs and escapements, which was distinctly audible, reproduced the genuine English pronunciation. This automaton, in short, was an accomplished gentleman, and nothing was wanting to render it completely human except a soul. But the English mechanician had not the power to bestow on his work this soul, and the poor creature, having become conscious of its imperfection, tormented its creator day and night with supplication for a soul. This request, daily repeated with growing urgency, became at last so insupportable to the poor artist that he took to flight in order to escape from his own masterpiece. But the automaton also took the mail coach, pursued him over the whole continent, travelled incessantly at his heels, frequently overtook him, and then gnashed and growled in his ears, *Give me a soul!* These two figures may now be met with in every country, and he only who knows their peculiar relationship to each other can comprehend their unwonted haste and their haggard anxiety. But as soon as we are made aware of their strange relationship, we at once discover in them something of a general character; we see how one portion of the English people is becoming weary of its mechanical existence, and is demanding a soul, whilst the other portion, tormented by such a request, is driven about in all directions, and that neither of them can endure matters at home any longer.

The story is a terrible one. It is a fearful thing when the bodies we have created demand of us a soul; but it is a far more dreadful, more terrible, more awful thing when we have created a soul, to hear that soul demanding of us a body, and to behold it pursuing us with this demand. The thought to which we have given birth is such a soul, and it leaves us no rest until we have endowed it with a body, until we have given it sensible reality. Thought strives to become action, the word to become flesh, and, marvellous to relate, man, like God in the Bible, needs only to express his thought and the world takes form; there is light or darkness; the waters separate themselves from the dry land; or it may even be that wild beasts are brought forth. The world is the sign-manual of the word.

Mark this, ye proud men of action; ye are nothing but unconscious hodmen of the men of thought who, often in humblest stillness, have appointed you your inevitable task. Maximilian Robespierre was merely the hand of Jean Jacques Rousseau, the bloody hand that drew from the womb of time the body whose soul Rousseau had created. May not the restless anxiety that troubled the life of Jean Jacques have caused such stirrings within him that he already foreboded the kind of accoucheur that was needed to bring his thought living into the world?

Old Fontenelle may have been right when he said : "If I held all the truths of the universe in my hand, I would be very careful not to open it." I, for my part, think otherwise. If I held all the truths of the world in my hand, I might perhaps beseech you instantly to cut off that hand; but, in any case, I should not long hold it closed. I was not born to be a gaoler of thoughts; by Heaven! I would set them free. What though they were to incarnate themselves in the most hazardous realities, what though they were to range through all lands like a mad bacchanalian procession, what though they were to crush with their thyrsus our most innocent flowers, what though they were to invade our hospitals and chase from his bed the old sick world—my heart would bleed, no doubt, and I myself would suffer thereby! For alas! I too am part of this old sick world, and the poet says truly, one may mock at his crutches yet not be able to walk any better for that. I am the most grievously sick of you all, and am the more to be pitied since I know what health is; but you do not know it, you whom I envy; you are capable of dying without perceiving your dying condition.   Yea, many of you are already long since dead, though maintaining that your real life is just beginning.   When I try to dispel such a delusion, then you are angry with me and rail at me, and, more horrible still, the dead rush upon and mock at me, and more loathsome to me than their insults is the smell of their putrefaction.   Hence, ye spectres! I am about to speak of a man whose mere name has the might of an exorcism; I speak of Immanuel Kant.

It is said that night-wandering spirits are filled with terror at sight of the headsman's axe.   With what mighty fear, then, must they be stricken when there is held up to them Kant's *Critique of Pure Reason!*   This is the sword that slew deism in Germany.

To speak frankly, you French have been tame and moderate compared with us Germans.   At most, you could but kill a king, and he had already lost his head before you guillotined him.   For accompaniment to such deed you must needs cause such a drumming and shrieking and stamping of feet that the whole universe trembled.   To compare Maximilian Robespierre with Immanuel Kant is to confer too high an honour upon the former.   Maximillian Robespierre, the great citizen of the Rue Saint Honoré, had, it is true, his sudden attacks of destructiveness when it was a question of the monarchy, and his frame was violently convulsed when the fit of regicidal epilepsy was on; but as soon as it came to be a question about the Supreme Being, he wiped the white froth from his lips, washed the blood from his hands, donned his blue Sunday coat with silver buttons, and stuck a nosegay in the bosom of his broad vest.

The history of Immanuel Kant's life is difficult to portray, for he had neither life nor history.   He led a mechanical, regular almost abstract bachelor existence in a little retired street of Königsberg, an old town on the north eastern frontier of Germany. I do not believe that the great clock of the cathedral performed in a more passionless and methodical manner its daily routine than did its townsman, Immanuel Kant.   Rising in the morning, coffee-drinking, writing, reading lectures, dining, walking, everything had its appointed time, and the neighbours knew that it was exactly half-past three o'clock when Immanuel Kant stepped forth from his house in his grey, tight-fitting coat, with his Spanish cane in his hand, and betook himself to the little linden avenue called after him to this day the "Philosopher's Walk." Summer and winter he walked up and down it eight times, and when the weather was dull or heavy clouds prognosticated rain, the townspeople beheld his servant, the old Lampe, trudging anxiously behind him with a big umbrella under his arm, like an image of Providence.

What a strange contrast did this man's outward life present to his destructive, world-annihilating thoughts! In sooth, had the citizens of Königsberg had the least presentiment of the full significance of his ideas, they would have felt a far more awful dread at the presence of this man than at the sight of an executioner, who can but kill the body. But the worthy folk saw in him nothing more than a Professor of Philosophy, and as he passed at his customary hour, they greeted him in a friendly manner and set their watches by him.

But though Immanuel Kant, the arch-destroyer in the realm of thought, far surpassed in terrorism Maximilian Robespierre, he had many similarities with the latter, which induce a comparison between the two men. In the first place, we find in both the same inexorable, keen, poesyless, sober integrity. We likewise find in both the same talent of suspicion, only that in the one it manifested itself in the direction of thought and was called criticism, whilst in the other it was directed against mankind and was styled republican virtue. But both presented in the highest degree the type of the narrow-minded citizen. Nature had destined them for weighing out coffee and sugar, but fate decided that they should weigh out other things, and into the scales of the one it laid a king, into the scales of the other a God . . . . . . And they both gave the correct weight!

The *Critique of Pure Reason* is Kant's principal work; and as none of his other writings is of equal importance, in speaking of it we must give it the right of preference. This book appeared in 1781, but, as already said, did not become generally known till 1789. At the time of its publication it was quite overlooked, except for two insignificant notices, and it was not till a later period that public attention was directed to this great book by the articles of Schütz, Schultz, and Reinhold. The cause of this tardy recognition undoubtedly lay in the unusual form and bad style in which the work is written. As regards his style, Kant merits severer censure than any other philosopher, more especially when we compare this with his former and better manner of writing. The recently published collection of his minor works con-

tains his first attempts, and we are surprised to find in these an excellent and often very witty style. These little treatises were trilled
forth while their author ruminated over his great work. There is
a gleefulness about them like that of a soldier tranquilly arming
for a combat in which he promises himself certain victory. Especially remarkable amongst them are his *Universal Natural History and Theory of the Heavens*, composed as early as 1755;
Observations on the Emotions of the Sublime and Beautiful
written ten years later; and *Dreams of a Ghostseer*, full of
admirable humour after the manner of the French essay. Kant's
wit as displayed in these pamphlets is of quite a peculiar sort. The
wit clings to the thought, and in spite of its tenuity is thus enabled
to reach a satisfactory height. Without such support wit, be it
ever so robust, cannot be successful; like a vine-tendril wanting a
prop, it can only creep along the ground to rot there with all its
most precious fruits.

But why did Kant write his *Critique of Pure Reason* in
such a colourless, dry, packing-paper style? I fancy that, having
rejected the mathematical form of the Cartesio-Leibnitzo-Wolfian
school, he feared that science might lose something of its dignity
by expressing itself in light, attractive, and agreeable tones. He
therefore gave it a stiff, abstract form, which coldly repelled all
familiarity on the part of intellects of the lower order. He wished
haughtily to separate himself from the popular philosophers of his
time, who aimed at the most citizen-like clearness, and so clothed
his thoughts in a courtly and frigid official dialect. Herein he
shows himself a true philistine. But it might also be that Kant
needed for the carefully measured march of his ideas a language
similarly precise, and that he was not in a position to create a
better. It is only genius that has a new word for a new thought.
Immanuel Kant, however, was no genius. Conscious of this defect, Kant, like the worthy Maximilian, showed himself all the
more mistrustful of genius, and went so far as to maintain, in his
Critique of the Faculty of Judgment, that genius has no business with scientific thought, and that its action ought to be rele-
gated to the domain of art.

The heavy, buckram style of Kant's chief work has been the
source of much mischief; for brainless imitators aped him in his
external form, and hence arose amongst us the superstition that no
one can be a philosopher who writes well. The mathematical
form, however, could not, after the days of Kant, reappear in

philosophy; he has mercilessly passed sentence of death upon it in his *Critique of Pure Reason*. The mathematical form in philosophy, he says, is good for nothing save the building of houses of cards, in the same way that the philosophic form in mathematics produces nothing but twaddle, for in philosophy there can be no definitions such as those in mathematics, where the definitions are not discursive but intuitive, that is to say, capable of being demonstrated by inspection; whilst what are called definitions in philosophy are only tentatively, hypothetically put forth, the real definition appearing only at the close, as the result.

How comes it that philosophers display so strong a predilection for the mathematical form? This predilection dates from the time of Pythagoras, who designated the principles of things by numbers. This was the idea of a genius: all that is sensible and finite is stripped off in a number, and yet it denotes something determined, and the relation of this thing to another determined thing, which last, designated in turn by a number, receives the same insensible and infinite character. In this respect numbers resemble ideas that preserve the same character and relation to one another. We can indicate by numbers in a very striking manner ideas, as they are produced in our mind and in nature; but the number still remains the sign of the idea, it is not the idea itself. The master is always conscious of this distinction, but the scholar forgets it, and transmits to other scholars at second hand merely a numerical hieroglyph, dead ciphers, which are repeated with parrot-like scholastic pride, but of which the living significance is lost. This applies likewise to the other methods of mathematical demonstration. The intellect in its eternal mobility suffers no arrest; and just as little can it be fixed down by lines, triangles, squares, and circles, as by numbers. Thought can neither be calculated nor measured.

As my chief duty is to facilitate in France the study of German philosophy, I always dwell most strongly on the external difficulties that are apt to dismay a stranger who has not already been made aware of them. I would draw the special attention of those who desire to make Frenchmen acquainted with Kant to the fact, that it is possible to abstract from his philosophy that portion which serves merely to refute the absurdities of the Wolfian philosophy. This polemic, constantly reappearing, will only tend to produce confusion in the minds of Frenchmen, and can be of no utility to them.

The *Critique of Pure Reason* is, as I have said, Kant's principal work, and his other writings are in a measure superfluous, or may at least be considered as commentaries. The social importance that attaches to his chief work will be apparent from what follows.

The philosophers who preceded Kant reflected, doubtless, on the origin of our cognitions, and followed, as we have seen, two different routes, according to their view of ideas as *a priori* or as *a posteriori;* but concerning the faculty of knowing, concerning the extent and limits of this faculty, they occupied themselves less. Now this was the task that Kant set before himself ; he submitted the faculty of knowing to a merciless investigation, he sounded all the depths of this faculty, he ascertained all its limits.   In this investigation he certainly discovered that about many things, wherewith formerly we supposed ourselves to be most intimately acquainted, we can know nothing. This was very mortifying ; but it has always been useful to know of what things we can know nothing. He who warns us against a useless journey performs as great a service for us as he who points out to us the true path. Kant proves to us that we know nothing about things as they are in and by themselves, but that we have a knowledge of them only in so far as they are reflected in our minds. We are therefore just like the prisoners of whose condition Plato draws such an afflicting picture in the seventh book of his Republic. These wretched beings, chained neck and thigh in such a manner that they cannot turn their heads about, are seated within a roofless prison, into which there comes from above a certain amount of light. This light, however, is the light from a fire, the flame of which rises up behind them, and indeed is separated from them only by a little wall. Along the outer side of this wall are walking men bearing all sorts of statues, images in wood and stone, and conversing with one another. Now the poor prisoners can see nothing of these men, who are not tall enough to overtop the wall ; and of the statues, which rise above the wall, they see only the shadows flitting along the side of the wall opposite them. The shadows, however, they take for real objects, and, deceived by the echo of their prison, believe that it is the shadows that are conversing.

With the appearance of Kant former systems of philosophy, which had merely sniffed about the external aspect of things, assembling and classifying their characteristics, ceased to exist. Kant led investigation back to the human intellect, and inquired what the latter had to reveal. Not without reason, therefore, did he compare his philosophy to the method of Copernicus. Formerly when men conceived the world as standing still, and the sun as revolving round it, astronomical calculations failed to agree accurately. But when Copernicus made the sun stand still and the earth revolve round it, behold! everything accorded admirably. So formerly reason, like the sun, moved round the universe of phenomena, and sought to throw light upon it. But Kant bade reason, the sun, stand still, and the universe of phenomena now turns round, and is illuminated the moment it comes within the region of the intellectual orb.

These few words regarding the task that presented itself to Kant will suffice to show that I consider that section of his book where he treats of *phenomena* and *noumena* as the most important part, as the central point, of his philosophy. Kant, in effect, distinguishes between the appearances of things and things themselves. As we can know nothing of objects except in so far as they manifest themselves to us through their appearance, and as objects do not exhibit themselves to us as they are in and by themselves, Kant gives the name *phenomena* to objects as they appear to us, and *noumena* to objects as they are in themselves. We know things, therefore, only as phenomena; we cannot know them as noumena. The latter are purely problematic; we can neither say that they exist nor that they do not exist. The word noumena has been correlated with the word phenomena merely to enable us to speak of things in so far as they are cognisable by us, without occupying our judgment about things that are not cognisable by us. Kant did not therefore, as do many teachers whom I will not name, make a distinction of objects into phenomena and noumena, into things that for us exist and into things that for us do not exist. This would be an Irish bull in philosophy. He wished merely to express a notion of limitation.

God, according to Kant, is a noumenon. As a result of his argument, this ideal and transcendental being, hitherto called God, is a mere fiction. It has arisen from a natural illusion. Kant shows that we can know nothing regarding this noumenon, regarding God, and that all reasonable proof of his existence is impossible. The words of Dante, "Leave all hope behind!" may be inscribed over this portion of the *Critique of Pure Reason*.

My readers will, I think, gladly exempt me from attempting a popular elucidation of that portion of his work in which Kant treats "of the arguments of speculative reason in favour of the existence of a Supreme Being." Although the formal refutation of these arguments occupies but a small space, and is not taken in hand till the second part of the book is reached, there is already a very evident intention of leading up to this refutation, which forms one of the main points of the work. It connects itself with the *Critique of all Speculative Theology*, wherein the last phantoms of deism are put to flight. I cannot help remarking that Kant, in attacking the three principal kinds of evidence in favour of the existence of God, namely, the ontological, the cosmological, and the physico-theological, whilst successful, according to my opinion, in refuting the latter two, fails with regard to the first. I am not aware whether the above terms are understood in this country, and I therefore quote the passage from the *Critique of Pure Reason* in which Kant formulates the distinction between them.

"There are but three kinds of proof possible to speculative reason of the existence of God. All the routes that may be selected with this end in view start, either from definite experience and the peculiar properties of the external world, as revealed by experience, and ascend from it according to the laws of causality up to the supreme cause above the world ; or, they rest merely on an indefinite experience, as, for example, on an existence or being of some kind or other ; or, lastly, they make an abstraction from all experience, and arrive at a conclusion entirely *a priori* from pure ideas of the existence of the supreme cause. The first of these is the physico-theological proof, the second the cosmological, and the third the ontological. Other proofs there are none, nor can other proofs exist."

After repeated and careful study of Kant's chief work, I fancied myself able to recognise everywhere visible in it his polemic against these proofs of the existence of God ; and of this polemic I might speak at greater length were I not restrained by a religious sentiment. The mere discussion by any one of the existence of God causes me to feel a strange disquietude, an uneasy dread such as I once experienced in visiting New Bedlam in London, when, for a moment losing sight of my guide, I was surrounded by madmen. "God is all that is," and doubt of His existence is doubt of life itself, it is death.

The more blameworthy any dispute regarding the existence of God may be, the more praiseworthy is meditation on the nature of

God. Such meditation is a true worship of God; the soul is
thereby detached from the perishable and finite, and attains to
consciousness of innate love and of the harmony of the universe.
It is this consciousness that sends a thrill through the heart of the
emotional man in the act of prayer or in the contemplation of the
sacred symbols; and the thinker realises this holy fervour in the
exercise of that sublime faculty of the mind called reason, a faculty
whose highest function is to inquire into the nature of God. Men
of specially religious temperament concern themselves with this
problem from childhood upwards; they are mysteriously troubled
about it even at the first dawnings of reason. The author of these
pages is most joyfully conscious of having possessed this early
primitive religious feeling, and it has never forsaken him. God
was always the beginning and the end of all my thoughts. If I
now inquire: What is God? what is his nature?—as a little child
I had already inquired: How is God? what is he like? In that
childish time I could gaze upwards at the sky during whole days,
and was sadly vexed at evening because I never caught a glimpse
of God's most holy countenance, but saw only the grey silly gri-
maces of the clouds. I was quite puzzled over the astronomical
lore with which in the "enlightenment period" even the youngest
children were tormented, and there was no end to my amazement
on learning that all those thousand millions of stars were spheres
as large and as beautiful as our own earth, and that over all this
glittering throng of worlds a single God ruled. I recollect once
seeing God in a dream far above in the most distant firmament.
He was looking contentedly out of a little window in the sky, a
devout hoary-headed being with a small Jewish beard, and he was
scattering forth myriads of seed-corns, which, as they fell from
heaven, burst open in the infinitude of space, and expanded to vast
dimensions till they became actual, radiant, blossoming, peopled
worlds, each one as large as our own globe. I could never forget
this countenance, and often in dreams I used to see the cheerful-
looking old man sprinkling forth the world-seeds from his little
window in the sky; once I even saw him clucking like our maid
when she threw down for the hens their barley. I could only see
how the falling seed-corns expanded into great shining orbs: but
the great hens that may by chance have been waiting about with
eager open bills to be fed with the falling orbs I could not see.

You smile, dear reader, at the notion of the big hens. Yet this
childish notion is not so very different from the view of the most

advanced deists.   In the attempt to provide a conception of an extra-mundane God, orient and occident have exhausted themselves in hyperbole.   The imagination of deists has, however, vainly tormented itself with the infinitude of time and space.   It is here that their impotence, the inadequacy of their cosmology, and the untenableness of their explanation of the nature of God becomes fully apparent.   We are not greatly distressed, therefore, at beholding the subversion of their explanation.   Kant has actually wrought this affliction upon them by refuting their demonstration of the existence of God.

Nor would the vindication of the ontological proof specially benefit deism, for this proof is equally available for pantheism. To render my meaning more intelligible, I may remark that the ontological proof is the one employed by Descartes, and that long before his time, in the Middle Ages, Anselm of Canterbury had expressed it in the form of an affecting prayer. Indeed, St. Augustine may be said to have already made use of the ontological proof in the second book of his work, *De Libero Arbitrio*.

I refrain, as I have said, from all popular discussion of Kant's polemic against these proofs.   Let it suffice to give an assurance that since his time deism has vanished from the realm of speculative reason.   It may, perhaps, be several centuries yet before this melancholy notice of decease gets universally bruited about; we, however, have long since put on mourning.   *De Profundis!*

You fancy, then, that we may now go home !   By my life, no ! there is yet a piece to be played; after the tragedy comes the farce.   Up to this point Immanuel Kant has pursued the path of inexorable philosophy ; he has stormed heaven and put the whole garrison to the edge of the sword ; the ontological, cosmological, and physico-theological bodyguards lie there lifeless; Deity itself, deprived of demonstration, has succumbed; there is now no All-mercifulness, no fatherly kindness, no other-world reward for renunciation in this world, the immortality of the soul lies in its last agony—you can hear its groans and death-rattle ; and old Lampe is standing by with his umbrella under his arm, an afflicted spectator of the scene, tears and sweat-drops of terror dropping from his countenance.   Then Immanuel Kant relents and shows that he is not merely a great philosopher but also a good man ; he reflects, and half good-naturedly, half ironically, he says : ''Old Lampe must have a God, otherwise the poor fellow can never be happy. Now, man ought to be happy in this world ; practical reason says so ;—well, I am quite willing that practical reason should also guarantee the existence of God." As the result of this argument Kant distinguishes between the *theoretical reason* and the *practical reason*, and by means of the latter, as with a magician's wand, he revivifies deism, which theoretical reason had killed.

But is it not conceivable that Kant brought about this resurrection, not merely for the sake of old Lampe, but through fear of the police ? Or did he act from sincere conviction ? Was not his object in destroying all evidence for the existence of God to show us how embarrassing it might be to know nothing about God ? In doing so, he acted almost as sagely as a Westphalian friend of mine, who smashed all the lanterns in the Grohnder Street in Göttingen, and then proceeded to deliver to us in the dark a long lecture on the practical necessity of lanterns, which he had theoretically broken in order to show how, without them, we could see nothing.

I have already said that on its appearance the *Critique of Pure Reason* did not cause the slightest sensation, and it was not till several years later, after certain clear-sighted philosophers had written elucidations of it, that public attention was aroused regarding the book. In the year 1789, however, nothing else was talked of in Germany but the philosophy of Kant, about which were poured forth in abundance commentaries, chrestomathies, interpretations, estimates, apologies, and so forth. We need only glance through the first philosophic catalogue at hand, and the innumerable works having reference to Kant will amply testify to the intellectual movement that originated with this single man. In some it exhibited itself as an ardent enthusiasm, in others as an acrid loathing, in many as a gaping curiosity regarding the result of this intellectual revolution. We had popular riots in the world of thought, just as you had in the material world, and over the demolition of ancient dogmatism we grew as excited as you did at the storming of the Bastille. There was also but a handful of old pensioners left for the defence of dogmatism, that is, the philosophy of Wolf. It was a revolution, and one not wanting in horrors. Amongst the party of the past, the really good Christians showed least indignation at these horrors. Yea, they desired even greater, in order that the measure of iniquity might be full, and the counter-revolution be more speedily accomplished as a necessary reaction. We had pessimists in philosophy as you had in politics. As in France there were people who maintained that Robespierre was the agent of Pitt, with us there were many who went so far in their wilful blindness as to persuade themselves that Kant was in secret alliance with them, and that he had destroyed all philosophic proofs of the existence of God merely in order to convince the world that man can never arrive at a knowledge of God by the help of reason, and must therefore hold to revealed religion.

Kant brought about this great intellectual movement less by the subject-matter of his writings than by the critical spirit that pervaded them, a spirit that now began to force its way into all sciences. It laid hold of all constituted authority. Even poetry did not escape its influence. Schiller, for example, was a strong Kantist, and his artistic views are impregnated with the spirit of the philosophy of Kant. By reason of its dry, abstract character, this philosophy was eminently hurtful to polite literature and the fine arts. Fortunately it did not interfere in the art of cookery.

The German people is not easily set in motion; but let it be once forced into any path and it will follow it to its termination with the most dogged perseverance. Thus we exhibited our character in matters of religion, thus also we now acted in philosophy. Shall we continue to advance as consistently in politics?

Germany was drawn into the path of philosophy by Kant, and philosophy became a national cause. A brilliant troop of great thinkers suddenly sprang up on German soil, as if called into being by magical art. If German philosophy should some day find, as the French revolution has found, its Thiers and its Mignet, its history will afford as remarkable reading as the works of these authors. Germans will study it with pride, and Frenchmen with admiration.

THE KANTIAN PHILOSOPHY.

(AFTER ARTHUR SCHOPENHAUER.[1])

KANT'S greatest merit is the distinction of the phenomenon from the thing in itself, based upon the proof that between things and us there still always stands the *intellect*, so that they cannot be known as they may be in themselves. He was led into this path through Locke (see *Prolegomena*, § 13, Note 2). The latter had shown that the secondary qualities of things, such as sound, smell, color, hardness, softness, smoothness, and the like, as founded on the affections of the senses, do not belong to the objective body, to the thing in itself. To this he attributed only the primary qualities, i. e., such as only presuppose space and impenetrability; thus extension, figure, solidity, number, mobility. But this easily discovered Lockeian distinction was, as it were, only a youthful introduction to the distinction of Kant. The latter, starting from an incomparably higher standpoint, explains all that Locke had accepted as *primary qualities*, i. e., qualities of the thing in itself, as also belonging only to its phenomenal appearance in our faculty of apprehension, and this just because the conditions of this faculty, space, time and causality, are known by us *a priori*. Thus Locke had abstracted from the thing in itself the share which the organs of sense have in its phenomenal appearance; Kant, however, further abstracted the share of the brain-functions (though not under that name). Thus the distinction between the phenomenon and the thing in itself now received an infinitely greater significance and a very much deeper meaning. For this end he was obliged to take in hand the important separation of our *a priori* from our *a posteriori* knowledge which before him had never been carried out with adequate strictness and completeness, nor with distinct consciousness. Accordingly this

---

[1] From the *World as Will and Idea*. Trans. by Haldane and Kemp. 3 vols. Third edition. London: Kegan Paul, Trench, Trübner & Co. 1896.

now became the principal subject of his profound investigations
Now here we would at once remark that Kant's philosophy has a
threefold relation to that of his predecessors. First, as we have
just seen, to the philosophy of Locke, confirming and extending
it; secondly, to that of Hume, correcting and making use of it, a
relation which is most distinctly expressed in the *Prolegomena*
(that most beautiful and comprehensible of all Kant's important
writings, which is far too little read, for it facilitates immensely
the study of his philosophy), thirdly, a decidedly polemical and
destructive relation to the Leibnitz-Wolfian philosophy. All three
systems ought to be known before one proceeds to the study of the
Kantian philosophy. Now as Kant's separation of the phenomenon from the thing in itself, arrived at in the manner explained
above, far surpassed all that preceded it in the depth and thought-
fulness of its conception, it was also exceedingly important in its
results. For in it he propounded, quite originally, in a perfectly
new way, found from a new side and on a new path, the same
truth which Plato never wearies of repeating, and in his language
generally expresses thus: This world which appears to the senses
has no true being, but only a ceaseless becoming; it is, and it is
not, and its comprehension is not so much knowledge as illusion.
This is also what he expresses mythically at the beginning of the
seventh book of the Republic, which is the most important passage
in all his writings. He says: "Men, firmly chained in a dark
cave, see neither the true original light nor real things, but only
the meagre light of the fire in the cave and the shadows of real
things which pass by the fire behind their backs; yet they think
the shadows are the reality, and the determining of the succession
of these shadows is true wisdom." The same truth, again quite
differently presented, is also a leading doctrine of the Vedas and
Puranas, the doctrine of Mâyâ, by which really nothing else is
understood than what Kant calls the phenomenon in opposition to
the thing in itself; for the work of Mâyâ is said to be just this
visible world in which we are, a summoned enchantment, an in-
constant appearance without true being, like an optical illusion or
a dream, a veil which surrounds human consciousness, something
of which it is equally false and true to say that it is and that it is
not. But Kant not only expressed the same doctrine in a completely new and original way, but raised it to the position of proved
and indisputable truth by means of the calmest and most tempe-
rate exposition; while both Plato and the Indian philosophers had

founded their assertions merely upon a general perception of the
world, had advanced them as the direct utterance of their consciousness, and presented them rather mythically and poetically
than philosophically and distinctly. In this respect they stand to
Kant in the same relation as the Pythagoreans Hicetas, Philolaus,
and Aristarchus, who already asserted the movement of the earth
round the fixed sun, stand to Copernicus. Such distinct knowledge and calm, thoughtful exposition of this dream-like nature of
the whole world is really the basis of the whole Kantian philosophy ; it is its soul and its greatest merit. He accomplished this
by taking to pieces the whole machinery of our intellect by means
of which the phantasmagoria of the objective world is brought
about, and presenting it in detail with marvellous insight and ability. All earlier Western philosophy, appearing in comparison with
the Kantian unspeakably clumsy, had failed to recognise that
truth, and had therefore always spoken just as if in a dream.
Kant first awakened it suddenly out of this dream ; therefore the
last sleepers (Mendelssohn) called him the "all-destroyer." He
showed that the laws which reign with inviolable necessity in existence, i. e., in experience generally, are not to be applied to deduce and explain *existence itself*; that thus the validity of these
laws is only relative, i. e., only arises after existence ; the world
of experience in general is already established and present ; that
consequently these laws cannot be our guide when we come to the
explanation of the existence of the world and of ourselves. All
earlier Western philosophers had imagined that these laws, according to which the phenomena are combined, and all of which—
time and space, as well as causality and inference—I comprehend
under the expression "the principle of sufficient reason,"—were
absolute laws conditioned by nothing, *æternæ veritates* ; that the
world itself existed only in consequence of and in conformity with
them ; and therefore that under their guidance the whole riddle of
the world must be capable of solution. The assumptions made
for this purpose, which Kant criticises under the name of the Ideas
of the reason, only served to raise the mere phenomenon, the work
of Mâyâ, the shadow world of Plato, to the one highest reality, to
put it in the place of the inmost and true being of things, and
thereby to make the real knowledge of this impossible ; that is, in
a word, to send the dreamers still more soundly to sleep. Kant
exhibited these laws, and therefore the whole world, as conditioned
by the form of knowledge belonging to the subject ; from which it

followed, that however far one carried investigation and reasoning under the guidance of these laws, yet in the principal matter, i. e., in knowledge of the nature of the world in itself and outside the idea, no step in advance was made, but one only moved like a squirrel in its wheel.   Thus, all the dogmatists may be compared to persons who supposed that if they only went straight on long enough they would come to the end of the world; but Kant then circumnavigated the world and showed that, because it is round, one cannot get out of it by horizontal movement, but that yet by perpendicular movement this is perhaps not impossible.   We may also say that Kant's doctrine affords the insight that we must seek the end and beginning of the world, not without, but within us.

AN ESTIMATE OF KANT BY A SWEDEN-
BORGIAN.

(AFTER THEODORE F. WRIGHT.[1])

IN all his metaphysical work Kant was not pursuing a religious
course and was in fact becoming less and less of a Christian.
He was, however, no more contracted in his philosophical view of
the limits of reason than he was in all the ways of his life. "His
body was extremely emaciated, and at last it was dried like a pot-
sherd," said one who knew him well. He was hollow-chested, and
one shoulder was too low. Not five feet high, his bones were
small and weak, and his muscles still weaker (Stückenburg, p. 93).
He had strong prejudice against the Jews (*Ibid.*, p. 116). He took
no interest in other philosophers (*Ibid.*, p. 124). Though he wrote
much in the field of theology, he knew almost nothing of theolo-
gians (*Ibid.*, p. 359). He did not answer letters (*Ibid.*, p. 127).
He held to his views after rebutting facts were shown him, and
would contradict foreigners who spoke of their own countries in a
manner to interfere with his preconceived ideas (*Ibid.*, p. 141).
He lived in the same small city with his two sisters, yet did not
speak to them for twenty-five years because of their inferior position (*Ibid.*, p. 182). He spoke contemptuously of women and was
especially hostile to those of any mental power (*Ibid* , p 184). One
of his jokes was that there can be no women in heaven, for it is
written that there was silence there for the space of half an hour
(*Ibid.*, p. 187),—and this from a man who always did the talking
wherever he was and who listened to another with marked impatience (*Ibid.*, p. 141). He did not desire friendships, for "it is a
great burden to be tied to the fate of others and to be loaded with
their needs" (*Ibid.*, p. 193). He said that he did not know the
meaning of the word "spirit" (*Ibid.*, p. 240). With Hume he held

[1]This amusing compilation of data concerning Kant's life and personality appeared in the *New Church Review* (Boston) of January, 1901.

that we have no knowledge of God (*Ibid.*, p. 290). He saw no use in revelation (*Ibid.*, p. 335). He identified religion with mere morality (*Ibid.*, p. 338). He never attended church and spoke of prayer as ridiculous (*Ibid*, p. 354). His views against religion led students to become mockers (*Ibid.*, p. 358). His old age was unhappy (*Ibid.*, p. 425), and his rigidity of habits became repulsive in the last degree (*Ibid.*, p. 435). He died February 12, 1804, after fifteen years of mental decline.

KANT'S LETTER TO HIS BROTHER.[1]

TRANSCRIPTION OF THE ORIGINAL.

Lieber Bruder!

Bei dem Besuche, den Ueberbringer dieses, Herr Reimer, ein Verwandter von Deiner Frau, meiner werthen Schwägerin, bei mir abgelegt hat, ermangle ich nicht, was sich meiner überhäuften Beschäftigungen wegen nur in ausserordentlichen Fällen thun lässt, mich bei Dir durch einen Brief in Erinnerung zu bringen. Unerachtet dieser scheinbaren Gleichgültigkeit habe ich an Dich, nicht allein so lange wir beiderseitig leben, oft genug, sondern auch für meinen Sterbefall, der in meinem Alter von 68 Jahren doch nicht mehr sehr entfernt sein kann, brüderlich gedacht. Unsere zwei übrigen, beide verwittweten, Schwestern sind, die älteste, welche fünf erwachsene und zum Theil schon verheirathete Kinder hat, gänzlich durch mich, die andere, welche im St. Georgenhospital eingekauft ist, durch meinen Zuschuss versorgt. Den Kindern der ersteren habe ich, bei ihrer anfänglichen häuslichen Einrichtung und auch nachher, meinen Beistand nicht versagt; so dass, was die Pflicht der Dankbarkeit, wegen der uns von unsern gemeinschaftlichen Eltern gewordenen Erziehung fordert, nicht versäumt wird. Wenn Du mir einmal von dem Zustande Deiner eigenen Familie Nachricht geben willst, so wird es mir angenehm sein.

Uebrigens bin ich, in Begrüssung meiner mir sehr werthen Schwägerin, mit unveränderlicher Zuneigung

Dein treuer Bruder

KÖNIGSBERG, den 26. Januar 1792.　　　　I. KANT.

TRANSLATION.

DEAR BROTHER:—

Taking advantage of the visit which the bearer of this letter Herr Reimer, a relative of your wife, my esteemed sister-in-law has paid me, I do not omit to recall myself to your memory, although owing to my over-burdening labors this is something that I allow myself only in extraordinary cases. Notwithstanding this apparent indifference, I have, however, frequently thought of you with brotherly regard, not only for this present life, but also in case of my death, which at my age of 68 years cannot be far distant. Of our two remaining widowed sisters, the eldest, who has five adult children, some of whom are married, has been entirely supported by me, and the younger, for whom admission to the St. George's Hospital has been purchased, is also provided for. I have also not refused assistance to the children of the former, on their establishing their first homes, and even afterwards; so that there has been no neglect of the duty of gratitude that we owe to our common parents for the education they gave us. If you will inform me of the condition of your own family, I shall be gratified.

With regards to my much-esteemed sister-in-law, I remain, with constant affection,

Your Faithful Brother,

I. KANT.

KÖNIGSBERG, January 26, 1792.

CHRONOLOGY OF KANT'S LIFE AND PUBLICATIONS.[1]

1724 Immanuel Kant born on April 22.
1728 Lambert born.
1729 Lessing born.
1729 Mendelssohn born.
1730 Hamann born.
1732 Kant enters the Fridericianum, an academy in Königsberg.
1735 Kant's brother Johann Heinrich born.
1737 Kant's mother dies.
1740 Kant matriculates at the University of Königsberg
1740 Frederick II. ascends the throne.
1740 Feder born.
1742 Garve born.
1744 Herder born.
1746 Kant's first publication: *Gedanken von der wahren Schätzung der lebendigen Kräfte* (Thoughts on the True Measurement of Living Forces).
1746 Kant's father dies.
1749 Goethe born.
1751 M. Knutzen dies.
1754 Christian Wolff dies.

1754 Investigation of the question, Whether the earth in its rotation about its axis has suffered any alterations.
1754. Investigation of the question, Whether the earth is growing old. (Both questions treated in the *Königsberger Nachr.*).
1755 *Allgem. Naturgeschichte und Theorie des Himmels* (General Natural History and Theory of the Heavens).
1755 Kant takes his degree with the treatise *De Igne*, and qualifies as a university lecturer with the treatise, *Principiorum primorum cognitionis metaphysicæ nova dilucidatio*.
1756–1763 Seven Years War. The Russians in Königsberg.
1756 Disputation on the treatise *Monadologia physica*.
1756 Three small essays in the *Königsberger Nachr.*,

1 From Paulsen's *Life of Kant*, Fromann's *Klassiker der Philosophie*, Stuttgart, 1898.

on Earthquakes. (Evoked
by the Lisbon earthquake
of 1755.)

1756 New notes in elucidation
of the Theory of the
Winds.

1757 Outline and Announcement
of a course of Lectures
on Physical Geography,
with a brief supplemen-
tary consideration of the
question whether the
west winds in our locality
are moist because of hav-
ing passed over a broad
stretch of sea.

1758 New Scientific Conception
of Motion and Rest.

1759 Some Tentative Considerations of Optimism.

1759 Schiller born.

1762 Fichte born.

1762 Publication of Rous-
seau's *Émile* and *Contrat
social.*

1762 *Die falsche Spitzfindig-
keit der vier syllogisti-
schen Figuren erwiesen*
(The Erroneous Sophis-
try of the Four Syllogistic
Figures Demonstrated).

1762 *Der einzig mögliche Be-
weisgrund zu einer De-
monstration vom Da-
sein Gottes* (The Only
Possible Basis of a Dem-
onstration of the Exist-
ence of God).

1762 *Untersuchung über die
Deutlichkeit der Grund-
sätze der natürlichen*

Theologie und Moral
(Researches on the Dis-
tinctness of the Princi-
ples of Natural Theology
and Morals). (*Preis-
schrift der Berliner
Akademie,* printed in
1764.)

1763 *Versuch, den Begriff der
negativen Grössen in
die Weltweisheit einzu-
führen* (Attempt to In-
troduce the Notion of
Negative Quantities into
Philosophy).

1763 F. A. Schultz dies.

1764 *Versuch über die Krank-
heiten des Kopfes* (Essay
on the Diseases of the
Head.) (*Königsb. Ztg.*).

1764 *Beobachtungen über das
Gefühl des Schönen und
Erhabenen* (Observa-
tions on the Feeling of
the Beautiful and the
Sublime).

1765 Information on the Plan
of his Lectures.

1766 *Träume eines Geister-
sehers, erläutert durch
Träume der Metaphysik*
(Dreams of a Spirit-Seer,
etc.).

1766 Gottsched dies.

1768 *Von dem ersten Grunde
des Unterschieds der
Gegenden im Raum* (On
the Fundamental Reason
for the Difference of Lo-
calities in Space). (*Kön.
Nachr.*)

1770 Kant obtains his full professorship in logic and metaphysics.

1770 *Disputatio de mundi sensibilis atque intelligibilis forma et principiis.*

1770 (Holbach) *Système de la nature.*

1775 *Von den verschiedenen Racen des Menschen (Ankündigung der Vorlesungen über physische Geographie).* (On the Different Races of Men.)

1776 *Ueber das Dessauer Philanthropie. (Kön. Ztg.)*

1776 North American Declaration of Independence.

1776 Hume dies.

1778 Voltaire dies.

1778 Rousseau dies.

1780 Joseph II. ascends the throne.

1781 Lessing dies.

1781 *Kritik der reinen Vernunft* (Critique of Pure Reason.

1783 *Prolegomena zu einer jeden künftigen Metaphysik, die als Wissenschaft wird auftreten können* (Prolegomena to Every Future Metaphysics, etc.).

1784 *Idee zu einer allgemeinen Gesch. in weltbürgerlicher Absicht* (Ideas for a Universal History, etc.).

1784 *Beantwortung der Frage Was ist Aufklärung?* (Both the preceding articles in the *Berliner Monatsschrift.*)

1785 *Criticisms of Herder's Ideen zur Philos. der Geschichte. (Jenaische Litteraturztg.)*

1785 *Ueber Vulkane im Monde* (On Volcanoes in the Moon).

1785 *Von der Unrechtmässigkeit des Büchernachdrucks* (On the Illegality of Literary Piracy).

1785 *Bestimmung des Begriffs einer Menschenrace* (Determination of the Concept of a Race of Men).

1785 *Grundlegung zur Metaphysik der Sitten* (Foundation of the Metaphysics of Morals).

1786 *Mutmasslicher Anfang der Menschengeschichte* (Presumable Origin of Human History). (*Berl Monatsschrift.*)

1786 *Was heisst sich im Denken orientieren?* (What is the Meaning of Orientation in Thinking?) (*Berliner Monatsschrift.*)

1786 *Metaphysische Anfangsgründe der Naturwissenschaften* (Metaphysical Rudiments of the Natural Sciences).

1786 Frederick the Great dies, Frederick William II. ascends the throne.

1788 Wöllner's religious edict.

1788 *Ueber den Gebrauch teleo-
logischer Prinzipien in
der Philosophie* (On the
Use of Teleological Prin-
ciples in Philosophy).
(*Deutsch. Merk.*).

1788 *Kritik der praktischen
Vernunft* (Critique of
Practical Reason).

1789 French Revolution.

1790 *Kritik der Urteilskraft*
(Critique of the Judg-
ment).

1790 *Ueber Philosophie überhaupt (erste Einl. zur
Kr. d. Urt.)* (On Philos-
ophy in General).

1790 *Ueber eine Entdeckung,
nach der alle neue Kri-
tik der reinen Vernunft
durch eine ältere ent-
behrlich gemacht wer-
den soll* (On a Discovery
by which, etc.). (Against
Eberhard).

1790 *Ueber Schwärmerei und
die Mittel dagegen* (On
Gushing and the Means
for its Prevention).

1791 *Ueber das Misslingen
aller philos. Versuche in
der Theodicee* (On the
Failure of all Philosoph-
ical Attempts in Theod-
icy). (*Berl. Mon.*)

1792 *Vom radikalen Bösen* (On
the Radically Bad).
(*Berl. Mon*)

1792 The continuation of
the foregoing articles is
prohibited by the Berlin
censorship.

1793 *Religion innerhalb der
Grenzen der blossen Ver-
nunft* (Religion within
the Bounds of Mere Rea-
son).

1793 *Ueber den Gemeinspruch.
Das mag in der Theorie
richtig sein, taugt aber
nicht für die Praxis* (On
the Maxim : Good in
Theory, but Bad in Prac-
tice). (*Berl. Mon.*)

1794 *Etwas über den Einfluss
des Mondes auf die
Witterung* (On the In-
fluence of the Moon on
the Weather). (*Berliner
Mon.*)

1794 *Das Ende aller Dinge*
(The End of all Things).
(*Berl. Mon.*)

1794 Cabinet order of the King
and Kant's promise to
write nothing more on re-
ligion.

1795 Peace of Basel.

1795 *Zum ewigen Frieden* (On
Universal Peace).

1796 Kant discontinues his lectures.

1796 *Von einem neuerdings er-
hobenen, vornehmen Ton
in der Philosophie* (On a
Recent Aristocratic Tone
in Philosophy). (*Berl.
Mon.*)

1796 Announcement of the approaching completion of

a tract on Universal
Peace in Philosophy.

1797 *Metaphysische Anfangsgründe der Rechtslehre*
(Metaphysical Rudiments
of Jurisprudence).

1797 *Metaphysische Anfangsgründe der Tugendlehre*
(Metaphysical Rudiments
of Morals).

1797 *Ueber ein vermeintes
Recht aus Menschenliebe
zu lügen* (On a Supposed
Right to Lie out of Love
for Man).

1797 Frederick William II.
dies and is succeeded by
Frederick William III.
Wöllner dismissed.

1798 *Ueber die Buchmacherei.
Zwei Briefe an Fr. Ni-*
colai (On Bookmaking
Two Letters to Fr. Nico-
lai).

1798 *Der Streit der Fakultäten*
(The Battle of the Facul-
ties).

1798 *Anthropologie in prag-
matischer Hinsicht.*

1800 *Logic*, edited by Jäsche.

1802 *Physical Geography*, edited by Rink.

1803 *Pedagogy*, edited by Rink.

1804 On the Prize Question of
the Berlin Academy:
What Real Progress has
Metaphysics made in Ger-
many, since the Times
of Leibnitz and Wolff?
Edited by Rink.

1804 Kant dies on February 12.

INDEX TO KANT'S PROLEGOMENA.

(Pages 1–163.)

INDEX TO THE ARTICLE ON KANT'S PHI-
LOSOPHY.

(Pages 167–240.)